Institutions and Norms in
Economic Development

CESifo Seminar Series
edited by Hans-Werner Sinn

See http://mitpress.mit.edu for a complete list of titles in this series.

Institutions and Norms in Economic Development

edited by
Mark Gradstein and
Kai A. Konrad

CESifo Seminar Series

The MIT Press
Cambridge, Massachusetts
London, England

© 2006 Massachusetts Institute of Technology

MIT Press books may be purchased at special quantity discounts for business or sales promotional use. For information, please email special_sales@mitpress.mit.edu.

This book was set in Palatino on 3B2 by Asco Typesetters, Hong Kong and was printed and bound in the United States of America.

Library of Congress Cataloging-in-Publication Data

Institutions and norms in economic development / edited by Mark Gradstein, Kai A. Konrad.
    p.   cm. — (CESifo seminar series)
Includes bibliographical references and index.
ISBN 978-0-262-07284-7 (hardcover : alk. paper)—978-0-262-52637-1 (pb)
1. Economic development. 2. Economic policy. I. Gradstein, Mark. II. Konrad, Kai A.
HD75.I564   2006
338.9—dc22   2006033790

Contents

Contributors

Daniel L. Chen   is a Postdoctoral Fellow at the University of Chicago and Research Affiliate at the Population Research Center. His main research interests are development economics and how beliefs interact with market forces and regulation.

Nicola Gennaioli   is an Assistant Professor at IIES, Stockholm University. His main research interests are law and economics, political economy, and contract theory.

Mark Gradstein   is a Professor of Economics at Ben Gurion University and is the department chair. His current research interests are political economy and development.

Stuti Khemani   is an Economist at the Development Research Group of The World Bank. Her research focuses on the political economy of public policy choices, and its implications for institutional reform to promote growth and human development outcomes.

Kai A. Konrad   is a Professor of Economics at the Freie Universität Berlin and Director of the unit "Market Processes and Governance" at the Social Science Research Center Berlin (WZB). His main fields of interest are public economics and political economy.

Michael Kremer   is the Gates Professor of Developing Societies at Harvard University in Cambridge. His main research interest is development economics.

Michael McBride   is an Assistant Professor of Economics at the University of California, Irvine. His research interests include the political economy of development and conflict.

Ilia Rainer   is an Assistant Professor of Economics at George Mason University and at the Center for the Study of Public Choice. His main field of interest is political economy of development.

Moses Shayo   is a Lecturer in Economics at the Hebrew University of Jerusalem. His main fields of interest are in behavioral economics and political economy.

Stergios Skaperdas   is a Professor of Economics at the University of California, Irvine. He is interested in the interaction of conflict, governance, and economic performance.

Pedro C. Vicente   is a Postdoctoral Research Fellow at the Department of Economics/Centre for the Study of African Economies, University of Oxford. His main research interest is microeconomics of institutions in developing countries.

Karl Wärneryd   is an Associate Professor of Economics at the Stockholm School of Economics. A number of his publications concern property rights, distributional conflict, and the theory of the firm.

Series Foreword

This book is part of the CESifo Seminar Series. The series aims to cover topical policy issues in economics from a largely European perspective. The books in this series are the products of the papers and intensive debates that took place during the seminars hosted by CESifo, an international research network of renowned economists organized jointly by the Center for Economic Studies at Ludwig-Maximilians University, Munich, and the Ifo Institute for Economic Research. All publications in this series have been carefully selected and refereed by members of the CESifo research network.

Hans-Werner Sinn

Preface

Even a cursory look at countries' development around the world reveals a picture of growth dynamics in recent decades that are almost unprecedented in their overall pace. Moreover it reveals a performance heterogeneity among these countries that is astounding. This picture easily eludes standard conclusions of investment-induced growth theories and establishes what could be called the development puzzle.

In recent search for explanations and sources of these growth dynamics, researchers have tended to view norms and institutional arrangements, alongside with factor accumulation, as important causal elements. The authors contributing to this book take this line of research even further, focusing their theoretical and empirical work on specific institutions and norms and exploring their implications for economic efficiency and growth performance. This book is consequently meant as a reader both for researchers and for policy makers who are puzzled by the divergence of countries' performance, and who seek for deeper explanations for the divergence of performance measures.

In the process of producing this book we accumulated considerable debt both to persons and to institutions, and we would like to thank them. Nina Bonge handled the manuscript speedily, reliably, and with great care. We would also like to thank Roisin Hearn, Marko Köthenbürger, Toke Aidt, Arye Hillman, Enrico Spolaore, and the referees of this book for their comments and encouragement throughout. We are very grateful to Dana Andrus, John Covell, and Elizabeth Murry at The MIT Press for their safe guidance through the production process. Last, but not least, we would like to thank CESifo and its staff for providing the financial support and human resources for bringing

together this group of researchers, and for creating a fruitful and stim-
ulating environment.

Beer-Sheva and Berlin, July 2006
Mark Gradstein
Kai A. Konrad

List of Tables

List of Figures

I

Setting the Stage

1   The Development Puzzle

Mark Gradstein and
Kai A. Konrad

1.1   Background

Beginning with the second half of the twentieth century, the average growth of income per capita in the world, at the annual rate of almost 2.5 percent, has been unprecedented by historical standards. In particular, economic growth has been much more rapid than in the United States in the half century between the Reconstruction and World War I (Maddison 2001). This overall extraordinary performance, however, hides a considerable variation in growth rates across countries as pointed out in several studies (e.g., see Pritchett 1997; Easterly and Levine 1997; Ndulu and O'Connell 1999). Thus the average growth rate of income per capita in East Asia and the Pacific in the period 1960 to 2004 was a remarkable 4.9 percent; among OECD countries it was 2.7 percent, but just about 0.5% in sub-Saharan Africa.[1] The examples of rapidly developing Korea and Taiwan since 1960s, the growth spurts in China since the late 1970s, and more recently, India, show that the adage "the rich (countries) stay rich, while the poor stay poor," need not hold in the absolute; staying behind is not a sealed fate. Yet the persistent underdevelopment in much of the world is troubling. Further Artadi and Sala-i-Martin (2003) document that the disappointing growth performance of sub-Saharan Africa is accompanied by an increase in inequality, and Kraay (2006) shows that economic growth is the most direct route out of poverty. Low growth rates therefore directly translate into desperate human conditions: extreme poverty and hunger, high infant mortality and low life expectancy, poor infrastructure and inability to cope with natural disasters, devastating conflicts and civil wars that inflict death and sow despair. These twin observations—an increasing pace of aggregate development and the unequal incidence of its benefits across countries and regions of the world—constitute some of the fascinating and pressing puzzles researchers have tried to grapple with.

When trying to understand the causes of development, the neoclassical economists of the post–World War II period traditionally looked for narrowly defined "economic" factors such as the accumulation of physical factors and resource endowments. Investment, in particular, was viewed as a key factor in boosting economic growth. Then there came the recognition that with diminishing returns to scale in production, the neoclassical view cannot possibly explain the existing gross differences in economic performance. This led to Solow's emphasis of the importance of technological progress as a source of long-run growth. Assuming free flows of technology, however, this theory has a problem in explaining persistent—and even growing—differences in growth performance across countries. Consequently the endogenous growth theories of the 1980s have drawn attention to the process of technological advance and of human capital accumulation. This literature focused on spillover effects pertinent to knowledge acquisition, and the resulting allocation inefficiencies were viewed as obstacles to development. Policies in the relevant areas of education, research, and innovation have become to be considered the means to achieving adequate levels of growth and development. Even more recently the profession seems to have recognized ever more acutely that political, social, geographical, and even historical factors cannot be ignored when trying to make sense of development. These factors, while potentially having an independent effect, are also likely to play an important role in shaping the accumulation of the production factors deemed crucial for development in the earlier literature. The shift in emphasis was also partly motivated by multiple country experiences that have been inconsistent with the established growth paradigms. For instance, achievements in the area of education are in themselves insufficient to guarantee economic progress, and the impact of human capital investment arguably depends on other institutional aspects—as is evidenced by the performance of east European countries under the communist regime. Similarly the relationship between actual physical investment and economic outcomes need not be a very close one, and it depends on the type of investment and the environment in which it takes place (Artadi and Sala-i-Martin 2003).

The recent report on *Prospects for the Global Economy* by the World Bank (2005) also confirms the picture according to which the high-income countries outperformed, whereas most developing countries, and in particular, sub-Saharan Africa, strongly underperformed in the 80th and 90th in terms of their growth rates compared to GDP growth rates in the world. The data show that this trend has reversed in the first half of the current decade, and the report's authors expect that developing countries will outperform the high-income countries and conjecture that even sub-Saharan Africa will have an annual growth of GDP of 1.6 percent. However, their account of the income distribution draws a gloomy picture of the current state of the world (see table 1.1).

This cursory review illustrates the frustrations of empirical growth analyses based on estimating a neoclassical production function— which tends to leave much of growth performance across countries unexplained by the standard production factors. This major challenge has haunted the researchers of development ever since the issue came to grab their attention. While the large unexplained, "residual" variance has been recognized since Solow's seminal work, its traditional interpretation tended to focus on technology and innovation. More recently some scholars—guided by the insights of economic historians (see North 1990)—have instilled in the residual a much broader interpretation as being related to a society's institutional quality (see Acemoglu et al. 2002; Hall and Jones 1999). In the evolution of developmental thought, political factors came to be seen as one of the factors reflecting and shaping this quality. In this view, political and economic forces interact in determining the societal outcomes.[2] In a related vein, rich models of political economy and their application to development-related issues such as corruption, comparative politics, the size, composition and structure of government have emerged from this research program. They allowed opening the black box of policies formation and how it is affected by the nature of political and social institutions. The study of the role of political institutions in the development process has been picking up momentum in recent years addressing issues such as the nexus of democracy, inequality, and growth; political obstacles to development-enhancing policies; weak institutions and corruption; social capital; political instability; and the political economy of trade openness. In many cases this was not just a reflection of academic curiosity but a response to and an interpretation of pressing developmental issues.

The chapters in this volume address some of the issues above. While by all means not exhaustive of the vast area of research in the political economy of development, they make a representative sample of topics

Table 1.1
Regional breakdown of poverty in developing countries

| | Millions of people living on | | | | | |
| | Less than $1 per day | | | Less than $2 per day | | |
Region	1990	2002	2015	1990	2002	2015
East Asia and Pacific China	472	21	14	1116	748	260
China	*375*	*180*	*11*	*825*	*533*	*181*
Rest of East Asia and Pacific	*97*	*34*	*2*	*292*	*215*	*78*
Europe and Central Asia	2	10	4	23	76	39
Latin America and Caribbean	49	42	29	125	119	106
Middle East and North Africa	6	5	3	51	61	40
South Asia	462	437	232	958	1091	955
Sub-Saharan Africa	227	303	336	382	516	592
Total	**1218**	**1011**	**617**	**2654**	**2611**	**1993**
Excluding China	*844*	*831*	*606*	*1829*	*2078*	*1811*

| | Percentage of population living on | | | | | |
| | Less than $1 per day | | | Less than $2 per day | | |
Region	1990	2002	2015	1990	2002	2015
East Asia and Pacific China	29.6	14.9	0.9	69.9	40.7	12.7
China	*33*	*46.6*	*1.2*	*72.6*	*41.6*	*13.1*
Rest of East Asia and Pacific	*21.1*	*10.8*	*0.4*	*63.2*	*38.6*	*11.9*
Europe and Central Asia	0.5	3.6	0.4	4.9	16.1	8.2
Latin America and Caribbean	11.3	9.5	6.9	28.4	22.6	17.2
Middle East and North Africa	2.3	2.4	0.9	21.4	19.8	10.4
South Asia	41.3	31.3	12.8	85.5	77.8	56.7
Sub-Saharan Africa	44.6	46.4	38.4	75	74.9	67.1
Total	**27.9**	**21.1**	**10.2**	**60.8**	**49.9**	**32.8**
Excluding China	*26.1*	*22.5*	*12.9*	*56.6*	*52.6*	*38.6*

Source: World Bank, 2005, Prospects for the Global Economy 2006: Economic Implications of Migration and Remittances, p. 9.

and approaches that are used in the literature. In particular, an exciting feature of much of the recent work is the methodological variety employed to seriously tackle and thoroughly understand the interaction between political, social, institutional, and economic factors in development. Thus the methodologies employed in the chapters range from carefully formulated mathematical models to statistical analyses of cross-country and panel data, from survey data analyses to subtly designed randomized policy experiments. This wealth of sometimes complementary, sometimes competing approaches should, so we hope, contribute to our better understanding of this complex area of research.

Many features of a society can possibly be included as ultimate determinants of economic development; among them, a few can be singled out as being of some significance: the *structure of governance*, the *quality of a country's governing bodies, including the degree of property rights protection*, and the *social norms* that govern collective decision making. The analyses in this book contribute precisely to these three features, which we will now discuss in some more detail. The focus on these areas implies, inter alia, that other equally important issues within the general domain of the political economy of development remain outside the scope of this volume.

1.2 Book Themes and Organization

Governance Structure

The division of responsibilities among various levels of government is an important issue, both in developed and developing countries, and as such this issue has received much attention in the literature. Early work, driven by Tiebout's (1956) insights and motivated primarily by intergovernmental relationship in industrialized countries, focused on the potential advantages of decentralized government structure as the means to allow local preferences to express themselves (Oates 1972). Riker (1964) emphasised the importance of clearly delineated responsibilities. More recent work on the political economy of federalism considers whether a federal structure increases or decreases the scope for making politicians accountable for their policy decisions, and how federal structures affect the process of evaluation and selection of politicians with respect to their competence or ability. Intuitively, for instance, competition among local communities is viewed as leading to superior decision making relative to centralized government, which could be subject to pressures by interest groups and thus state capture. However, the theory results on accountability paint a more complex picture, and the policy recommendations that result from this literature are not clear-cut.[3]

Decentralization has been claimed more generally to be an important variable factor for improving political accountability also by political scientists (Weingast 1995; Qian and Weingast 1997), and the World Bank has routinely promoted decentralization as a desirable direction of policy reform. More recent research, however, generates a much deeper and nuanced view of the relationship between decentralization and development. Motivated by the comparison of China's economic achievements with Russia's failure, some have argued that the quality of government, namely its ability to commit, is a key factor in explaining the success of decentralization. Jin, Qian and Weingast (2005) compare China and Russia and conclude that there is a positive relationship between credible financial incentives given to the lower level governments and local economic performance. Similarly Qian and Roland (1998) attribute performance differences to weak incentives of local governments to be efficient in the centralized structure. Because many developing countries (Brazil, China, India, Russia) happen to have a federal, multiple-layer governance structure, issues of economic and political decentralization, its fiscal aspects vis-à-vis administrative control and accountability, have featured prominently in recent years.

Vertical decentralization gives some scope for uncoordinated behavior or strategic rivalry between different tiers of government, and this is a potentially important source of serious inefficiencies of federalism. This holds, in particular, in the context of developing countries that are characterized by institutions that are too weak for correcting for such incentives. Some of these problems have been highlighted, for example, by Treisman (1999a) and Cai and Treisman (2005) and Kessing, Konrad, and Kotsogiannis (2006). Many of the advantages of decentralization emerge in a theory where a benevolent government or a government directly responsive to voter's preferences is assumed. Some more recent research, focusing more narrowly on the experience of developing countries, with either weaker mechanisms for disciplining government or less benevolent government, suggests, in contrast, that decentralization may result in a "local capture" and may perform less well than a centralized government for other reasons.[4]

While theoretical debates on the advantages and deficiencies of decentralization versus central government structure has been in full swing, there have been relatively few empirical tests of the theoretical arguments.[5] Three chapters in the volume purport to fill this vacuum by dealing empirically with this issue. **Gennaioli and Rainer** (chapter 2) set to test the economic advantages of decentralization in the context of sub-Saharan Africa, focusing on the provision of public goods such as education, health, and infrastructure. Their identification strategy is based on using the pre-colonial degree of decentralization. They find that countries that had a more centralized government structure at that stage do better in terms of public goods provision than decentralized countries. Their interpretation of these findings is that centralization may undermine local capture and lead to better accountability.

Khemani (chapter 3) focuses on intergovernmental relationship in India and accomplishes two objectives. First, she provides an indirect test of the soft budget constraint hypothesis using a panel data of 15 Indian states. She finds that when the national government and a state government are controlled by the same party, the state tends to have a larger budget deficit than otherwise; the interpretation of this finding is that this occurs in anticipation of a future bail out. Additionally Khemani argues that relegating fiscal authority in this regard to an independent agency tends to alleviate the problem. The recent Indian experience with such an independent authority seems to support such policy.

Kremer (chapter 4) examines this same issue in the context of the Kenyan education systems. In Kenya, teachers are hired by the central government, but many other educational choices such as decisions on school constructions are made locally. Kremer finds that this system is inefficient, generating in particular an excessive school building with small classes as well as overspending on teachers at the expense of non-teacher inputs so that the resulting school fees are excessively high. He argues that the absence of alignment in incentives at the central and the local levels caused the Kenyan educational system to stagnate, despite some features which are considered as potentially enhancing its quality such as parents' ability to exercise school choice. Kremer also reports on the results of a donor intervention that helped improve the allocation of educational funds and argues that allocative distortions, not necessarily low level of spending on education, have been the main culprits behind the failures of the school system in Kenya.

Institutional Quality, Property Rights, and Appropriation

The quality of institutions, their stability, transparency, predictability, enforceability of rules, and the ability to commit are also likely to influence—directly or indirectly—economic performance, and the recognition of its importance for development came to the fore in some recent writings.[6] A key aspect in this context is corruption and a large research program evaluates the direct and indirect consequences of corruption (Aidt 2003), typically based on data that describe corruption as a subjectively assessed rather than an objectively measured variable. The effect of such corruption measures on growth is typically considered to be negative in general, and also specifically for the performance of African countries.[7]

The contribution by **Vicente** (chapter 5) considers a so far neglected cause of corruption: a country's stock of natural resources. As is well known, a country's natural resource wealth may retard rather than promote economic development. Sachs and Warner (1997) report a negative and robust correlation between GDP growth and natural resource wealth of a country and between growth and the share of natural resource exports in GDP and these stylized facts illustrate what is sometimes called the "natural resource curse." Several explanations for this phenomenon have been discussed. Torvik (2002) and Mehlum, Moene, and Torvik (2006) emphasize the role of rent-seeking activities and the importance of the institutional setup, which explains why the natural resource curse is more likely to show up in a country with weakly developed institutions. Empirical work suggests that resource wealth may interact with the development of institutional quality.[8] Vicente constructs an analytical model of a repeated interaction between a country's elite and its population, where the former determine the level of corruption and the latter can possibly revolt. This framework enables the author to study the effect of a windfall in natural resources on corruption incentives. Vicente also presents, consistent with the model's analysis, some tentative empirical evidence on the positive relationship between natural resource windfalls and corruption.

In the context of African (laggard) development, several scholars drew our attention to the detrimental effects of violent conflict. Much of this work concentrates on the conflict between various social groups for political leadership and how it can potentially be mitigated.[9] The impacts of social pressure, peer groups, religious and ethnic factors in shaping political identities and thereby economic outcomes, have increasingly come into play in recent research.[10]

In this context, causal factors of violent conflicts have attracted researchers' attention (Collier and Hoeffler 2004).[11] The relationship between political stability and the governmental incentives to promote economic prosperity and growth is most likely a key issue for understanding the poor growth performance of many developing countries. Olson (1993) and McGuire and Olson (1996) compared the incentives of a political leader to use current revenue for investments in public goods or to delay the extraction of rents to those of the owner of a business company. Incentives to invest are there only where there are expectations of reaping the benefits from such investment, which suggests a positive relationship between political stability and a country's economic development. However, as reported in Robinson (1999) there is a large number of dictators who were in office for a very long period of time and, at the same time, extracted revenue but disinvested in infrastructure and other public investment goods; the list of examples includes the Somoza family in Nicaragua who governed from 1937 to 1979, Ferdinand Marcos in Philippines, who governed from 1965 to 1986, the Duvaliers who ruled in Haiti from 1957 to 1981, and Mobutu who ruled in Zaire from 1965 to 1997. These cases either falsify the theory or show that the observed office duration of country leaders is a poor indicator of political stability. Konrad (2002) considers a theoretical explanation whereby the effort required to fend off contenders and the resulting expected tenure are endogenous to country leaders' investments in the development of his country. Country leaders typically have an incumbency advantage when competing with rival contenders, and the size of this incumbency advantage may determine a certain upper prosperity threshold that may not be surpassed for an incumbent leader to stay in office. Accordingly, institutions that determine the size of incumbency advantages turn out to be key factors for economic development.

Two contributions in this volume relate to appropriation conflict. As discussed, empirically, poor countries seem to be the countries in which property rights conflict between private investors and government representatives is most pronounced. **McBride and Skaperdas** (chapter 6) provide an important explanation why this is a consequence of countries' income levels. They show how violent conflict is more likely to emerge in low-income countries. If the future is bright and resourceful compared to the present situation, it may be valuable for opponents to avoid enduring conflict and to fight things out in the present. Accordingly, violent conflict is more likely to emerge in countries with rival political forces when the national income of the country is still low. In richer countries, the cost of conflicts that occur today is higher, and the cost is less likely to be justified by the savings in future, enduring conflict.

The second contribution focuses on the potential appropriation conflict between government officials and agents in the private sector. Work that traces back at least to the analyses on the expropriation waves in the 1960s and 1970s drew attention to the possible relationship between an investor's chances to recover at least a major share in the returns in his investment and his unwillingness to undertake the investment if he cannot expect to recover a reasonable return.[12] The holdup problem in foreign direct investment, by which the ex post incentives of the host government to extract rents or to expropriate deter the investor to make use of investment opportunities that could generate considerable rents, has attracted considerable interest in the literature.[13] To a large extent this literature essentially assumes that it is up to the decision of the government whether an investor can keep the returns on his investment, or whether these are partially or fully confiscated. A central question is then what are the conditions under which repeated interaction—for instance, in terms of repeated decisions about the re-investment of depreciated capital—can sustain tacit collusion. Indeed, as becomes clear from considering particular cases and going into the deeper structure of expropriation cases, it turns out that this view is probably too simplistic. An extensive body of work shows that appropriation and the allocation of assets or returns of assets is the outcome of a conflict between different parties.[14]

Wärneryd (chapter 7) uncovers an important information aspect in such appropriation conflicts that feeds back on individuals' investment incentives and particularly applies to developing countries. An investor who anticipates that he must defend the returns of his investment against shareholders or other stakeholders and who can increase the uncertainty about the actual value of the returns of his investment will benefit from pursuing such a policy, even if this policy reduces the expected gross returns of his investment. This trade-off emerges only if the investor has to fight for protecting the returns of his investment from appropriation. Hence the trade-off emerges only in states in which investors are not well protected from attempts to confiscate the investment returns.

Norms and Culture

Social characteristics such as social norms, identity, and trust have for some time featured as relevant for economic performance.[15] More recent literature documents this empirically, identifying robust economic effects of these "softer" factors.[16] Two chapters in this volume tackle these effects from different perspectives.

Chen (chapter 8) focuses on the relationship between religious intensity and social violence. Using the differential effect of the Indonesian financial crisis across regions as an identifying variable, he illustrates an increase in both, depending on the region's vulnerability. He then goes on to argue for a causal effect from religiosity to social violence. In other words, the intensity of religious sentiments seems to have increased in Indonesia in response to the financial crisis and, in turn, to have caused an increase in social violence. The availability of social insurance acted, however, to mitigate this effect. One of the chapter's conclusions therefore is that people tend to resort to deeper religious identification and religious extremism in times of crisis, especially in the absence of a well-organized social insurance scheme.

Shayo (chapter 9) sets to study the determinants of identification with one's nation and its effects on attitudes toward redistribution using the data from several surveys of individual attitudes in most of the world's countries. He finds that income is negatively related to the intensity of such identification, so the poor are more likely to identify with the nation than the rich. Moreover national identification reduces the support for income redistribution. The chapter provides one argument why redistributional demands by the poor are often quite limited: while fiscal considerations would appear to cause an increase in these demands, social dimensions seem to moderate them.

The Organization of the Volume

While the issues above form just a relatively small subset of the relationship between political, social and economic factors in development, each constitutes an important research area with well advanced literature both theoretical and empirical. The growing data availability both at a macro, country level and at a micro level of individual or small aggregate units has led to a mounting insistence on measurability of theoretical concepts and on making them ever more operational. Consequently the volume is organized around the themes reviewed above. It begins with the section on governance structure (Gennaioli and Rainer, Khemani, and Kremer), continues with the section on institutional quality and property rights (Vicente, McBride and Skaperdas, and Wärneryd), and concludes with the section on social and cultural norms as the main driving forces for development (Chen and Shayo).

The issues being vast and the literature evolving fast, it is impossible to expect from a volume like this to do full justice to the existing body of work and the variety of approaches pursued, all the more to solve the development puzzle. A more modest aim is to stimulate a discussion and, perhaps, provide a fertile ground for further work. Indeed our hope is that this collection will be useful both for continuing academic efforts in the area of economic development as well as to its many dedicated practitioners.

Notes

1. Calculations based on World Development Indicators.

2. See Acemoglu (2005) for an example of this approach.

3. For instance, Besley and Case (1995), Seabright (1996), Hendriks and Lockwood (2005).

4. See Bardhan and Mookherjee (2006), Blanchard and Shleifer (2001), Treisman (1999b, 2000a).

5. See, for instance, Kessing, Konrad, and Kotsogiannis (2007) for a discussion and empirical evidence regarding the detrimental role of vertical decentralization for countries' ability to attract foreign direct investment.

6. For instance, Acemoglu et al. (2002), Hall and Jones (1999), and Rodrik et al. (2004).

7. See Mauro (1995) for an example of the former, and Gyimah-Brempong (2002) for the latter. Gyimah-Brempong (2002) estimates the direct and indirect effect of an increase in the corruption index by one unit to cause a reduction in the growth rates of GDP in a large set of African countries by three quarter to 0.9 percentage points per year.

8. Sala-i-Martin and Subramanian (2003) and Bulte, Damania, and Deacon (2003).

9. Easterly and Levine (1997), Collier (2000), and Collier and Hoeffler (2004).

10. Akerlof and Kranton (2000), Alesina et al. (1999), Barro and McCleary (2003).

11. A key insight emerging from this work is that the relationship between conflict and fractionalization is unlikely to be monotonic, or even linear (Collier 2001). Two large ethnic groups may struggle much more forcefully with each other than a much more fractionalized country.

12. Andersson (1991) contains an empirical account on confiscatory taxation and nationalization.

13. Examples are Eaton and Gersovitz (1983), Cole and English (1991), and Thomas and Worrall (1994).

14. For instance, Grossman and Kim (1995), Hirshleifer (1995), Müller and Wärneryd (2001), and Skaperdas (1992, 2003).

15. See Adelman and Morris (1967).

16. Thus Zak and Knack (2001) find that trust enhances growth prospects; Easterly and Levine (1997) emphasize the significance of ethnic cleavages in explaining poor economic performance of African countries; Hall and Jones (1999) develop measures of social infrastructure that they find extremely relevant for economic growth across countries.

References

Acemoglu, D. 2005. *Modelling inefficient institutions*, mimeo.

Acemoglu, D., S. Johnson, and J. Robinson. 2002. Reversal of fortune: Geography and institutions in the making of the modern world distribution. *Quarterly Journal of Economics* 117(4): 1231–94.

Adelman, I., and C. T. Morris. 1967. *Society, Politics and Economic Development: A Quantitative Approach*, 2nd ed. Baltimore: Johns Hopkins Press.

Aidt, T. S. 2003. Economic analysis of corruption: A survey. *Economic Journal* 113(491): F632–F652.

Akerlof, G. A., and R. E. Kranton. 2000. Economics and identity. *Quarterly Journal of Economics* 115(3): 715–53.

Alesina, A., R. Baqir, and W. Easterly. 1999. Public goods and ethnic divisions. *Quarterly Journal of Economics* 114(4): 1243–84.

Andersson, T. 1991. *Multinational Investment in Developing Countries: A Study of Taxation and Nationalization*. London: Routledge.

Artadi, E. V., and X. Sala-i-Martin. 2003. The economic tragedy of the XXth century: Growth in Africa. NBER Working Paper 9865.

Bardhan, P., and D. Mookherjee. 2006. Decentralization and accountability in infrastructure delivery in developing countries. *Economic Journal* 116: 101–27.

Barro, R. J., and R. M. McCleary. 2003. Religion and economic growth. *American Sociological Review* 68(5): 760–81.

Besley, T. J., and A. C. Case. 1995. Incumbent behavior: Vote-seeking, tax-setting, and yardstick competition. *American Economic Review* 85(1): 25–45.

Blanchard, O., and A. Shleifer. 2001. Federalism with and without political centralization: China vs. Russia. *IMF Staff Paper* 48 (special issue): 171–79.

Bulte, E. H., R. Damania, and R. T. Deacon. 2003. Resource abundance, poverty and development. University of California at Santa Barbara, Economics Working Paper 1173.

Cai, H. B., and D. Treisman. 2005. Does competition for capital discipline governments? Decentralization, globalization and public policy. *American Economic Review* 95(3): 817–30.

Cole, H. L., and W. B. English. 1991. Expropriation and direct investment. *Journal of International Economics* 30(3–4): 201–27.

Collier, P. 2000. Ethnicity, politics and economic performance. *Economics and Politics* 12(3): 225–45.

Collier, P. 2001. Implications of ethnic diversity. *Economic Policy* 16(32): 127–55.

Collier, P., and A. Hoeffler. 2004. Greed and grievance in civil war. *Oxford Economic Papers* 56(4): 563–95.

Easterly, W., and R. Levine. 1997. Growth tragedy: Policies and ethnic divisions. *Quarterly Journal of Economics* 112(4): 1203–50.

Eaton, J., and M. Gersovitz. 1983. Country risk, economic aspects. In R. J. Herring, ed., *Managing International Risk*. Cambridge: Cambridge University Press, pp. 75–108.

Grossman, H. I., and M. Kim. 1995. Swords or plowshares? A theory of the security of claims to property. *Journal of Political Economy* 103(6): 1275–88.

Gyimah-Brempong, K. 2002. Corruption, economic growth, and income inequality in Africa. *Economics of Governance* 3(3): 183–209.

Hall, R. E., and C. I. Jones. 1999. Why do some countries produce so much more output per worker than others? *Quarterly Journal of Economics* 114(1): 83–116.

Hendriks, J., and B. Lockwood. 2005. Decentralization and electoral accountability: Incentives, separation, and voter welfare. Warwick Economic Research Paper 729.

Hirshleifer, J. 1995. Anarchy and its breakdown. *Journal of Political Economy* 103(1): 26–52.

Jin, H., Y. Quian, and B. R. Weingast. 2005. Regional decentralization and fiscal incentives: Federalism, Chinese style. *Journal of Public Economics* 89(9–10): 1719–42.

Kessing, S., K. A. Konrad, and C. Kotsogiannis. 2006. Federal tax autonomy and the limits of cooperation. *Journal of Urban Economics* 59(2): 317–29.

Kessing, S., K. A. Konrad, and C. Kotsogiannis. 2007. Foreign direct investment and the dark side of decentralization. *Economic Policy* 43: 7–70.

Konrad, K. A. 2002. Investment in the absence of property rights; the role of incumbency advantages. *European Economic Review* 46(8): 1521–37.

Kraay, A. 2006. When is growth pro-poor? Evidence from a cross-section of countries. *Journal of Development Economics* 80: 198–227.

Maddison, A. 2001. *The World Economy: A Millennial Perspective*. OECD Development Center, Paris.

Mauro, P. 1995. Corruption and growth. *Quarterly Journal of Economics* 110(3): 681–712.

McGuire, M. C., and M. Olson, Jr. 1996. The economics of autocracy and majority rule. *Journal of Economic Literature* 34(1): 72–96.

Mehlum, H., K. Moene, and R. Torvik. 2006. *Institutions and the resource curse. Economic Journal* 116: 1–20.

Müller, H., and K. Wärneryd. 2001. Inside versus outside ownership: A political theory of the firm. *RAND Journal of Economics* 32(3): 527–41.

Ndulu, B. J., and S. A. O'Connell. 1999. Governance and growth in sub-Saharan Africa. *Journal of Economic Perspectives* 13(3): 41–66.

North, D. C. 1990. *Institutions, Institutional Change and Economic Performance*. Cambridge: Cambridge University Press.

Oates, W. 1972. *Fiscal Federalism*. London: Harcourt Brace Jovanovich.

Olson, M. 1993. Dictatorship, democracy, and development. *American Political Science Review* 87(3): 567–76.

Pritchett, L. 1997. Divergence, big time. *Journal of Economic Perspectives* 11(3): 3–17.

Qian, Y., and B. R. Weingast. 1997. Federalism as a commitment to preserving market incentives. *Journal of Economic Perspectives* 11(4): 83–92.

Qian, Y., and G. Roland. 1998. Federalism and a soft budget constraint. *American Economic Review* 88(5): 1143–62.

Riker, W. 1964. *Federalism*. Boston: Little.

Robinson, J. A. 1999. When is a state predatory? CES Working Paper 178.

Rodrik, D., A. Subramanian, and F. Trebbi. 2004. Institutions rule: The primacy of institutions over geography and integration in economic development. *Journal of Economic Growth* 9(2): 131–65.

Sachs, J. D., and A. M. Warner. 1997. *Natural Resource Abundance and Economic Growth*. Cambridge: Center for International Development and Harvard Institute of Development.

Sala-i-Martin, X., and A. Subramanian. 2003. Addressing the natural resource curse: An illustration from Nigeria. NBER Working Paper W9804.

Seabright, P. 1996. Accountability and decentralization in government: An incomplete contracts model. *European Economic Review* 40(1): 61–91.

Skaperdas, S. 1992. Cooperation, conflict and power in the absence of property rights. *American Economic Review* 82(4): 720–39.

Skaperdas, S. 2003. Restraining the genuine homo economicus: Why the economy cannot be divorced from its governance. *Economics and Politics* 15(2): 135–62.

Thomas, J., and T. Worrall. 1994. Foreign direct investment and the risk of expropriation. *Review of Economic Studies* 61(1): 81–108.

Tiebout, C. M. 1956. A pure theory of local expenditures. *Journal of Political Economy* 64(5): 416–24.

Torvik, R. 2002. Natural resources, rent seeking and welfare. *Journal of Development Economics* 67(2): 455–70.

Treisman, D. 1999a. Russia's tax crisis: Explaining falling revenues in a transitional economy. *Economics and Politics* 11(2): 145–69.

Treisman, D. 1999b. Political decentralization and economic reform: A game theoretic analysis. *American Journal of Political Science* 43(2): 488–517.

Treisman, D. 2000. *Decentralization and the quality of government.* Mimeo.

Weingast, B. R. 1995. The economic role of political institutions: Market-preserving federalism and economic development. *Journal of Law, Economics and Organization* 11(1): 1–31.

World Bank. 2005. *Prospects for the Global Economy 2006: Economic Implications of Migration and Remittances.* Washington: World Bank.

Zak, P. J., and S. Knack. 2001. Trust and Growth. *Economic Journal* 111(470): 295–321.

II

Governance Structure

2

Precolonial Centralization and Institutional Quality in Africa

Nicola Gennaioli and Ilia Rainer

2.1 Introduction

Sub-Saharan Africa is populated by several hundreds ethnic groups. Before the large-scale colonization undertaken by European powers toward the end of the nineteenth century, those groups varied tremendously in their political institutions. Colonial powers, and later the international community, superimposed on top of these precolonial institutions new state organizations borrowed from the Western historical experience that are identified with today's African countries. Yet these developments did not prevent precolonial institutions to exert a profound influence across the African continent. Political scientists noticed the presence of a dual authority structure in Africa, where central governments (be they colonial or independent) had to confront with the power of precolonial leaders (e.g., Sklar 1993; Mamdani 1996; Boone 2003). More specifically, historians document that precolonial institutions heavily shaped the quality of government, and hence the success of modernization efforts, in colonial and postcolonial Africa (e.g., Abubakar 1980; Falola 1999). Anthropologists and historians stress that the main distinction in Africa is that between more and less centralized precolonial political systems (Fortes and Evans-Pritchard 1940) and report that African ethnic groups characterized by more centralized institutions were better able to modernize (e.g., Low 1965; Pratt 1965; Schapera 1970).

In recent years we undertook a research project aimed at evaluating, theoretically and empirically, the impact of precolonial institutions on the performance of colonial and postcolonial African countries. In our earlier paper, "The Modern Impact of Precolonial Centralization in Africa" (Gennaioli and Rainer 2005), we used an anthropological dataset to measure the degree of precolonial political centralization of African ethnic groups. We then built a country-level index of precolonial centralization and documented that African countries with a larger share of population belonging to ethnic groups with centralized (rather than fragmented) precolonial institutions display superior capacity to provide public goods such as health, education, and infrastructure between 1960 and 2002. Furthermore our analysis showed that a plausible explanation for this finding lies in the greater ability of centralized systems to hold local elites accountable. Such accountability led local elites to foster the implementation of public policies aimed at expanding productive inputs such as health, education, and infrastructure.

In this chapter we use the index of precolonial centralization we developed in Gennaioli and Rainer (2005) but ask a different question. Our goal here is to assess whether, in addition to fostering the provision of basic public goods, precolonial centralization also helped African governments to create an institutional environment supportive of private sector initiative. There is a near consensus in economics around the notion that market friendly institutions are of fundamental importance for economic development (Smith 1776; North 1981; Acemoglu et al. 2001). In addition a longstanding intellectual tradition views the extent of centralization as a crucial determinant of institutional quality.

The argument that decentralization should improve institutional quality evokes the idea that competition among different jurisdictions should enhance the quality of government (Tiebout 1956). Local officials who overtax or expropriate will lose their residents to other districts. Also greater monitoring ability on the part of voters may increase political accountability under decentralization (Besley and Case 1995). Conversely, by giving enormous power to an arbitrary or corrupt government, centralization is likely to foster expropriation. Hence, according to this view, decentralized precolonial systems should have led to higher institutional quality. A different strand of theories holds instead that centralization boosts the quality of government (Riker 1964). Localism may be a threat to an effective rule of law, which requires a great deal of coordination among jurisdictions (Oates 1972). Not to mention the possibility that local politics may easily be captured by local regressive interests (Blanchard and Shleifer 2001). According to this view, the accountability mechanisms (Gennaioli and Rainer 2005) of centralized precolonial systems should have improved institutional quality by restraining the arbitrariness of local elites.

To give a concrete example, consider the case of corruption. Insofar as corruption is an illegal form of taxation, it represents a violation of property rights and a threat to the private sector.[1] On the role of centralization in the control of corruption, Shleifer and Vishny (1993) offer an illuminating discussion. They argue that under centralization the level of corruption is determined by the center, who maximizes joint profits from bribe collection. Under decentralization, instead, each of the relevant authorities independently sets its level of bribes to maximize own profits while taking the others' bribes as given.

As a result, under centralization, the level of corruption is positive, and it equals the monopoly solution. Under decentralization, the level of corruption depends on the interaction among different authorities. For example, if in Tiebout fashion different authorities set bribes competitively, then corruption is zero. Unfortunately, this competitive mechanism is unlikely to work in many real world circumstances. For instance, in Africa many quasi-independent authorities have the ability to stop a project, and may use this power to set bribes shielded from competitive forces (Klitgaard 1990). Shleifer and Vishny (1993) argue that in this situation—as in a standard problem of double marginalization—the uncoordinated bribe taking by independent monopolists enhances the level of bribes to such an extent that the presence of a centralized authority reduces corruption. The same reasoning, which can easily be extended to other property rights' violations, may help explain the role of precolonial centralization in Africa. Being so weak, the African national governments are unable to penalize provincial authorities running their own expropriation rackets. As a result centralized precolonial institutions could have helped reduce expropriation and improve institutional quality by enforcing collusion among multiple authorities.

Our empirical results are indeed consistent with this view and show that precolonial centralization helped enhance institutional quality. We measure institutional quality using the indexes of Control of Corruption and Rule of Law. The Control of Corruption index measures the exercise of public power for private gain, while the index of Rule of Law summarizes the quality of contract enforcement, the police and the courts as well as the likelihood of crime and violence. Overall, these measures reflect the key institutional dimensions required for the proper working of a private economy.

We find that African countries where a larger share of the population belongs to ethnic groups with centralized (rather than fragmented) precolonial institutions have lower corruption and better rule of law. Our results are very robust to the two main alternative explanations of our finding. We control for proxies capturing the view that centralized ethnic groups were just economically more advanced and thus more effective—regardless of centralization—at dealing with government failures. But we also control for proxies capturing the view that only colonial or postcolonial national institutions mattered, while precolonial centralization only indirectly affected institutional quality. The robustness of our results points, in line with historical accounts, to a direct beneficial effect of precolonial centralization on institutional quality in Africa. This suggests that precolonial institutions are essential to explain the performance of former colonies. Our results also contribute to the empirical literature on centralization and institutional quality (Fisman and Gatti 2002; Treisman 2000, 2003) and suggest that centralization can lead to better government when unaccountable local elites capture local politics for private gain.

The chapter is organized as follows: Section 2.2 reviews the historical evidence on the role of precolonial centralization in Africa. Section 2.3 summarizes our earlier findings on the modern impact of precolonial centralization in Africa (see Gennaioli and Rainer 2005). Section 2.4 presents the new empirical results of the current chapter. Section 2.5 concludes.

2.2 Historical Background

As hinted above, historians document that African precolonial institutions shaped modernization in Africa, thanks to their continuity in the periphery and especially in rural areas. Such continuity dates back to the end of the nineteenth century, when the massive European colonization of Africa began, and emerges from historical accounts of Angola (e.g., White 1959), Nigeria (e.g., Abubakar 1980), Botswana (e.g., Schapera 1970), Lesotho (Ashton 1967), West Africa (Boone 2003), and of sub-Saharan Africa more generally (Mamdani 1996). Because of the paucity of European officers on African soil, colonialists sought the cooperation of traditional chiefs to administer the colonies more effectively (Low 1965). But precolonial institutions continued to exert an important role also in postcolonial Africa (e.g., Van Rouveroy van Nieuwaal 1987; Herbst 2000).[2]

The history of Uganda provides a good illustration of the role of precolonial institutions during the colonial period. Uganda was colonized by England between 1890 and 1910. The British understood the importance of traditional chiefs and heavily relied on them for building roads, organizing schools, improving sanitation, and many other activities (Pratt 1965). The British administrative personnel never spread below the district commissioner and his assistants. Beneath them a purely African infrastructure was employed and reliance was placed almost entirely on hierarchies of African chiefs (Low 1965).

The British dealt with centralized groups by signing agreements with native authorities who accepted to pay tribute to the British administration. In exchange, their indigenous system of government was upheld. For example, the Kabaka (traditional king) and his ministers remained at the top of the Ganda hierarchy of government, which continued to administer the kingdom of Buganda. A similar strategy was followed in the kingdoms of Bunyoro, Ankole, Toro, and Busoga. In traditionally fragmented districts the British yielded local power to appointed chiefs, selected from men of local prestige and power (clan heads, village headmen). Such chiefs were the direct subordinates of the colonial administration. Hence during the colonial period the administration of local affairs reflected the precolonial patterns: more centralized in areas inhabited by centralized groups, more fragmented in areas inhabited by fragmented groups.

Historians forcefully stress the beneficial role played by precolonial centralization in colonial Uganda for the introduction of new agricultural technologies (Richards 1960; Ehrlich 1965), religion and education (Low 1965), and health improvements (Pratt 1965). The evidence on centralized groups contrasts with that on fragmented ones. In his study of the Lango, a fragmented group from northern Uganda, Tosh (1978) notices that traditional authorities could not effectively implement reforms aimed at expanding education and raising agricultural productivity and severely distorted the administration of justice. This picture is confirmed by the history of all Ugandan fragmented groups (Low 1965; Burke 1964). Figure 2.1 and table 2.1 are taken from Gennaioli and Rainer (2005) and show, respectively, the variation of precolonial institutions within Uganda and the distribution of various public goods across Ugandan regions circa 2000. The numbers confirm the historical accounts. Areas inhabited by centralized groups such as the central and the western regions display better provision of public goods than the north of the country, inhabited by fragmented groups; the "mixed" eastern region tends to have intermediate values.

To summarize, due to their continuity, precolonial institutions crucially shaped modernization efforts in colonial Uganda. Furthermore the key dimension of precolonial institutions was the degree of their centralization, with politically centralized areas being better able to

Figure 2.1
Distribution of centralized and fragmented ethnic groups across Uganda regions

modernize than fragmented ones. The key role of precolonial centralization emerges from historical accounts of many other African countries. To mention just a few examples, Abubakar (1980) and Falola
(1999) stress the disappointing performance of native authorities
among the fragmented Ibo and Ibibio of Nigeria, while Boone (2003)
discusses the political isolation and poor performance of the fragmented Diola in Senegal.

Overall, in contrast with the economic literature on institutions (e.g.,
La Porta et al. 1999; Acemoglu et al. 2001), African history suggests
that the quality of government in colonial and postcolonial Africa did
not only depend on the institutions set up by the colonizers. Abundant
historical evidence stresses the importance of precolonial factors, in

Table 2.1
Precolonial centralization and public goods in Uganda

Region *Precolonial institutions of* *ethnic groups*	Central Central- ized	Western Central- ized	Eastern Mixed	Northern Frag- mented
Percentage of roads paved in 2002	13.4	10.3	10.9	1.3
Infant mortality in 2001 (per 1,000 live births)	71.9	97.8	89.3	105.9
Percentage of children under five years with diarrhoea in 2001	14.5	16.0	23.3	26.7
Availability of sewerage system in 2000 (% of households)	15.0	14.0	9.0	6.0
Piped water inside house in 2000 (% of households)	10.0	10.0	8.0	5.0
Availability of latrine or human waste disposal service in 2000 (% of households)	96.0	86.0	77.0	67.0
Adult literacy rate in 1997 (%)	72.0	61.0	54.0	54.0
Adequacy of facility and equipment at primary schools in 2000 (% of households satisfied)	62.0	72.0	55.0	51.0

Sources: Uganda Bureau of Statistics (1999, 2003); Uganda Bureau of Statistics and ORC Macro (2001).

particular, of the precolonial institutions of African ethnic groups. Thus, to fully understand the determinants of the quality of government in Africa, we must understand how and through which channels did precolonial centralization interact with modernization.

In order to delve into these issues, in our 2005 paper "The Modern Impact of Precolonial Centralization in Africa," we built an index of precolonial centralization and studied its association with the provision of basic public goods such as health, education, and infrastructure. The analysis aimed at understanding the effect of precolonial institutions on the ability of colonial and postcolonial African governments to implement policies directly fostering the accumulation of basic productive factors such as human and physical capital.

By focusing on measures of corruption and rule of law, our goal here is instead to study the extent to which precolonial centralization helped African countries set up an institutional infrastructure facilitating private sector transactions. Because we use the index of precolonial institutions built in our previous work, it is worth at this point rehearsing the main ingredients and results of the latter. The detour also helps us contextualize our new findings within the broader role of precolonial centralization in Africa.

2.3 "The Modern Impact of Precolonial Centralization in Africa"

The subtitles of this section summarize the building blocks of our 2005 paper, "The Modern Impact of Precolonial Centralization in Africa." We refer the interested reader to that paper for details.

The Centralization Index

We built a cross-country measure of centralization of African precolonial institutions because the lack of comparable subnational data on public goods prevents us from performing the study at the ethnic-group level. We use the *Ethnographic Atlas*, which is a database of around 60 variables describing the social, economic, and political traits of 1,270 ethnic groups around the world. The data summarize the information of a multitude of individual field-studies done by anthropologists between 1850 and 1950. Every ethnic group is pinpointed to the earliest period for which satisfactory data existed in order to avoid the acculturative effects of contacts with Europeans. In the *Ethnographic Atlas*, the "jurisdictional hierarchy" variable measures the degree of centralization of ethnic groups' precolonial polities. Using this variable, we define an ethnic group as "fragmented" or "centralized" depending on the number of jurisdictional levels transcending the local community, where more jurisdictional levels correspond to more centralized groups. Our "fragmented" category includes groups lacking any political integration above the local community such as the Tonga of Zambia, and groups such as the Alur of eastern Africa where petty chiefs rule over very small districts. Our "centralized" category comprises large kingdoms such as the Swazi in southern Africa as well as the less centralized Yoruba city-states in southern Nigeria and the Ashanti confederation in Ghana. Having classified more than 300 African ethnic groups, we matched them to the groups listed in the *Atlas Narodov Mira*, which provides the most comprehensive division of the world population into different ethnic groups. We used the countries' ethnic composition from the Soviet atlas to calculate the share of each country's non-European population belonging to centralized ethnic groups. This share represents our country-level index of precolonial political centralization, and we call it "centralization." We excluded Europeans to focus on indigenous African institutions, but their inclusion in the index does not affect our results.

The Basic Empirical Finding

The basic finding of "The Modern Impact of Precolonial Centralization in Africa" (Gennaioli and Rainer 2005) is a strong and positive association across African countries between centralization and public goods. African countries where a larger share of the population belongs to centralized (rather than fragmented) ethnic groups showed superior capacity to provide public goods such as health, education, and infrastructure between 1960 and 2002. Infant mortality and percentage of infants immunized against DPT (diphtheria, pertussis, and tetanus) represent our health outcomes, adult illiteracy rate and average school attainment are our proxy for education, and the percentage of roads paved (as a share of total roads) is our measure of infrastructure.

This empirical association does not in itself document the impact of precolonial centralization on public goods, as two alternative hypotheses may explain our finding. According to the first, centralized ethnic groups were just socioeconomically more "advanced," thus being more effective at adopting western technologies; in this view, precolonial institutions did not matter, but precolonial endowments did. The second hypothesis holds that precolonial centralization played an important but indirect role by improving colonial and postcolonial political outcomes at the national level. We extensively control in our regressions for proxies capturing these alternative hypotheses. Ethnic-group and country-level proxies capture the key attributes of socioeconomic advancement: fixity of residence, dependence on agriculture, urbanization, and population density, easiness of transportation, use of writing, technological level, use of money, and absence of slavery. As for national politics, we control for national political outcomes in the colonial and postcolonial periods. Our results are remarkably robust and point to a direct effect of precolonial centralization on public goods in Africa. In line with historical accounts, this evidence confirms the crucial role of precolonial centralization in fostering the adoption of European policies and technologies in Africa.

The next question we ask is: Why was precolonial centralization so beneficial? In line with the political economy literature on centralization and public goods provision (see Bardhan 2002), our results are inconsistent with the "central capture" view, holding that *decentralization* fosters public goods provision by *increasing* the accountability of local administrators (Tiebout 1956; Besley and Case 1995; Seabright 1996). Our findings support instead the opposite "local capture" view, holding that in developing countries democratic mechanisms often fail at the local level, leading to policy capture by local elites interested in blocking socioeconomic reforms (Riker 1964; Bardhan and Mookherjee 2000; Blanchard and Shleifer 2001).

Centralization and Accountability: A View from African Colonial History

Colonial history of Uganda supports the "local capture" view, suggesting that greater accountability of local chiefs was a crucial factor behind the success of centralized systems (Apter 1961; Burke 1964). We already discussed how in fragmented groups local chiefs behaved as tyrants, distorting public goods provision to their own advantage. In contrast, the accountability of local chiefs in centralized systems emerges from accounts on the Buganda, Bunyoro, Toro, and other centralized Ugandan groups (Apter 1961; Richards 1960; Burke 1964). Local chiefs abusing their power and blocking modernization were promptly replaced by higher traditional authorities. In the kingdom of Buganda, for instance, local chiefs were appointed by the Kabaka (the king), or by lower level administrators, and could be abruptly dismissed if the performance of their district was not satisfactory (Apter 1961; Low 1971).

Interestingly the accountability in centralized systems did not simply reflect the preference of traditional central rulers for greater provision of public goods as in Blanchard and Shleifer (2001). It was instead a product of political competition, which resulted from the process of administrators' appointment followed by the central apparatus. For example, the history of the Buganda illustrates the pervasive struggle between local power holders in order to influence the king's appointment decisions and make their way up the chiefly hierarchy. In this struggle the political support of a man (the number of his followers) was a major factor determining his power and status.[3] A man with a larger following could better influence the king through bribes or protest.[4]

Since the size of his constituency determined a man's prestige and hence his chance to be appointed, it ultimately behooved him to rule in the interest of his community (Apter 1961). In short, Buganda centralization increased competition between local power holders and enhanced their accountability to local communities (and hence the quality of government). It did so by expanding the political arena and by creating a hierarchy of chiefly offices to compete for. In contrast, abusive behavior of chiefs in Ugandan fragmented groups, such as Lango, was a direct result of the fragmented nature of local politics (Tosh 1978). This message is confirmed by the history of other African centralized groups such as the Tswana of Botswana (Schapera 1970; Wylie 1990), the Sotho of Lesotho (Ashton 1967; Breytenbach 1975), or the Swazi of Swaziland among others (Schapera 1956).

More broadly, Bates (1983, pp. 41–42) viewed the intense political competition as a general feature of traditionally centralized African societies. He also hinted at the economic benefits it could bring: "But, to win and retain political power, political aspirants must attract followers, and to do so they must offer advantages, such as the opportunity to prosper." To summarize, historians document that the greater accountability of local administrators in centralized systems was a key factor behind their success and that such accountability resulted from the stiffer political competition faced by local power holders in centralized systems, which undermined local capture, the plague of decentralization.

The Model and the Empirical Test of "Local Capture"

Having reviewed the empirical and historical evidence on the role of precolonial centralization, in "The Modern Impact of Precolonial Centralization in Africa" we scrutinize the "local capture" view. We build a model of centralization that allows us to formulate an empirical test to identify the benefits of precolonial centralization in reducing local capture.

Our model builds on two key assumptions borrowed from African colonial history. First, we assume that for providing local public goods such as education, health, and infrastructure, colonizers relied on the indigenous institutions they found upon their arrival. Second, we assume that precolonial centralization created a competition for higher office among local elites that was won by the elite with wider popular support. Under these assumptions we find that precolonial centralization leads to the formation of local pressure groups that hold local elites accountable and induce them to provide more public goods thus curing the two costs of decentralization stressed by Riker (1964): the conflict between local elites and the center or "lack of coordination" (responsible for the underprovision of public goods involving large interdistrict spillovers) and the conflict between local elites and local masses or "local tyranny" (responsible for the underprovision also of public goods without spillovers). Crucially, our model predicts that centralization benefits local communities depending on their level of social stratification. In stratified communities, where the conflict between local elites and local masses is acute, centralization boosts the provision of all public goods, that is, those with and without spillovers. In egalitarian communities, where the problem of local tyranny is small, centralization only boosts the provision of goods with large spillovers. We test these predictions by using another dimension of African ethnic groups coded in our anthropological dataset: the degree of social stratification at the local level. In line with our theory we find that for goods with large spillovers such as roads and immunization, the benefit of centralization is large in both stratified and egalitarian groups. Conversely, for education and infant mortality, centralization benefits stratified groups more than egalitarian ones. Indeed spillovers should be relatively less important for the public goods behind these outcomes (local schools and clinics).

The consistency between these results and the theoretical predictions of our model suggests that the benefits of precolonial centralization come at least in part from its ability to reduce local capture. In fact the results of the estimation of our model are hard to reconcile with the alternative hypotheses that centralized groups were simply more "advanced" or that their institutions only improved national politics.[5] Moreover, by showing that centralization not only fostered interdistrict coordination but also softened local tyranny, our results are new to the empirical literature (Fisman and Gatti 2002; Treisman 2000, 2003), which has only looked at the overall effect of centralization on public policies, without identifying the nature of its costs or benefits.

Overall, our analysis of African indigenous institutions in "The Modern Impact of Precolonial Centralization in Africa" parallels Riker's (1964) classic work on federalism. The lack of accountability in politically fragmented ethnic groups is in line with Riker's assertion that, rather than encouraging freedom, federalism may lead to local tyranny. Moreover our emphasis on the disciplining effect of interelite competition for higher office is analogous to his idea that a strong party system can improve the effectiveness of government by providing career incentives to local politicians.

Having reviewed the impact of precolonial centralization on the provision of basic inputs such as education, health, and infrastructure, we can now accomplish the main goal of the chapter, which is to study the impact of precolonial centralization on institutional quality.

2.4 Precolonial Centralization and Institutional Quality

Our country-level measure of precolonial centralization is the Centralization index developed in Gennaioli and Rainer (2005) for 42 countries in sub-Saharan Africa. Our country-level measures of institutional quality are the indexes of Control of Corruption and Rule of Law constructed by Kaufmann, Kraay, and Mastruzzi (2005). These indexes are based on dozens of individual variables measuring perceptions of governance and drawn from several separate data sources. The Control of Corruption index measures perception of corruption defined as the exercise of public power for private gain. It incorporates information on the frequency of "additional payments to get things done" and more generally reflects the effects of corruption on business environment. The index of Rule of Law measures the extent to which agents have confidence in and abide by the rules of society. It includes perceptions of the incidence of crime, effectiveness of the judiciary, and the enforceability of contracts. More generally, it reflects the government's ability to protect property rights and establish fair and predictable rules for private transactions. Both indexes are scaled between −2.5 and +2.5, with higher scores corresponding to better outcomes.

We compute the average values of the two indexes for the entire 1996 to 2004 period for which the data are available and use these values as dependent variables in our analysis. Tables A2.1 and A2.2 show summary statistics and pairwise correlations between Centralization and our controls. Our basic regression specification is

$$Y_i = \alpha_0 + \alpha_1 * Centralization_i + \varepsilon_i.$$

Y_i is one of our institutional measures in country i and $Centralization_i$ is the value of Centralization for that country. Parameter α_1 captures the association between precolonial centralization and institutional quality.

Table 2.2
Precolonial centralization and institutional quality

	Control of corruption in 1996–2004	Rule of law in 1996–2004
	(1)	(2)
Centralization	0.593***	0.659**
	(0.205)	(0.246)
Constant	−1.009***	−1.11***
	(0.113)	(0.147)
Observations	42	42
R^2	0.16	0.15

Notes: (1) OLS estimations. (2) Robust standard errors are shown in parentheses. *** denotes significance at the 1 percent level, ** at the 5 percent level, * at the 10 percent level.

Empirical Findings

Table 2.2 shows the bivariate relationship between Centralization and our measures of institutional quality. Figures 2.2 and 2.3 show the same results graphically. Precolonial centralization is positively associated with control of corruption (column 1) and the rule of law (column 2). Both relationships are statistically significant and economically large. A change from 0 to 1 in Centralization (i.e., a move from a country only populated by fragmented groups to a country only populated by centralized groups) is associated with an increase of 0.593 in the anticorruption index and an increase of 0.659 in the index of Rule of Law. This improvement in institutional quality is equivalent to more than one standard deviation in our sample.[6]

The comparison between Lesotho and Liberia is telling. In 1996 to 2004 Lesotho on average scored 0.03 and −0.12 in the Control of Corruption and Rule of Law indexes, respectively. Liberia lies at the other extreme, having the average values of −1.31 and −1.77 for the same institutional measures. But while our Centralization index gives 1 for Lesotho, populated by the centralized Sotho and Zulu, it gives 0 for Liberia, whose population comes from the fragmented Kru and Peripheral Mande. Thus differences in precolonial institutions may capture almost half the difference in institutional quality between these two countries.

Overall, table 2.2 shows that countries inhabited by centralized groups enjoy better institutional quality. These results are in line with

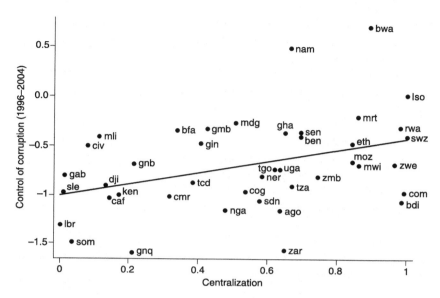

Figure 2.2
Precolonial centralization and control of corruption

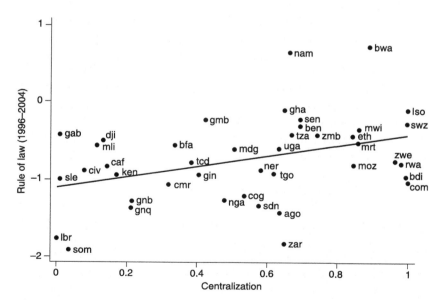

Figure 2.3
Precolonial centralization and rule of law

the argument developed by Shleifer and Vishny (1993) that the presence of a centralized authority should help coordinate bribe taking and hence reduce corruption. As discussed at the start of this chapter, they are also consistent with the view that centralization boosts the quality of government more broadly defined (Riker 1964; Blanchard and Shleifer 2001; Gennaioli and Rainer 2005).

Notice that reverse causality is not a problem for our analysis. The political organization of African ethnic groups certainly evolved over centuries but was predetermined at the end of the nineteenth century, when the massive European colonization began. It is then difficult to see how recent differences in institutional quality could have affected our Centralization index. Cross-country studies of centralization (e.g., Treisman 2000; Fisman and Gatti 2002) use measures of centralization that, being contemporaneous to public goods outcomes, may be endogenous. Our index is far less prone to this problem, and thus improves on this empirical literature.

However, the mere absence of reverse causation does not necessarily imply that our results are driven by precolonial centralization per se. In particular, our findings may be explained by two alternative hypotheses. First, centralized ethnic groups may just be economically more advanced and thus more effective—regardless of centralization—at dealing with government failures. Second, precolonial institutions may have affected institutional quality only indirectly, by affecting colonial institutions or by shaping national political outcomes after independence. In order to check for these possibilities, we pick proxies for our alternative hypotheses and introduce them one at a time in our basic regression specification. Table 2.3 reports the values and the standard errors of the coefficient for the Centralization index, as well as those for the relevant proxy.

First Alternative Hypothesis: Economic Advancement

The economic advancement of traditional societies is likely to favor centralization (Braudel 1972), but it may also lead to the creation of more efficient institutions (Demsetz 1967). In order to check for this possibility, we pick two proxies of economic advancement: a country's per capita GDP in 1960 and the collection of climate type dummies, capturing differences in agricultural productivity across countries. Rows 2 and 3 of table 2.3 show the results of regressions including these controls. The effect of Centralization remains large and (at least

Table 2.3
Robustness to alternative hypotheses: Economic advancement and indirect effects

Specifications	Dependent variables			
	Control of corruption in 1996–2004		Rule of law in 1996–2004	
	(1)		(2)	
Centralization	0.593***	(0.205)	0.659**	(0.246)
No controls				
Centralization	0.569**	(0.218)	0.73***	(0.259)
Log of GDP/cap in 1960	0.114	(0.169)	0.17	(0.204)
Centralization	0.614**	(0.256)	0.558	(0.332)
p-Value for climate types	[0.495]		[0.614]	
Centralization	0.672***	(0.214)	0.758***	(0.245)
Population of European descent in 1960 (%)	3.313	(2.864)	6.113***	(2.225)
Centralization	0.581***	(0.205)	0.627**	(0.261)
English legal origin	0.079	(0.145)	0.211	(0.174)
Centralization	0.591***	(0.215)	0.617**	(0.262)
Catholics	−0.016**	(0.007)	−0.019**	(0.007)
Muslims	−0.008	(0.006)	−0.013**	(0.006)
Other religions	−0.004	(0.007)	−0.011	(0.007)
Centralization	0.418**	(0.193)	0.551**	(0.24)
Constraints on the executive in 1970–1994	0.146***	(0.046)	0.16***	(0.051)
Centralization	0.52**	(0.238)	0.673**	(0.293)
Ethnolinguistic fractionalization	−0.237	(0.31)	0.046	(0.345)

Notes: (1) The table shows coefficients and robust standard errors for *Centralization* index and controls introduced one at a time. (2) All regressions have 42 observations, except those including *Log of GDP/cap* (40 observations), *% of Europeans* (41) and *Constraints on the executive* (40). *** denotes significance at the 1 percent level, ** at the 5 percent level, * at the 10 percent level.

marginally) significant, while neither the early level of per capita income nor the climatic conditions seem to have any impact on institutional quality in sub-Saharan Africa.

Second Alternative Hypothesis: Indirect Effects

The indirect effect of precolonial centralization can be formulated in two broad versions. The first deals with the possibility that precolonial centralization mainly affected colonial institutions. For example, indigenously centralized areas could have facilitated European settlement, thus leading to better institutions (Acemoglu et al. 2001), or attracted English colonizers, which could have also led to better institutions (La Porta et al. 1999). To account for these possibilities, we control in our regressions for the fraction of a country's population of European descent in 1960 and for the English legal origin variable. But precolonial centralization may have also facilitated the arrival of missionaries, who may have brought efforts aimed at improving local governance. We thus control for the share of a country's population belonging to Catholic, Muslim, Protestant, or other religions.

The second version of the indirect effects hypothesis deals with the possibility that precolonial centralization may have affected postcolonial national political outcomes. For example, in postindependence Africa, centralized groups could provide mechanisms of political participation and representation, putting constraints on the behavior of national political elites (Boone 2003). At the same time indigenously centralized political organization could reduce the scope for distinctive cultural differences, thus reducing the ethnolinguistic fractionalization and its costs. In order to capture these indirect channels, we control in our regressions for the Constraints on the Executive index (measuring national checks and balances) and for the Ethnolinguistic Fractionalization index of Easterly and Levine (1997).

Rows 4 through 8 of table 2.3 show the results of the regressions controlling for these indirect effects. In all the specifications the coefficient of Centralization remains large and significant, indicating a strong direct effect of precolonial institutions. The data also suggest that the Protestant religion and stronger national checks and balances are conducive to better economic institutions. However, it is unlikely that precolonial centralization had an additional, indirect, effect operating through these channels, given the low and insignificant correlation of Centralization index with these intermediate variables (see table A2.2).

The robustness analysis tends to reject the hypotheses that centralized groups fared better just because they were more advanced or because precolonial centralization had only an indirect effect working through colonial or postcolonial national political outcomes. The data are instead broadly consistent with the presence of a direct impact of precolonial centralization on institutional quality.

2.5 Conclusions

We document the importance of the precolonial political institutions for the quality of government in colonial and postcolonial Africa. We find that African countries with a larger share of their population belonging to ethnic groups with centralized institutions have less corruption and better rule of law.

Our analysis contributes to the economic literature on institutions with two main ideas. First, differently from existing work in this field, which stress the impact of colonial institutions (La Porta et al. 1999; Acemoglu et al. 2001), we view *precolonial* institutions as a key determinant of the quality of government in former colonies. Second, the evidence presented in this chapter that centralization may be conducive to a framework supportive of private sector initiative complements our previous finding (Gennaioli and Rainer 2005) that centralization can reduce the abusive power of local elites and foster public goods provision.

This brings us to the general implications of our work for the decentralization debate. The arguments in favor of political decentralization ultimately rely on the crucial assumptions that the local political system is able to maintain a meaningful democratic process and that the main threat to institutional quality is represented by a corrupt and arbitrary central government. Yet the evidence from around the world—from Russia to India to Latin America[7]—shows how local power holders may subvert and distort the implementation of private and public initiatives to their own advantage. We suggest that in such circumstances political *centralization* is desirable because it constitutes a way to hold local elites more accountable.

Appendix

Table A2.1
Summary statistics

Variable	Obser-vations	Mean	Standard deviation	Mini-mum	Maxi-mum
Dependent variables					
Corruption in 1996–2004	42	−0.69	0.477	−1.59	0.72
Rule of law in 1996–2004	42	−0.756	0.554	−1.91	0.71
Main independent variable					
Centralization	42	0.537	0.321	0	1
Controls					
Log of GDP/cap in 1960	40	6.559	0.456	5.549	7.49
Population of European descent in 1960 (%)	41	0.014	0.03	0.001	0.141
English legal origin	42	0.405	0.497	0	1
Catholics	42	23.457	22.22	0	78.3
Muslims	42	31.536	34.802	0	99.8
Protestants	42	13.812	14.886	0	64.2
Other religions	42	31.195	19.736	0.1	64.1
Constraints on the executive in 1970–1994	40	2.458	1.548	1	7
Ethnolinguistic fractionalization	42	0.639	0.271	0	1

Table A2.2
Pairwise correlations between precolonial centralization and controls

	Centralization
Controls	
Log of GDP/cap in 1960	−0.21
Population of European descent in 1960 (%)	−0.048
English legal origin	0.098
Catholics	0.134
Muslims	−0.193
Protestants	0.171
Other religions	0.061
Constraints on the executive in 1970–1994	0.164
Ethnolinguistic fractionalization	−0.363**

Notes: *** denotes significance at the 1 percent level, ** at the 5 percent level, * at the 10 percent level.

Table A2.3
Data and sources

Dependent variables

Control of corruption in 1996–2004	Average of the control of corruption index for the years 1996–2004. Control of corruption index measures perceptions of corruption defined as the exercise of public power for private gain. Aspects of corruption measured include the frequency of "additional payments to get things done," the effects of corruption on the business environment, "grand corruption" in the political arena or the tendency of elites to engage in state capture. Scale from −2.5 to 2.5, with higher scores corresponding to lower corruption. Source: Kaufmann, Kraay, and Mastruzzi (2005).
Rule of law in 1996–2004	Average of the index of rule of law for the years 1996–2004. Index of rule of law measures perceptions of the quality of contract enforcement, the police, and the courts, as well as the likelihood of crime and violence. Scale from −2.5 to 2.5, with higher scores corresponding to better rule of law. Source: Kaufmann, Kraay, and Mastruzzi (2005).

Main independent variable

Centralization	For each country measures the share of the non-European population that belongs to precolonially "centralized" ethnic groups. Scale is 0 to 1. An ethnic group is defined as "centralized" if it has 2, 3 or 4 jurisdictional levels above the local community according to Murdock's (1967) *Jurisdictional Hierarchy* variable. (It is defined as "fragmented" if it has 0 or 1 levels.) Source: Gennaioli and Rainer (2005). Originally based on Murdock (1967) and Atlas Narodov Mira (1964).

Controls

Log of GDP per capita in 1960	Logarithm of GDP per capita in constant 1985 dollars (international prices). Source: Global Development Network Growth Database, based on Penn World, Table 5.6.
Climate types	Climate types are tropical wet, tropical monsoon, tropical wet and dry, steppe (low latitude), desert (low latitude), subtropical humid, dry steppe wasteland and highland. Source: Parker (1997).
Population of European descent in 1960 (%)	Percentage of population of European descent in 1960. "European" includes all whites. Scale from 0 to 1. Source: Morrison et al. (1989).
English legal origin	Dummy variable taking value 1 for countries with English legal origin, 0 otherwise. Source: La Porta et al. (1999), originally based on *Foreign Laws: Current Sources of Basic Legislation in Jurisdictions of the World* (1989) and CIA World Factbook (1996).

Table A2.3
(continued)

Religion shares	Identify the percentage of the population of each country that belonged to the three most widely spread religions in the world in 1980. The numbers are in percent (scale from 0 to 100). The three religions identified are Roman Catholic, Protestant and Muslim. The residual is called "other religions." Source: La Porta et al. (1999), originally based on Barrett (1982), *Worldmark Encyclopedia of Nations* (1995), *Statistical Abstract of the World* (1995), United Nations (1995), CIA (1996).
Constraints on the executive in 1970–1994	Average of constraints on the executive for the years 1970 to 1994. Constraints on the executive are measured on a seven-category scale, from 1 to 7, with a higher score indicating more constraints. Score of 1 indicates unlimited authority; score of 3 indicates slight to moderate limitations; score of 5 indicates substantial limitations; score of 7 indicates executive parity or subordination. Scores of 2, 4 and 6 indicate intermediate values. Source: Polity III dataset.
Ethnolinguistic fractionalization	Average value of five different indices of ethnolinguistic fractionalization. Its value ranges from 0 to 1. Source: La Porta et al. (1999), originally from Easterly and Levine (1997).

Notes

We thank Mark Gradstein, Kai Konrad, Moses Shayo, and participants to the 2005 CESifo Venice conference on Political Economy and Development for useful comments.

1. Some political scientists (e.g., Leff 1964) argue that the optimal level of corruption is positive because it helps removing inefficient regulations. Yet even in such a case, corruption signals the presence of inefficient regulations and hence is a symptom of bad government. Indeed, the evidence does not support the view that corruption is beneficial (Svensson 2005).

2. See Potholm (1977) and Picard (1987) for evidence on Botswana and Swaziland.

3. The central apparatus tested a chief's popularity by consulting the local people (Richards 1960).

4. A crucial source of influence was local lords' ability to satisfy the king's need for soldiers (Apter 1961).

5. A general version of these views predicts that—either for their advancement or for their better national politics—centralized groups *uniformly* enjoy more public goods, regardless of local stratification. Although in more nuanced versions of these hypotheses local stratification may matter, they are still incapable of explaining the different patterns obtained for public goods with high and low spillovers.

6. To check for presence of influential observations that could bias our results, we computed the DFbetas (e.g., see Belsley, Kuh, and Welsch 1980, p. 28) from the regressions in table 2.2, but we did not find any cases of $abs(DFbeta) > 1$. If we more conservatively

drop all the observations with $abs(DFbeta) > 2/\sqrt{\#obs}$, the centralization coefficient slightly decreases but remains highly significant statistically.

7. See Shleifer and Treisman (1999) on Russia, Lieten (1996) and Mathew and Nayak (1996) on India, and Fox (1990) on Latin America.

References

Abubakar, S. 1980. Northern provinces under colonial rule. In O. Ikime, ed., *Groundwork of Nigerian History*. Ibadan, Nigeria: Historical Society of Nigeria/Heinemann Educational Books.

Acemoglu, D., S. Johnson, and J. Robinson. 2001. The colonial origins of comparative development: An empirical perspective. *American Economic Review* 91: 1369–1401.

Apter, D. E. 1961. *The Political Kingdom in Uganda: A Study in Bureaucratic Nationalism*. Princeton: Princeton University Press.

Ashton, H. 1967. *The Basuto: A Social Study of Traditional and Modern Lesotho*. Oxford: Oxford University Press.

Atlas Narodov Mira (Atlas of the Peoples of the World). 1964. Moscow: Glavnoe Upravlenie Geodezii i Kartografii.

Bardhan, P., and D. Mookherjee. 2000. Capture and governance at the local and national levels. *American Economic Review* 90(2): 135–39.

Bardhan, P. 2002. Decentralization of governance and development. *Journal of Economic Perspectives* 16: 185–205.

Bates, R. 1983. *Essays on the Political Economy of Rural Africa*. Berkeley: University of California Press.

Belsley, D. A., E. Kuh, and R. E. Welsch. 1980. *Regression Diagnostics: Identifying Influential Data and Sources of Collinearity*. New York: Wiley.

Besley, T., and A. Case. 1995. Incumbent behavior: Vote seeking, tax-setting and yard-stick competition. *American Economic Review* 85: 25–45.

Blanchard, O., and A. Shleifer. 2001. Federalism with and without political centralization: China versus Russia. IMF Staff Working Paper.

Boone, C. 2003. *Political Topographies of the African State: Territorial Authority and Institutional Choice*. Cambridge: Cambridge University Press.

Braudel, F. 1972. *The Mediterranean and the Mediterranean World in the Age of Philip II*. New York: Harper and Row.

Breytenbach, W. J. 1975. *Crocodiles and Commoners in Lesotho: Continuity and Change in the Rulemaking System of Lesotho*. Pretoria: African Institute.

Burke, F. G. 1964. *Local Government and Politics in Uganda*. Syracuse: Syracuse University Press.

Demsetz, H. 1967. Toward a theory of property rights. *American Economic Review Papers and Proceedings* 57: 347–59.

Easterly, W., and R. Levine. 1997. Africa's Growth Tragedy: Policies and Ethnic Divisions. *Quarterly Journal of Economics* 112: 1203–50.

Ehrlich, C. 1965. The Uganda economy, 1903–1945. In V. Harlow and E. M. Chilver, eds., *History of East Africa*, vol. 2. Oxford: Oxford University Press.

Falola, T. 1999. *The History of Nigeria*. Westport, CT: Greenwood Press.

Fisman, R., and R. Gatti. 2002. Decentralization and corruption: Evidence across countries. *Journal of Public Economics* 83: 325–45.

Fortes, M., and E. Evans-Pritchard, ed. 1940. *African Political Systems*. London: Oxford University Press.

Fox, J. 1990. Editor's introduction in special issue on The Challenge of Rural Democratization: Perspectives from Latin America and the Philippines. *Journal of Development Studies* 26(4): 1–19.

Gennaioli, N., and I. Rainer. 2005. The modern impact of precolonial centralization in Africa. Mimeo.

Herbst, J. 2000. *States and Power in Africa: Comparative Lessons in Authority and Control*. Princeton: Princeton University Press.

Jaggers, K., and T. R. Gurr. 1996. *Polity III: Regime Change and Political Authority, 1800–1994*. Computer File. Ann Arbor, MI: Inter-university Consortium for Political and Social Research.

Kaufmann, D., A. Kraay, and M. Mastruzzi. 2005. Governance matters IV: Governance indicators for 1996–2004. The World Bank mimeo.

Klitgaard, R. 1990. *Tropical Gangsters*. New York: Basic Books.

La Porta, R., F. Lopez-de-Silanes, A. Shleifer, and R. Vishny. 1999. The quality of government. *Journal of Law, Economics, and Organization* 15: 222–79.

Leff, N. 1964. Economic development through bureaucratic corruption. *American Behavioral Scientist* 8: 8–14.

Lieten, G. K. 1996. Panchayats in Western Uttar Pradesh. *Economic and Political Weekly*, 2700–5.

Low, D. A. 1965. Uganda: The establishment of the protectorate, 1894–1919. In V. Harlow and E. M. Chilver, eds., *History of East Africa*, vol. 2. New York: Oxford University Press.

Low, D. A. 1971. *Buganda in Modern History*. Berkeley: University of California Press.

Mathew, G., and R. Nayak. 1996. Panchayats at Work. *Economic and Political Weekly* 31: 1765–71.

Morrison, D. G., R. Mitchell, and J. Paden. 1989. *Black Africa Handbook*, 2nd ed. New York: Paragon Press.

Mamdani, M. 1996. *Citizen and Subject: Contemporary Africa and the Legacy of Late Colonialism*. Princeton: Princeton University Press.

Murdock, G. P. 1967. *Ethnographic Atlas*. Pittsburgh: University of Pittsburgh Press.

North, D. 1981. *Structure and Change in Economic History*. New York: Norton.

Oates, W. 1972. *Fiscal Federalism*. New York: Harcourt Brace.

Parker, P. M. 1997. *National Cultures of the World: A Statistical Reference, Cross Cultural Statistical Encyclopedia of the World*, vol. 4. Westport, CT: Greenwood Press.

Picard, L. A. 1987. *The Political Development in Botswana: A Model for Success?* Boulder CO: Lynne Rienner.

Potholm, C. P. 1977. The Ngwenyama of Swaziland: The dynamics of political adaptation. In R. Lemarchand, ed., *African Kingships in Perspective: Political Change and Modernization in Monarchical Settings*. London: Frank Cass.

Pratt, R. C. 1965. Administration and politics in Uganda, 1919–1945. In V. Harlow and E. M. Chilver, eds., *History of East Africa*, vol. 2. New York: Oxford University Press.

Richards, A. I., ed. 1960. *East African Chiefs: A Study of Political Development in Some Uganda and Tanganyika Tribes*. London: East African Institute of Social Research/Faber and Faber.

Riker, W. 1964. *Federalism: Origins, Operation, Significance*. Boston: Houghton Mifflin.

Rouveroy van Nieuwaal, E. A. B. van. 1987. Modern states and chieftaincy in Africa. *Journal of Legal Pluralism* 25: 1–41.

Schapera, I. 1956. *Government and Politics in Tribal Societies*. London: Watts.

Schapera, I. 1970. *Tribal Innovators: Tswana Chiefs and Social Change, 1795–1940*. London: Athlone Press.

Seabright, P. 1996. Accountability and decentralization in government: An incomplete contracts model. *European Economic Review* 40: 61–89.

Shleifer, A., and R. Vishny. 1993. Corruption. *Quarterly Journal of Economics* 108: 599–617.

Shleifer, A., and D. Treisman. 1999. *Without a Map: Political Tactics and Economic Reform in Russia*. Cambridge: MIT Press.

Sklar, R. L. 1993. The African frontier for political science. In R. H. Bates, V. Y. Mudimbe, and J. O'Barr, eds., *Africa and the Disciplines: The Contributions of Research in Africa to the Social Sciences and Humanities*. Chicago: University of Chicago Press.

Smith, A. 1776. *The Wealth of Nations*. London: Dent (1977).

Svensson, J. 2005. Eight questions about corruption. *Journal of Economic Perspectives* 19: 19–42.

Tiebout, C. 1956. A pure theory of local expenditures. *Journal of Political Economy* 64(5): 416–24.

Tosh, J. 1978. *Clan Leaders and Colonial Chiefs in Lango: The Political History of an East African Stateless Society c. 1800–1939*. New York: Oxford University Press.

Treisman, D. 2000. The causes of corruption: A cross-national study. *Journal of Public Economics* 76: 399–457.

Treisman, D. 2003. Decentralization and the quality of government. Unpublished paper. UCLA.

Uganda Bureau of Statistics. 1999. *Uganda National Household Survey, 1997*: Summary Analytical Report.

Uganda Bureau of Statistics and ORC Macro. 2001. *Uganda Demographic and Health Survey, 2000–2001*.

Uganda Bureau of Statistics. 2003. *Statistical Abstract*.

White, C. M. N. 1959. Northern Rodhesia: Luvale political organization and the Luvale lineage. In R. Apthorpe, ed., *From Tribal Rule to Modern Government, The Thirteenth Conference Proceedings of the Rhodes-Livingstone Institute for Social Research*. Lusaka.

Wylie, D. 1990. *A Little God: The Twilight of Patriarchy in a Southern African Chiefdom*. Hanover, NH: University Press of New England.

3

Can Delegation Promote Fiscal Discipline in a Federation? Evidence from Fiscal Performance in the Indian States

Stuti Khemani

3.1 Introduction

One of the more prominent issues in recent development policy is the risk of fiscal indiscipline and macroeconomic instability in developing countries that are rapidly decentralizing fiscal powers to subnational governments. The concern lies explicitly in the domain of political economy—that political incentives will change with fiscal decentralization in a manner detrimental to fiscal stability. Evidence from individual country experience is being garnered to understand what forms of institutions can address problems of fiscal indiscipline arising from political incentives. One institution has received particular attention and support in policy circles—delegating authority to the national political executive of oversight and regulation of subnational borrowing and debt. Can such delegation successfully address political distortions to fiscal discipline? In this chapter I provide evidence on this question from the long-term experience of one of the largest federations in the developing world, India. I argue that such delegation has limited success when the political incentives of the national government are such that it is unwilling or unable to enforce hard budget constraints on subnationals. In light of this evidence, I explore the role of an alternate form of delegation, to an independent fiscal agency, of monitoring and oversight of consolidated government debt, again providing evidence from India on the functioning of such an institution to support its arguments.

The risk of fiscal indiscipline in a federation (or in any system with extensive fiscal decentralization) was raised by Alesina and Perotti (1995) in a review article on the political economy of budget deficits. They suggested that fiscal decentralization or federal arrangements are prone to a classic "common-pool" problem, when spending decisions taken at local levels are financed by transfers from the national government, which raises taxes. This insight for fiscal federalism was drawn from a model of legislative bargaining on how representatives from geographically based constituencies overestimate the benefits of public spending in their districts relative to its financing costs, leading to above optimal levels of spending (Weingast, Shepsle, and Johnsen 1981). Although these models typically address the *size* of budgets, they can be made dynamic so that they also address the *balance* of government budgets. Persson and Tabellini (2000) provide a simple dynamic extension of the common-pool problem and show that both spending and borrowing are higher than optimal, when different groups in the government are given decision power over parts of the budget, but no one is given authority for the aggregate outcome. Velasco (1999) presents a more detailed dynamic political economy model where government resources are a "common property" from which interest groups can finance expenditures on their preferred areas. Fiscal deficits and debt accumulation result in this model even when there are no reasons for intertemporal tax and consumption smoothing.

The salience of interest groups in overfishing the common property of public resources has been measured through the political party composition of a government. Alesina and Perotti (1995) emphasize the importance of coalition governments, consisting of several political parties, in delaying fiscal adjustments and more rapid accumulation of public debt. That is, bargaining among multiple political parties is likely to proxy for bargaining among multiple interest groups over public resources. Beginning with the seminal contribution of Roubini and Sachs (1989) a large empirical literature has found a positive correlation between deficits and "type of government," an indicator variable that typically ranks governments in ascending order of political fragmentation, from single-party majority governments to coalitions and minority governments. Perotti and Kontopoulos (2002) have recently pointed out that this set of results is sensitive to the subjective coding of the "type of government" indicator, and they instead test the impact of a more objective measure—the number of political parties in a government. Using panel data for 19 OECD countries from 1970 to 1995, they find that although coalition size is a significant determinant of government spending and deficits, a stronger more robust association is revealed with the size of the cabinet, or the number of spending ministers in a cabinet.

Consistent with these theoretical ideas and empirical evidence, countries seem to have explored solutions to the common-pool problem by concentrating decision power over aggregate budgets to central agencies. An established literature on the role of fiscal institutions in promoting fiscal performance has argued that such hierarchical institutions that centralize decision power over fiscal aggregates, such as deficit and debt, can make a difference for better outcomes (Poterba and von Hagen 1999). In the context of fiscal decentralization it is the delegation of authority to the national political executive of oversight and regulation of subnational borrowing and debt. At least in two regions of the world where subnational fiscal profligacy has been credited with contributing to macroeconomic crises, Russia and Latin America, many scholars and policy makers, among them Ordeshook (1996), Dillinger and Webb (1999), Samuels (2000), Stepan (2000), and Blanchard and Shleifer (2001), have advocated a disciplining role for strong, centralized national political parties that can force subnational governments to internalize the costs of their policies.

However, this line of thinking is at odds with that in an earlier literature where the institutions of decentralization were viewed as potentially solving the problem of political distortions in public resource allocation. Qian and Weingast (1997) review their idea of "market-preserving federalism," where interjurisdictional competition among governments attract private economic activity would tie the hands of governments from interfering in market forces. Specifically, they argue that if decentralization to locally elected governments creates competition among them, then this competition serves to commit governments to not bail out agencies, projects, or enterprises that fail. Qian and Roland (1998) use this story to interpret the success of China in transitioning to a market economy—that decentralization to local governments created conditions for hard budget constraints on economic activity and thereby promoted good resource allocation decisions that led to growth.[1]

In the market-preserving view of federalism, there is doubt about whether a central political authority that is strong enough to impose discipline on subnational governments would be itself disciplined by market considerations of efficiency (Wibbels 2003; Weingast 1995). Specifically, limiting central government information about and power over subnational finances reinforces the credible commitment to "hard budget constraints" provided by competition between subnational governments. Qian and Weingast (1997) support this argument through an example from China, where the central government allows local governments to maintain various "extra-budget" and "off-budget" accounts of which it has limited knowledge, precisely as a commitment device to not intervene to tax nor bail them out, which in turn encourages local governments to invest in profitable activity.

Blanchard and Shleifer (2001), however, offer a counterargument by comparing the experiences of China and Russia, that the degree of political centralization in China allowed the central government to discipline local governments into favoring growth, whereas the waning power of central political authorities in Russia prevented them from doing the same. They invoke Riker (1964), one of the earliest thinkers on federalism, for stating that if federalism is to function and endure, it must come with political centralization.

The review above thus shows that the importance of a single and strong national ruling party controlling the national government has been emphasized in both the literature on fiscal federalism and in a general literature on common-pool problems in public resource allocation. The idea appears to be that a strong national party at the center is likely to be held accountable by voters for overall macroeconomic outcomes and hence have the right incentives for fiscal discipline. However, the critique of the market-preserving view of governments suggests that more analysis is needed to understand the political incentives of national parties, before any conclusion on the potential fiscal benefits of political centralization can be reached.

India provides a valuable laboratory to study this issue because for much of its history as an independent, democratic country, it has seen one dominant national political party at the helm of fiscal policy, and federal institutions characterized both by dependence of states on national transfers, and national regulation of subnational borrowing. Some of the literature reviewed above would therefore predict that with this combination of political and federal institutions India is not likely to suffer from subnational fiscal profligacy. Indeed in recent years, when the strength of the national political parties declined, and subnational fiscal deficit simultaneously increased, contributing to an overall increase in the consolidated government deficit, many interpreted this correlation as confirming the importance of single-party national governments in promoting fiscal discipline in a federation. In this chapter I test whether delegation of subnational debt oversight to the national political executive, at a time when there was a strong national political party, indeed served to strengthen subnational fiscal discipline, by exploring the correlation between center-state political relations and state fiscal deficits.

I define political conditions whose variation across states are a good proxy for the variation in political costs of the national government of withholding a bailout when a state requires additional financing. I find large effects of political partisanship on subnational deficits and argue that this suggests significant political incentives problems for fiscal discipline, even when the center is dominated by a single national party. When such political distortions exist, I argue that delegation to the national political executive is likely to be insufficient or ineffective in promoting fiscal discipline in a federation. Instead I explore a new institutional solution—delegation of debt oversight to an independent fiscal agency, much in the same spirit as delegation of monetary policy to an independent central bank—that has hitherto not been deliberated in the literature, and present evidence from India to inform this idea.[2]

After trying several specifications to test the impact of politics, as suggested by a large literature, I find that party affiliation between the national and state governments in India emerges as the single-most significant political determinant of state deficits. Using a panel dataset for 15 major states of India over the period 1972 to 1995, I find that when a state government is controlled by the same party that controls the national government, the state has higher than average fiscal deficit. This partisan effect is large, with deficits in politically affiliated states being 11 percent higher than deficits in nonaffiliated states, calculated at the sample average. Among co-partisan states, those where the national ruling party controls a larger proportion of seats allotted to the state in the national legislature may be characterized as "core support" states, whereas those where the party controls a smaller proportion of seats may be characterized as "swing" states. I find that deficits are greater in the latter, that is, the "swing" states. Affiliated states where the ruling party controls close to zero of the state's seats in the national legislature have deficits that are more than 25 percent higher than the sample average. Nonaffiliated states have lower deficits compared to affiliated states, regardless of their representation in the national legislature.

The evidence for the Indian states shows that partisan affiliation between the national and state governments stands out as the only significant political determinant of variation in deficits across and within states over time, to the exclusion of other plausible political and institutional determinants at the state level that have been tested in the received literature, such as election cycles (Alesina et al. 1997; Khemani 2004), fragmented or divided legislatures (Roubini and Sachs 1989; Poterba 1994; Alt and Lowry 1994; Perotti and Kontopoulos 2002), and dependence on intergovernmental transfers (Jones, Sanguinetti, and Tommasi 2000; Rodden 2002). I find no evidence of impact on state deficits of the timing of state elections, the existence of a coalition government at the state level, nor the extent of dependence of a state on federal revenue transfers. I interpret this pattern of evidence as suggesting that while delegation to the national political executive of subnational debt oversight might allow it to discipline states governed by rival political parties, it does not prevent the national ruling party from using deficit financing to further its own political objectives. That is, the mere existence of a single and strong national party at the helm of government does not guarantee that the underlying process of electoral competition that got the party there will necessarily provide strong incentives for fiscal discipline.

I review the literature on multi-party electoral competition in India, and use the evidence provided here on the effect of center-state political relations on fiscal discipline, to argue that the fundamental political problem with fiscal profligacy in developing countries like India might not be fiscal decentralization to multiple spending entities but rather the platform of multi-party electoral competition at all tiers of government. This platform is characterized by emphasis on spending programs that target benefits to specific groups, out of generalized taxation, and therefore consistent with the common-pool problem of fiscal discipline analyzed early on in the literature on political economy of budget deficits.

This insight has a particular policy implication, which is topical for India and other rapidly decentralizing developing countries, given recent concern over burgeoning deficits. Instead of focusing on strengthening the hands of the national political executive to control subnational governments, which is what current policy debates do, policy makers could fruitfully explore delegation of consolidated government debt oversight to a nonpartisan, independent fiscal agency, as a commitment device that reduces costly political bargaining between multiple interest groups over public resources. An independent fiscal agency already exists in India—the Finance Commission—and is delegated power over the distribution of national revenue transfers. Recent evidence shows that it indeed functions to curb the partisan influence of the national executive (Khemani 2003), and that it is therefore an agency that might be credible to diverse political groups in the country. The Finance Commission could become the means to a more cooperative bargaining equilibrium where the costs of noncooperation are reduced.

Section 3.2 describes the methodological approach used in the chapter to test for political distortions to fiscal discipline in a federation. Section 3.3 provides a brief description of Indian fiscal and political institutions. Section 3.4 describes the data used for our empirical analysis, and reports the evidence on the impact of national-state political relations on state fiscal deficit. Section 3.5 reviews insights from the political science literature on electoral competition in the country to interpret the empirical evidence provided here, and discusses delegation to an independent fiscal agency as an innovative policy solution to the problem of fiscal deficits. Section 3.6 concludes with some open questions.

3.2 Methodological Approach

Typically, to answer the question of whether the existence of a particular institution leads to particular outcomes, the empirical methodology employed is to measure either differences in outcomes across jurisdictions where some have the institutions, and some don't, or differences over time, before and after the institution is operational, or both, which is termed the difference-in-differences approach. However, such a methodology is difficult to apply to the question of interest here, because the institution of delegation of certain oversight powers to the national political executive is invariant across jurisdictions within a country. Changes measured at the aggregate level of one country over time, before and after the strength of the national political executive declined, usually imply very few observations from which to draw generalizations, and the "event" of substantial political weakening at the national level around which changes are measured, is likely to be confounded by many other underlying changes that simultaneously impact other outcomes. Variations across countries would be useful to explore and some have attempted it (Rodden and Wibbels 2002 is a prominent and successful example to be reviewed below), but cross-country analysis is constrained by measurement and comparability problems.

The approach taken in this chapter is to exploit variation across states and over time within a country, in states' political relations with the center that would proxy for political costs to the center of not bailing-out a state, estimate correlations between center-state political relations and state fiscal deficit, and use the pattern of results to deduce the incentives of the national political executive in its fiscal dealings with states. The null hypothesis is therefore that center-state political relations should have no impact on state fiscal deficits if delegation to the national political executive solves the problem of perverse subnational incentives.

The literature on intergovernmental fiscal relations identifies several political factors, variation in which would determine whether the national government is able to discipline subnational governments. Dependence of subnationals on national revenue transfers has been identified as perhaps the single most important factor in determining whether the national government has inescapable obligations to respond to states in need. In states where the governments are more dependent on central transfers for their spending programs, voters might find it harder to distinguish whether fiscal problems and economic hardships are due to unsustainable actions taken by their state government or to inaction by the central government during times of negative economic shocks, and therefore more likely to punish the center for withholding bailouts to the state (Rodden 2002).

Indeed in many developing countries the basic condition of the market-preserving view of federalism, that subnational government actions be driven by competition with other jurisdictions, is unlikely to hold because local government accountability for its own actions is clouded by its dependence on federal revenue transfers (rather than relying on own-revenue bases). Various articles in Rodden, Eskeland, and Litvack (2001) argue that fiscal decentralization institutions "soften" subnational budget constraints because the center cannot credibly commit to withhold a bailout from a subnational government in financial trouble. If it did not, it would share in the political costs of the financial failure, and knowing this, subnationals would have incentives to overspend in expectation of future bailouts. Rodden and Wibbels (2002) and Rodden (2002) find that greater regulation and oversight of subnational borrowing by the national government is correlated with lower deficits, when subnational taxing autonomy is limited, and spending is largely financed by federal transfers. Rodden and Wibbels (2002) further speculate upon one measure of political centralization, the existence of strong national parties with representation at both national and subnational tiers of government. Thus this literature on fiscal decentralization joins the literature on political conditions for fiscal discipline of national governments in emphasizing the importance of national political parties.

Second, party affiliation between the central and state governments is likely to matter. Dillinger and Webb (1999), Jones, Sanguinetti, and Tommasi (2000), Rodden and Wibbels (2002), among others, hypothesize that the center is likely to have leverage in affiliated states through internal party disciplinary mechanisms, and might be able to preempt state fiscal profligacy, leading to lower deficits for affiliated states. Subnational governments that are politically affiliated with the center are more likely to internalize the effect of spending an additional unit of national resources due to internal party discipline to protect the party's national reputation, and should therefore have lower spending and deficits. Consistent with this hypothesis Jones et al. (2000) find empirical evidence that provinces in Argentina whose governors belong to the same political party as that of the national president have lower spending than provinces that are not affiliated with the president's party.

However, co-partisanship can have the opposite effect, depending on the nature of electoral competition, if the center bears political costs for not bailing out a state only in those states where its own party controls the government. In politically affiliated states the center might bear relatively greater costs of no bailout from the damage done to the reputation of the political party due to poor performance of the state government. In unaffiliated states, the direct costs to the center might be mitigated by costs to the rival political party controlling the state, if voters punish the rival political party ruling the state for subsequent ill-effects of fiscal mismanagement. That is, the central ruling party might actually stand to gain from its rival party's discomfiture due to fiscal retrenchment, while it loses by supporting additional spending on local public goods whose political benefits would accrue to the rival party.

Another measure of bargaining power of states is their representation in the national legislature. States that have greater representation in the national legislature, in terms of the absolute number of representatives elected from a state to the national legislature, might be harder for the national government to ignore (à la Weingast et al. 1981). In addition to, or instead of absolute representation, partisan affiliation of the legislators elected from the state's constituencies might matter— states whose constituencies return a larger proportion of legislators from the national ruling party might receive more resources. Or conversely, if the national ruling party can discipline its own legislators, then states sending a higher proportion of legislators from rival political parties might be the ones with the bargaining power for greater resources to their state (Riker 1964).

A prolific and ongoing discussion in the literature centers around the conditions under which voters that are "core supporters" of a ruling political party receive more or less public resources than voters that are "swing," with empirical evidence on both sides of the issue (Schady 2000; Case 2001; Johansson 2003; Miguel and Zaidi 2003). Thus the extent to which a state has "swing" voters or "core supporters" of the national political party might matter for whether it is likely to be bailed out when in financial trouble.

All these variables in the empirical analysis are defined below, and their relative impact on states' fiscal deficit tested. If any of these variables are significant determinants of subnational deficits, then we can conclude that central political discretion is being exercised in the allocation of subnational debt; that is, there are political distortions in subnational fiscal performance in the federation.

Moreover the pattern of impact would have implications for how strong the incentives of the national ruling party are for fiscal discipline. The key variable in this regard is the party affiliation between the center and a state. If there is any impact of political partisanship, then co-partisan states should have lower deficits if the party's political incentives are aligned with greater fiscal discipline. However, if the party's own interests are served through greater deficits, then co-partisan states should have higher deficits. If co-partisan states have higher deficits, then this could be either because of the center opportunistically and deliberately distributing deficit financing across states to further the party's political objectives or because state party leaders have bargaining power within the party and hold the central party leadership hostage through their actions. I will discuss both interpretations in the analysis below.

3.3 Political and Fiscal Institutions in India

Government in India has been a Westminster-style parliamentary democracy since the adoption of a constitution in 1950, with direct elections based on universal adult suffrage to the Lok Sabha, or the House of the People, the lower house at the national level, and to the Vidhan

Sabhas, the individual legislative assemblies at the state level. The country is divided into 4,061 single-member districts for state assembly elections; the districts are grouped together, separately within each state, to form 543 single-member districts for the national assembly. The party that wins a majority of districts distributed in any manner across the states[3] is invited to form the government, headed by a prime minister and a cabinet of ministers.[4] Analogous to the national executive, the party or coalition of parties with a majority of seats in an individual state's legislative assembly forms the state-level executive government headed by a chief minister and a state cabinet of ministers.

The Indian states are constitutionally assigned broad fiscal powers, the nature of which is typical of federal nations, with the central government responsible for macroeconomic and any other policies involving extensive spillovers across state boundaries. Expenditure responsibilities for most local public goods are assigned to the states. Between 1960 and the present state governments have been undertaking around 50 to 60 percent of total government expenditures in India (Rao and Singh 2000).

Relative to their expenditure responsibilities, the revenue generation powers of state governments are more limited, with high yielding taxes such as personal income tax, corporation taxes, and customs duty assigned to the center. State governments collect tax revenues from agricultural income, from property and capital transactions, and from the production and sale of commodities. Between 1960 and the present state governments collected around 30 percent of total revenues (Rao and Singh 2000).

The constitutional assignment of expenditure responsibilities and revenue authority between the central and the state governments in India is intentionally imbalanced to give the central government a role in regional redistribution.[5] A large part of state expenditures is financed by general-purpose revenue transfers, including both untied grants and share in centrally collected taxes. Federal transfers to state governments constitute about 30 to 40 percent of state revenues, and 5 percent of the national GDP (Rao and Singh 2000).

An independent fiscal agency was created for the explicit purpose of curbing partisan influence on the sharing of national revenues between national and state governments—the Finance Commission of India. It was established by the Indian Constitution of 1950, which mandates the appointment of new members to the Commission every five years, with the primary purpose of determining the sharing of centrally collected tax proceeds between the central and state governments, and the distribution of grants in aid of revenues across states.

The rules of membership are detailed in the Finance Commission Act of 1951—it is to consist of a chairman and four other members who are either qualified to be justices in High Courts, or have technical expertise in public financial matters. The appointments are formally made for a fixed term by the constitutional head of India, the president, upon the recommendation of the prime minister's office, in consultation with Parliament. Once appointed, the members of the Commission cannot be replaced at the discretion of the political executive. The Commission has general powers of summoning and requisitioning, and its recommendations with regard to tax devolution and grants-in-aid are legally binding, and cannot be overridden by the central cabinet of ministers or the legislature.

The Terms of Reference (TOR) of successive Commissions can be expanded by order of Parliament, but must include the determination of tax devolution and grants-in-aid. The overarching objectives of Finance Commission transfers are described in every TOR in terms of promoting economic efficiency and regional equity. Thus the powers of the agency over tax sharing and grants are based on constitutional authority and cannot easily be reversed by an act of parliament.

Interestingly, and perhaps revealingly, soon after the provision of this independent agency, the national government established another agency with access to very similar instruments of resource distribution across states, but with far fewer constraints on partisan manipulation. The Planning Commission was set up by a resolution of the government of India in 1950, as a government agency within the central executive, with the prime minister as chairman. Its purpose is to supplement the annual budget process with a medium- and long-term planning process to determine the allocation of national resources across competing needs. Its technical members are appointed directly by the prime minister and serve as advisors to the government, working under the general guidance of the National Development Council, which is chaired by the prime minister and includes all central cabinet ministers and state chief ministers. In particular, the formula for distribution of Planning Commission transfers across states is determined by the National Development Council and its political representatives.[6]

In the sample of 15 major states studied here, from 1972 to 1995, tax devolution and grants by the independent agency makes up about 24 percent of state revenues, while grants from central government agencies constitute about 14 percent. The Planning Commission also makes regular loans to the states.

Hence, while transfers made by the Planning Commission are amenable to the discretion of explicitly political agents, transfers made by the Finance Commission are at least designed to be protected from political discretion through constitutional rules. Whether these constitutional rules indeed make a difference is, however, an empirical question, because the members of the Finance Commission are ultimately appointed upon the recommendation of the prime minister, and are therefore open to some degree of central political control.[7] However, since new commissions are appointed according to a constitutionally established cycle, the tenure of the Finance Commission is not congruent with the electoral cycle that changes the executive government.

Khemani (2003) tests whether delegation to an independent agency does make a difference by contrasting the impact of partisan politics on the fiscal transfers determined by the two agencies. She finds that while the distribution of transfers by the Planning Commission is consistent with the political concerns of the national political executive, the distribution of transfers by the Finance Commission counteracts the partisan influence of the national government. This is evidence that delegation to an independent agency can be effective in controlling central partisan influence.

Fiscal deficits of states are defined as the difference between total spending (on the current account, on capital project investments, on net loans to other agencies, especially state-owned enterprises) and total revenues of a state (including own-generated and tax devolution and grants made by all central agencies). Fiscal deficits of state governments are largely financed by loans from the central government, constituting more than 65 percent of total borrowing by the 15 major states in the sample studied here.

Borrowing autonomy of state governments from other market sources is limited and subject to approval by the center. There is widespread belief that these regulations can be easily circumvented, largely by off-budget borrowing through state-owned public enterprises, although the burden ultimately falls on the state (Anand, Bagchi, and Sen 2001; McCarten 2001). The center therefore has a dominant role to play in determining deficit financing for states, both directly through a large volume of loans and indirectly through bailouts of state-owned enterprises and approval of market loans. Hence, interpreting any evidence of political impact on deficits as stemming from political incentives to provide bailouts makes specific sense in the Indian context because some of the largest pressures on the state budget come from financial losses of state-owned enterprises.

3.4 Data, Empirical Specification, and Results

Data

The data set for this study are compiled from diverse sources for 15 major states of India over the period 1972 to 1995. The political data are compiled from Butler, Lahiri, and Roy (1995). The public finance data on deficits, revenues, expenditures, and intergovernmental transfers are available since 1972 from relevant volumes of the *Reserve Bank of India Bulletin*, a quarterly publication of the central bank of India with annual issues on details of finances of state governments. State demographic and economic characteristics and a state-level price index to convert all variables into real terms are available from an Indian data set put together at the World Bank. A detailed description of these variables is available in Ozler, Datt, and Ravallion (1996). Table 3.1 provides summary statistics for each of the variables included in the analysis.[8] Of the 360 state-year observations in the sample studied here, only 2 have shown a small fiscal surplus; that is, state finances in India are always likely to be in deficit. This is presumably because of the inherent vertical fiscal imbalance in India's federal structure, and the role of the center in providing loans to states for planned economic development.

Specification

We begin with a simple model to estimate the effect of absolute representation of the state in the national legislature, and the political affiliation of its government. The basic model is

$$DEFICIT_{it} = \beta AFFILIATION_{it} + \alpha REPRESENTATION_{it}$$

$$+ \eta Z_{it} + \delta_t + \varepsilon_{it}, \tag{3.1}$$

where $DEFICIT_{it}$ is real per capita fiscal deficit in state i in year t; $AFFILIATION_{it}$ is an indicator of political affiliation that equals 1 when the governing party in state i at time t belongs to the same party as that governing at the center at time t, and 0 otherwise; $REPRESENTATION_i$

Table 3.1
Summary statistics

Variable	Number of obser- vations	Mean	Standard deviation
Real fiscal deficit[a]	360	193.41	118.62
Real state income	360	4,803.73	1,807.98
Total population (in thousands)	360	47,396.79	28,163.28
Political affiliation (= 1 if center and state government belong to same political party)	360	0.62	0.49
Absolute number of seats allotted to a state in the national legislature	360	33.55	18.91
Proportion of seats in the national legislature (allotted to the state) controlled by state ruling party	360	0.62	0.31
Proportion of seats controlled by national ruling party	360	0.62	0.31
Affiliation * State ruling party seats	360	0.47	0.41
(1 − Affiliation) * State ruling party seats	360	0.15	0.26
Vertical fiscal imbalance (Total grants/ Total revenues, in %)	360	37.22	13.93
Tax sharing and grants determined by the independent agency (Nondiscretionary grants)	352	173.32	64.80
Grants determined by central political agencies (Discretionary grants)	352	105.98	64.45

Note: Fiscal variables and state domestic product are in per capita 1992 Indian rupees.
a. Fiscal deficit = Total current expenditure + Total capital expenditure − Total revenue + (Loans by state government − Recovery of loans).

is the number of districts allotted to a state in the national legislature. There is large variation across states in absolute representation in the national legislature, with the sample average number of seats allotted to a state being 34, and the sample standard deviation being 19. The largest state, Uttar Pradesh, contributed over 80 seats to the national legislature over the period under study, while the smallest state, Haryana, contributed only 9 to 10 seats. Since there is little or no variation over time within a state in the number of seats allotted to it in the national legislature, we estimate the impact of state representation in the national legislature without state fixed effects. Time-variant economic and demographic characteristics of states (real per capita state domestic product and total population) are included in the vector Z_{it}, and a time effect for each year, δ_t, is included to control for various shocks to the state economy in any given year.

In order to account for the partisan identity of individual legislators from a state in the national assembly, we include the number of legislators in the national parliament belonging to the state ruling party, as a proportion of the total seats allotted to the state, distinguishing between their impact in affiliated and unaffiliated states. This yields the following specification where $StatePartySEATS_{it}$ is the proportion of seats (allotted to the state in the national legislature) controlled by the state ruling party:

$$DEFICIT_{it} = \beta AFFILIATION_{it} + \phi AFFIL * State/NationalPartySEATS_{it}$$

$$+ \gamma(1 - AFFIL) * StatePartySEATS_{it}$$

$$+ \eta Z_{it} + \alpha_i + \delta_t + \varepsilon_{it}. \tag{3.2}$$

Specification (3.2) includes state fixed effects, α_i, so that β, the coefficient on political affiliation, is identified from variation within a state from its own average deficit when it is affiliated and not affiliated with the center.

This specification also allows us to measure the impact of "swing" states. Measuring the extent to which a state is "swing," defined in much of the theoretical literature (Cox and McCubbins 1986; Dixit and Londregan 1998) as the extent to which more voters in a state are more likely to be influenced by public spending policies, and less likely to be ideologically driven, when making their choices between rival political candidates, is difficult, because of the level of aggregation involved at the state level. Johansson (2003) has most closely followed the theoretical literature in her study of distribution of grants across Swedish municipalities, by using Swedish voter surveys to directly measure the density of voters in a municipality that exhibit characteristics of "swing" voters. But the rest of the literature has used tightness of political races (margin of victory in single-member-first-past-the-post constituencies, or distance from 50 percent mark for two-candidate constituencies) as the basis for characterizing a constituency as "swing" or not (Schady 2000; Case 2001).

However, in the Indian system, national political parties do not have to pass a certain threshold of votes from a state in order to "win" the state—they can win a majority of seats in the national legislature distributed in any manner across the states in order to form the government. It is therefore difficult to identify a particular criterion for measuring "tightness" of a political race at the level of aggregation of the state. We argue that the proportion of seats allotted to a state that a party wins can be used to control for "swing" characteristics, especially when interacted with the party affiliation of the state government. If a party sweeps a state, that is, wins all or almost all the seats allotted to the state in the national legislature, and is also in power at the state government, it would imply the political race in that state is not tight, from the perspective of the party. If a party controls a very small proportion of seats from a state in the national legislature, but is in power at the state level, the state is likely to be "swing," in that there is room for political gains using the fiscal instruments of the state at the party's disposal. If a party controls a small proportion of seats from a state, and is not in power in the state, the state is least likely to be "swing" from the party's perspective, because the state might have an ideological preference for the rival political party. If a party sweeps a state in national elections, even when a rival party is in power at the state level, then the state is likely to be "swing" from the party's perspective, in that it is "up for grabs" in the next state election.[9] Thus in both nonaffiliated and affiliated states (but for different reasons), those where the state ruling party controls a smaller proportion of seats in the national legislature are likely to be swing.

If overall representation of a state matters for its bargaining power, we would have $\alpha > 0$ (from equation 3.1); if the central ruling party can only discipline its co-partisan states (as in the evidence from the Argentine provinces), we would have $\beta < 0$ (in both equations 3.1 and 3.2); conversely, if the center only bears political costs for not bailing out a state in co-partisan states, then we would have $\beta > 0$. Among affiliated states, if "swing" states are more important than "core support" states, we would have $\phi < 0$ (in equation 3.2).

Among nonaffiliated states, the impact of "swing" status of a state (i.e., whether the state ruling party controls a smaller proportion of seats in the national legislature) will be linked to what relation is observed on β. If $\beta > 0$, then the center does not bear direct costs of not bailing out a state when a rival political party is in power at the state level, because the losses are likely to be borne by the governing rival political party in the state. In this case nonaffiliated states that are swing (where the state's voters have not shown a clear preference for the rival political party by also voting for them in national elections) might have even lower deficits as the center tries to inflict greater damage on its rival political party in "swing" states, by withholding resources from the state governing party, that is, $\gamma < 0$. If $\beta < 0$, then nonaffiliated states have bargaining power for greater resources; their bargaining power might increase with the proportion of seats the rival political party controls in the national legislature, in which case we would have $\gamma > 0$.

If partisan identity of the state government does not matter and only bargaining power of national legislators belonging to rival political parties matters, then β and ϕ would be indistinguishable from 0, and we would have $\gamma > 0$. If national legislators belonging to the national ruling party are the ones bargaining for greater spending in their states of origin, again regardless of the partisan identity of the state government, then we would have β indistinguishable from 0, but $\phi > 0$ and $\gamma > 0$.

In section 3.4 below I discuss how specification (3.2) can be augmented to include dependence of states on central transfers. If transfer dependence is what matters for state deficits (and the partisan effect is driven by correlation between transfer dependence and partisan identity), then this inclusion can serve to test this alternate hypothesis.

Endogeneity Concerns

Estimating the potential effect of election outcomes on public expenditures (and hence deficits) is rather obviously subject to an endogeneity problem. If we believe that politicians use election outcomes to determine allocation of public resources, then we must also believe that public expenditure policies have an effect on elections; that is, election outcomes are influenced by expenditures in past periods. Schady (2000) explains that the coefficients on election outcomes (β, ϕ, and γ in equation 3.2 of this chapter) are biased and inconsistent when two conditions are simultaneously met—there is serial correlation in the error term and expenditures affect election outcomes.

In the absence of any valid instruments for political affiliation and seat share of ruling parties, we can address this problem by controlling for serial correlation in the regression specifications and including lagged values of the dependent variable. In particular, since political affiliation and seat share can only change in value in election years, we are likely to correctly identify the effect of political variables once we control for lagged deficit. That is, if an election occurs in year t, the electoral outcomes of year t can be treated as predetermined with respect to the fiscal deficit in years $t+1$, $t+2$, etc., until the next elections, once the deficit of year t, which is likely to influence election outcomes in year t, has been included in the specification. Since state elections in India have usually taken place exactly at the end of the fiscal year, in an election year t, equations (3.1) and (3.2) actually regress $DEFICIT_{it}$ during the course of year t, on outcomes of the previous election, that is, on values of $AFFILIATION_{it-1}$ and $SEATS_{it-1}$, that were obtained from the previous year.

Results

Table 3.2 reports the results of estimating specifications (3.1) and (3.2) using a variety of estimation strategies that have been commonly used in this literature—the first column reports ordinary least squares (OLS) estimates of the simple specification (3.1) without state fixed effects, with panel corrected standard errors that account for heteroskedasticity, autocorrelation, and contemporaneous correlation across panels; the second column reports OLS estimates of specification (3.2), with state fixed effects; the third column reports OLS estimates including the lag of the dependent variable; and the fourth column reports results from a generalized method of moments (GMM) estimator derived by Arellano and Bond (1991) for consistent parameter estimates in a fixed effects model with a lagged dependent variable.

All estimates show that state governments that belong to the same political party as the central government have significantly higher fiscal deficits. Among affiliated states, those that control a small proportion of seats to the national legislature tend to have significantly higher deficits than those that control a higher proportion of seats. In fact, if an affiliated state government controls all the state's seats to the national legislature (i.e., the proportion $= 1$), then its net benefit from affiliation can be negative, since the coefficient on the interaction term is greater than the coefficient on the affiliation indicator in many specifications. Hence it is really those affiliated states where the center receives greater political gains at the margin that seem to be particularly favored in terms of being allowed to run higher deficits.

The effect of political affiliation is substantial—the smallest estimated effect shows that deficits in affiliated states (where the proportion of seats controlled by the ruling party is at the sample average,

Table 3.2
Effect of partisanship on state fiscal deficit

Variable	(1) OLS (w/out fixed effects)	(2) OLS (w/fixed effects)	(3) OLS (w/lagged fiscal deficit)	(4) GMM
Seats allotted to state in national legislature	−0.09 (2.23)			
Political affiliation (= 1 if center and state government belong to same political party)	20.22** (10.09)	53.41** (27.50)	63.27*** (23.38)	62.93** (29.29)
Affiliation * State ruling party seats		−69.67** (29.61)	−66.69*** (24.47)	−53.58** (22.48)
(1 − Affiliation) * State ruling party seats		−22.56 (24.80)	−3.23 (20.79)	8.85 (17.58)
Lagged fiscal deficit			0.43*** (0.08)	0.41*** (0.05)
Real state income per capita	0.02*** (0.004)	0.01 (0.01)	0.01 (0.01)	0.01 (0.01)
Total population	−0.001 (0.002)	−0.001 (0.001)	−0.001 (0.001)	−0.001 (0.001)
	$N = 360$ $R^2 = 0.49$	$N = 360$ $R^2 = 0.65$	$N = 360$ $R^2 = 0.82$	$N = 360$

Notes: Standard errors are in parentheses. Dependent variable is real fiscal deficit per capita. *** Significant at 1 percent; ** significant at 5 percent; * significant at 10 percent. Columns 1, 2, and 3 report OLS regressions with panel corrected standard errors, for heteroskedasticity, autocorrelation, and contemporaneous correlation across panels. Year effects are included, and state fixed effects are in all but column 1. Column 4 reports the Arellano-Bond GMM estimates, one-step robust estimates.

which is about half) are greater than in other states by 11 percent of the average per capita fiscal deficit in the sample. If an affiliated state controls close to zero of the seats in the national parliament, then its deficit is greater by more than 25 percent of the average per capita fiscal deficit in the sample. Nonaffiliated states even when the rival party controls a larger proportion of state seats in the national legislature do not appear to bargain for higher deficits.[10] The result that among affiliated states those where the national ruling party controls a smaller number of seats have higher deficits is interesting in its own right, and suggestive of the importance of "swing" states as contrasted with "core-support" states.

Various types of alternate explanations, including those based on efficient fiscal responses to macroeconomic shocks, can be imagined for why changes in state governments might be correlated with state deficits, casting doubt on the interpretation that party affiliation represents political bargaining power in a federation and distorts allocation of government debt. In fact the variation in affiliation in the data derives largely from whether voters in a state elect a particular party, the Congress party, or not. The Congress party dominated national government in India until the 1990s, although it was frequently unseated from state governments. The Congress was driven out of power from the center by a coalition of opposition parties in the general elections of 1977 and 1990, and the states from where the non-Congress parties won the majority of their seats to the national legislature were also the states where these opposition parties defeated the incumbent Congress state government and tool control of the state. Thus a state is likely to be affiliated with the center if its voters elect Congress to the state, except in the years 1977 to 1979 and 1990 when the opposite was true.

We address these potential sources of endogenous variation in overall state government affiliation in a variety of ways. First, we include the share of votes cast for the Congress party in specification (3.2) to control for voter taste for the dominant national political party. These results are shown in column 1 of table 3.3, and do not change the impact of affiliation. Second, we test whether the impact of affiliation is different in the years 1977 to 1979 and in 1990 when non-Congress parties controlled the national parliament, in column 2 of table 3.3. There is no difference in the overall pattern of impact of political affiliation, but the non-Congress national ruling parties in 1977 to 1979 and 1990 appear to target more vigorously those affiliated states from where they control a lower proportion of seats in the national legislature.

Other political and institutional determinants of deficits at the state level that have been tested in the received literature might also be correlated with affiliation, and be driving the results, such as election cycles (Alesina et al. 1997; Khemani 2004), and fragmented or divided legislatures (Roubini and Sachs 1989; Poterba 1994; Alt and Lowry 1994; Perotti and Kontopoulos 2002). Column 3 of table 3.3 includes an additional indicator variable $COALITION_{it}$, which equals 1 when there is no clear majority in the state legislature, and the executive is formed of a coalition of various political parties, and an indicator for the state

Table 3.3
Effect of partisanship on state fiscal deficit when controlling for other political determinants

Variable	(1)	(2)	(3)
Political affiliation (= 1 if center and state government belong to same political party)	63.19** (30.87)	46.93** (23.70)	66.43** (31.52)
Affiliation * State ruling party seats	−57.67*** (21.52)	−37.95** (19.40)	−57.13** (24.01)
(1 − Affiliation) * State ruling party seats	7.73 (18.24)	23.63 (16.99)	8.03 (17.03)
Affiliation * Years 1977–80 & 1990		90.35** (45.74)	
Affiliation * State ruling party seats * Years 1977–80 & 1990		−106.81*** (41.98)	
(1 − Affiliation) * State ruling party seats * Years 1977–80 & 1990		−39.12 (37.91)	
Percentage of votes received by Congress party in state elections	−2.47* (1.49)		
Congress votes squared	0.04* (0.02)		
Coalition government (= 1 if state executive consists of a coalition government)			−3.87 (7.52)
State election year (= 1 in the year preceding a state election)			−11.62** (5.59)
Lagged fiscal deficit	0.40*** (0.05)	0.40*** (0.04)	0.40*** (0.05)
Real state income per capita	0.01 (0.01)	0.01 (0.01)	0.01 (0.01)
Total population	−0.001 (0.001)	−0.001 (0.001)	−0.001 (0.001)
	N = 360	N = 360	N = 360

Notes: Standard errors are in parentheses. Dependent variable is real fiscal deficit per capita. *** Significant at 1 percent; ** significant at 5 percent; * significant at 10 percent. Arellano-Bond GMM estimates and one-step robust estimates are reported.

election cycle.[11] Coalition politics at the state level and the state election cycle are not significantly or substantially correlated with state deficits, and including them in the regression does not affect the coefficients of interest. If anything, the estimated effects of partisanship become even larger once controls are included for these other political effects.

These results of the non-effect or small effect of other political variables are interesting in their own right because they seem to indicate that state-level political variables have no discernable effect on deficits, although they might on the composition of spending and revenues (as reported by Khemani 2004). It is instead the state's political relation with the center that accounts for significant variation in its deficit.

Dependence on federal grants is another variable that is likely to contribute to perverse incentives for fiscal profligacy (according to the argument in Rodden 2002). In fact the results on partisanship might be driven by this alternate hypothesis of dependence on federal transfers, if affiliated states receive greater transfers, and transfers exacerbate the credibility problem. Table 3.4 reports results when we include vertical fiscal imbalance, that is, the proportion of intergovernmental grants in total state revenues (total intergovernmental grants/total revenues) as a measure of transfer dependence. Since vertical fiscal imbalance is largely stable within a state over time, most of the variation in transfer dependence measured this way comes from variation across states. Hence results are reported both with and without state fixed effects, in columns 1 and 2 respectively. The GMM estimates in columns 3 and 4 include respectively vertical fiscal imbalance in first difference and in levels. The coefficient on vertical fiscal imbalance is not statistically significant; the sign is negative, suggesting that contrary to conventional wisdom greater transfer dependence might be correlated with *lower* deficits. The effect of partisanship is unchanged even after controlling for transfer dependence.[12]

Table 3.5 simultaneously estimates the effect of the *level* of transfers (in per capita real terms) on state fiscal deficit and the determinants of transfer distribution across states, using three-stage least squares. There is an inherent simultaneity problem in identifying the effect of transfers on deficits because both are presumably determined in equilibrium under general economic conditions. Unfortunately, this endogeneity could not be addressed in a satisfactory manner because of lack of good instruments that only impact transfers and not state fiscal behavior directly. However, my attempt to compensate is to use lagged values of transfers as instruments. To the best of my knowledge, this is

Table 3.4
Effect of intergovernmental grants on state fiscal deficit

Variable	(1) OLS (w/state fixed effects)	(2) OLS (w/out state fixed effects)	(3) GMM (grants/rev. differenced)	(4) GMM (grants/ rev. in levels)
Vertical fiscal imbalance (grants/revenues)	−0.07 (1.11)	−0.21 (0.34)	−0.46 (1.41)	−0.11* (0.06)
Political affiliation (= 1 if center and state government belong to same political party)	63.11*** (23.35)	56.22*** (21.90)	61.31** (27.21)	60.68** (28.99)
Affiliation * State ruling party seats	−66.42*** (24.57)	−55.39*** (22.59)	−52.50** (22.22)	−55.40** (23.01)
(1 − Affiliation) * State ruling party seats	−3.18 (20.80)	−6.63 (19.65)	7.73 (17.02)	10.48 (17.58)
Lagged fiscal deficit	0.43*** (0.08)	0.58*** (0.08)	0.40*** (0.05)	0.38*** (0.05)
Real state income per capita	0.01 (0.01)	0.01 (0.004)	0.01 (0.01)	−0.01 (0.01)
Total population	−0.001 (0.001)	−0.0002** (0.0001)	−0.001 (0.001)	−0.001 (0.001)
	$N = 360$ $R^2 = 0.82$	$N = 360$ $R^2 = 0.81$	$N = 360$	$N = 360$

Notes: Standard errors are in parentheses. Dependent variable is real fiscal deficit per capita. *** Significant at 1 percent; ** significant at 5 percent; * significant at 10 percent. Columns 1 and 2 report OLS regressions with panel corrected standard errors, for heteroskedasticity, autocorrelation, and contemporaneous correlation across panels; year fixed effects are included. Columns 3 and 4 report the Arellano-Bond GMM estimates, onestep robust estimates. Column 3 includes grants/revenues in first difference, while column 4 includes grants/revenues in levels.

the first time a rigorous test has been undertaken of the conventional wisdom that the design of intergovernmental transfers in India creates perverse incentives for state governments to run higher deficits (Rao 1998; Rao and Singh 2000).

I distinguish between the specifications for the distribution of the two types of transfers—those determined by the independent agency and those determined under political discretion—based on the results reported in Khemani (2003) of contrasting political effects across these two types. Lagged transfers are used in each specification for the deter-

Table 3.5
Effect of intergovernmental grants on state fiscal deficit in terms of 3-stage least squares

Variable	(1) Fiscal deficit	(2) Nondiscretionary grants	(3) Discretionary grants
Nondiscretionary grants	−0.44** (0.21)		
Discretionary grants	−0.76*** (0.23)		
Nondiscretionary grants (lag 1)		0.65*** (0.04)	
Discretionary grants (lag 1)			0.49*** (0.05)
Political affiliation (= 1 if center and state government belong to same political party)	84.22*** (29.51)	−28.89*** (7.37)	27.16** (11.35)
Affiliation ∗ State ruling party seats	−93.23*** (23.06)	8.34 (7.66)	−15.75* (9.79)
(1 − Affiliation) ∗ State ruling party seats	−4.76 (26.36)	−8.99 (8.88)	12.11 (11.44)
Real state income per capita	−0.003 (0.01)	0.002 (0.002)	−0.01* (0.003)
Total population	−0.003*** (0.001)	−0.0001 (0.0003)	−0.0004 (0.0004)
	$N = 335$ $R^2 = 0.75$	$N = 335$ $R^2 = 0.89$	$N = 335$ $R^2 = 0.83$

Notes: Standard errors are in parentheses. *** Significant at 1 percent; ** significant at 5 percent; * significant at 10 percent. Three-stage least squares estimates, state fixed effects, and year effects are included.

mination of transfers, and omitted from the deficit equation, to identify the impact of transfers on deficits. Political effects on the distribution of transfers across states are identical to those reported in Khemani (2003)—while discretionary transfers are targeted to those affiliated states where the ruling party controls a smaller proportion of seats in the national legislature (to maximize the party's representation in the legislature); transfers determined by the independent agency are consistent with promoting equity across states by curbing political influence.

The level of transfers received by state governments has a negative effect on fiscal deficit—a 1 percent increase in either category of per capita transfers is associated with a fall in deficit of 0.4 percent, calculated at the sample average. Hence, although the effect is not elastic, it runs counter to the received wisdom that greater transfer dependence is associated with higher deficits. Greater transfer receipts in this case appear to be indicative of greater resources available to state governments and so lower their need for deficit financing. There is no apparent evidence of perverse political incentives for fiscal profligacy as a result of greater transfer dependence.

3.5   Interpretation of Results and Implications for Policy

The Indian evidence hence suggests that while delegation to the national political executive of oversight authority for subnational debt can make a difference (which is why, perhaps, transfer dependence does not have a negative effect on deficits in India), national party political incentives can still lead to fiscal profligacy at the state level. Interpreting the evidence here in light of insights from the political science literature on electoral competition in India, we learn that these political incentives are likely to be arising from the pressure of multiple interest groups on public resources, as identified in the literature on the political economy of budget deficits.

There exists a large political science literature analyzing party competition in India from which comes the following brief description.[13] A single political party dominated electoral competition in the early years of India's democracy, namely the Indian National Congress (hereafter referred to as the Congress), largely due to the historical legacy of being the leader of the independence movement against British colonial rule. However, in the late 1960s the Congress party began to face stiff challenges from rival political parties in state assembly elections. Several of the parties that emerged were regional parties with limited national standing. These regional parties began to replace the Congress as the governing party at the state level.

The Congress lost control of the national Parliament for the first time in the national elections of 1977, when a new national-level opposition political party was forged through alliances between political leaders previously belonging to disparate political groups. However, Congress came back to power in an early election in 1980. It similarly lost control of the national parliament in the 1989 elections to a new political party created for the explicit purpose of organizing a unified opposition to the Congress, only to return quickly to power in 1991 with early elections. By the 1990s, seat control in the national parliament became increasingly fragmented across different political parties, including regional parties with their power bases at the state level. Since 1989, multi-party competition for the national parliament appears firmly established, with national parties like the Congress and BJP (Bharatiya Janata Party) leading coalition governments that depend upon the support of regional political parties.[14]

The emergence of regional parties in India can be attributed to the nature of electoral competition along the lines of caste, religion, and linguistic identities that vary systematically across states (Weiner and Field 1974). Chhibber (1995) and Weiner and Field (1974) suggest that there are limited ideological differences among parties along the lines of economic policy; party identity is instead driven by social, ethnic, and regional differences.[15] Electoral competition between these parties has been characterized as revolving around access to the instruments of government and appropriation of public resources by different groups (Chhibber 1995).

In addition to social identity based politics, specific electoral institutions in India emphasize the importance of geographically defined interest groups, which is a central feature of fiscal models with common-pool problems. India's first-past-the-post voting system is based on contests among individual candidates in single-member constituencies where the seat is won by the candidate that gets more votes than any other. This simple plurality electoral law in practice implies a tenuous link between the percentage of popular votes received by a party and the probability of winning the majority of seats in the legislature, because of fragmented electoral competition at the constituency level. In many electoral districts it is possible for a candidate to win with just about 20 percent of the popular vote (Butler, Lahiri, and Roy 1995). Butler et al. (1995) also indicate that once a party crosses a particular threshold in votes, around 30 to 35 percent, it can move to a landslide victory in seats by gaining just a few percentage points in popular support.

The spending instruments available to state governments have direct impact on people's lives, such as provision of education, health, water services, and construction of local roads. There are three large chunks that account for the bulk of central government spending—defense, debt-servicing, and various agricultural subsidies that are actually distributed through state governments (Varshney 1995). Thus the politically influential fiscal instruments available to the center, subsidies, depend on the states' political machinery for distribution. If a party loses control of a state government, it loses control over public instruments to buy political support through targeted provision of benefits. Hence it is not surprising to note that if a party comes to power in a state (by winning a majority of seats in the state legislature), then in the next national elections that party also tends to win seats to the national legislature from that state.[16] Additional spending by state governments can yield benefits in the form of additional seats for the political party in power in the state, in both state and national elections.

I have argued that the evidence above of the impact of federal politics on state fiscal deficits should be interpreted as evidence of limited ability of the national political executive in enforcing subnational fiscal discipline. However, as I mentioned at the end of section 3.2, the impact of co-partisanship on deficits could be because of the center opportunistically and deliberately distributing deficit financing across states to further the party's political objectives, or because state party leaders have bargaining power within the party and hold the central party leadership hostage through their actions. It is not possible to distinguish empirically between these two interpretations.

Which of the two is appropriate is likely to depend on the extent of control of national party leaders on state party leaders. There is quite a bit of political science literature on the bargaining power of state leaders of the Congress party, which is the party most likely to be driving the incidence of affiliation. In the late 1960s power within the Congress party has been described as resting in the hands of powerful state leaders, commonly called the Syndicate (Kochanek 1968; Frankel 1978; Rudolph and Rudolph 1987). From 1971 to 1977 and again from 1980 to 1985, Prime Minister Indira Gandhi tried to bypass state leaders to forge direct ties with local elites that helped as power "brokers" during elections (Kochanek 1976). After 1985, her son, and then prime minister, Rajiv Gandhi, has been described as unable to control the various factions within the Congress party (Frankel 1987; Weiner 1987; Manor 1988). This literature is therefore consistent with a story of bargaining by affiliated states for bailouts from the center.

This received description of Indian politics thus suggests that interest group politics can be played out within political parties, making even single-party dominant national governments unable to withstand electoral pressure for spending. The key therefore is to understand the nature of electoral competition, and whether the national party is primarily being held accountable for overall macroeconomic outcomes and national public goods or for private benefits targeted to disperse interest groups. If the latter, then the issue for concern is not just fiscal decentralization to multiple subnational spending authorities but rather consolidated government resource allocation decisions.

In many developing countries political competition is typically described as "clientelistic"—the exchange of votes for targeted, private resource transfers—rather than based on providing broad public goods. Such competition is likely to be appropriately represented in simple noncooperative bargaining games between multiple players, and therefore likely to lead to Nash-style equilibria where the final outcome is suboptimal from the perspective of each player. This suggests therefore a role for an independent agency, whose nonpartisan identity is credible to all players, to impose constraints on the overall size of fiscal aggregates for consolidated government accounts. In fact, if an independent agency were only delegated authority over the determination of overall fiscal aggregates that are consistent with the national public good of fiscal sustainability, without any powers of interfering in decisions of resource distribution within the overall envelope, then theoretically it might play the role of enforcing a cooperative equilibrium where outcomes are more efficient, leaving bargaining over distribution in the political arena.

An independent agency, whose nonpartisan identity is credible to all players, and with the legal authority to impose constraints on the overall size of government deficit and debt, could make a difference in two ways: (1) by announcing constraints early, it could bring political parties to the negotiating table early and hasten stabilization, and (2) it could help voters distinguish between government incompetence and actual need for a fiscal adjustment. Opposition parties would be constrained in placing all the blame for adjustment on the ruling party because they face the same rules of the game under the independent agency, and because of the credibility of the independent agency itself. Delegation to an independent agency of consolidated government borrowing and debt regulation can therefore serve as a commitment device for all political parties to reign-in populist promises.

Eichengreen, Hausmann, and von Hagen (1999) have already initiated this idea by outlining a blueprint for delegation of decisions over consolidated government debt ceilings to an independent agency in the Latin American region. The Finance Commission in India has a track record of success in checking the impact of partisan influence on general-purpose revenue transfers to states, and the Commission is therefore a promising candidate for delegation of consolidated government debt oversight. Ironically, it might be important for the Commission to relinquish its former authority over deciding interregional resource distribution to the national legislative assembly. This way the national assembly would have more instruments at its disposal for political bargaining, and overall fiscal aggregates could be credibly placed above the fray, giving all parties incentives to comply with its rulings.

Why have delegation and not formal fiscal rules targeting particular levels of debt and deficits? An increasing number of countries in both developed and developing regions have adopted various forms of fiscal rules, mainly balanced budget requirements and debt limits, with the primary objective of conferring credibility on their fiscal policies. Hallerberg and von Hagen (1999) show that countries with majoritarian electoral systems (where national legislatures are more likely to be dominated by a single political party) have chosen to delegate power to the finance minister in the budget process, while countries with proportional electoral systems (where the national legislature is likely to be fragmented across political parties) have tried to adopt formal budget targets. The research literature evaluating the efficacy of these rules has by and large concluded that they can make a difference for fiscal performance (Poterba and von Hagen 1999). Specifically, the evidence suggests that formal fiscal rules do impact short-run taxes and expenditures, and promote faster adjustment to fiscal shocks; however, they do not prevent extreme outcomes and the substitution of non-transparent debt for restricted debt instruments (von Hagen 1991). It is generally agreed in this literature on fiscal institutions that rules, in order to be effective, have to be simple (Tanzi 1993), leading to a trade-off between effectiveness and flexibility. If rules are to be flexible, they require accompanying institutions of transparency to enforce them and prevent their circumvention through creative accounting and counterproductive actions on the side. Thus an independent fiscal agency is likely to serve a useful purpose even if to simply monitor and ensure transparent compliance with fiscal rules, or to determine contingency conditions under which rules should be made flexible. In this spirit Eichengreen et al. (1999) describe the idea of an independent fiscal agency as the logical culmination of the approach of formal budgetary procedures and fiscal rules as institutional restraints on fiscal performance.

If this seems rather obvious, then the question arises why delegation to an independent fiscal agency has not yet been seriously pursued in wider policy circles, or in the mainstream research literature, given that similar steps have been taken for monetary policy, through the creation of independent central banks, for the same objective of promoting macroeconomic stability? Wyplosz (2002) raises this question as well and tentatively answers it as follows: Since fiscal policy is a powerful tool for income redistribution, democratic rule implemented through political representatives has been viewed as the more appropriate or just form of decision-making. However, he argues, although democratic control might be viewed as essential for decision-making over the size of government, the distribution of spending, and the structure of taxation, it should not be considered crucial for fiscal aggregates such as debt and deficit. Once this distinction is understood by policy makers, they might be open to considering the role of independent fiscal agencies. Blinder (1997) has advocated a role for independent agencies even more broadly, drawing from his experience of the functioning of the US Federal Reserve.

3.6 Conclusion

This chapter has provided new empirical evidence on political incentives of national governments to impose fiscal discipline on subnationals. It has argued from this evidence that the national political party itself does not have strong incentives for fiscal discipline, and that hence delegation to the national political executive of oversight authority of subnational debt has had limited success. Instead, in light of the overall common-pool problem of consolidated government finances, the chapter has suggested an innovative policy area that might be explored—delegation to an independent fiscal agency of oversight of consolidated government debt and borrowing.

Although such a policy recommendation is relevant for India, the country case considered here, because of the existence and demonstrated effectiveness of an independent fiscal agency, it is difficult to generalize to other countries. The reason is that there is no systematic research on the political conditions under which such agencies can be created and sustained, and it is not clear that they can be created everywhere. Even within India it is difficult to address counterfactuals such as whether political authorities will agree to delegate powers over debt oversight to the independent agency, and whether the agency will continue to effectively curb national partisan influence even after this delegation. There is no specific experience from any country of independent agencies with oversight authority for consolidated government debt. Independent agencies do exist in other developing countries for determining intergovernmental resource transfers. The Commonwealth Grants Commission in Australia and the National Finance Council in Malaysia are some other prominent examples, with other developing countries that are rapidly decentralizing beginning to experiment with the establishment of similar agencies. But there is no evidence from these countries on whether the agencies are effective in curbing political influence.

The immediate purpose of this chapter is to argue through new evidence on costly political bargaining and fiscal indiscipline, that the creation of independent fiscal agencies and delegation of debt oversight to them is a fruitful policy agenda to explore, much in the spirit of an earlier agenda pursuing independent central banks. Additional research on the political conditions under which effectively independent fiscal agencies can be created, and delegated sufficient authority would usefully serve this agenda.

Notes

The findings, interpretations, and conclusions expressed in this paper are entirely those of the author, and do not necessarily represent the views of the World Bank, its Executive Directors, or the countries they represent.

1. An enterprise or any organization was described by Kornai (1980, 1986) as having a "soft budget constraint" when it expects to be bailed out by external sources in case of financial trouble.

2. Only two other papers, to the best of my knowledge, have floated the idea of delegation of fiscal aggregates such as deficits and debt to an independent fiscal agency—Eichengreen, Hausman, and von Hagen (1999) and Wyplosz (2002)—but neither has provided empirical evidence on how such delegation might be effected and whether it would make a difference.

3. That is, a party does not have win a critical number of votes in each state in order to win the districts allotted to a state in the national legislature. Districts are won on an individual basis.

4. In the event of a single party not winning more than 50 percent of Lok Sabha seats, a ruling coalition is formed amongst different parties on the basis of a vote of confidence in parliament.

5. Detailed analysis of the history of fiscal federalism and intergovernment transfers in India, with exhaustive references, can be found in Rao and Chelliah (1991) and Rao and

Singh (2000). The main reason behind the imbalanced assignment of revenue authority and expenditure responsibility was to provide the central authorities with a fiscal instrument to promote unity amongst the disparate nationalities residing within one country. Overall fiscal control at the center was expected to reign-in regional secessionist tendencies and promote regional equality.

6. Many scholars of Indian fiscal federalism have described transfers made by the Planning Commission as unconstitutional, because the Finance Commission was envisioned in the Constitution as the only agency with decision authority over regular, general-purpose transfers to the states.

7. We scrutinized the membership of individual Finance Commissions from 1951 to the present and found that every one of them included one Justice (either sitting on a State High Court or the Supreme Court of India, or retired from one) and one technical expert with no political experience. However, the remaining members tended to have had a political careers either in the national or state legislature, or to have held senior positions in the central or state administration. In addition there have been a few instances when an individual member resigned from the Commission in the middle of tenure to accept a post in a state or central government. These instances might lead us to suspect the actual independence of the Commission from the political process, but there does not appear to be a systematic bias toward either the central or individual state governments from the identity of the members.

8. These 15 states of India account for 95 percent of the total population. India consists of 28 states at present of which 3 were newly created in 2000, 2 were recently converted to statehood from Union Territories, and 8 are designated "special" states, largely because of separatist tensions, and provided extraordinary central transfers. Of the 15 states under study, 11 have existed since the organization of the federation in 1956. An additional two were created for linguistic reasons out of a single large state—Maharashtra and Gujarat—in 1960; and two in 1966—Pubjab and Haryana—also for ethnic and linguistic reasons. Hence, in order to avoid issues of endogenous state boundaries, and of special transfers to some smaller states, I focus only on the 15 major states that have existed from the early days of the federation. These 15 states are Andhra Pradesh, Assam, Bihar, Gujarat, Haryana, Karnataka, Kerala, Madhya Pradesh, Maharashtra, Orissa, Punjab, Rajasthan, Tamil Nadu, Uttar Pradesh, and West Bengal.

9. Affiliation with the state government is a nonlinear way of measuring representation of the party in the *state* legislature. I did estimate the more general model of including a party's representation in both the state and national legislatures, and found that once the affiliation indicator was included, other measures of state legislature representation had no separate effect.

10. None of the main results are affected by including or excluding the control variables, expressing deficit as a percentage of state domestic product, or dropping individual states one at a time. The Arellano-Bond one-step model performs well. I was able to reject the presence of second order autocorrelation.

The sign of the coefficient on the affiliation and seats interaction is identical when the absolute number of national legislators belonging to the state ruling party is used instead of as a proportion of the total seats allotted to a state.

11. There is an emerging literature on political budget cycles that finds evidence of expansionary fiscal policies in election years in developing countries. However, in Khemani (2004), I find no effect of such cycles in overall spending and deficits in the Indian

states—only the composition of spending and revenues changes, possibly to target special interest groups for campaign support.

12. There is no effect of transfer dependence on fiscal deficits even when we distinguish between dependence on those transfers that are determined at the discretion of the central political executive and on those determined by the independent agency. These results are not reported here in the interests of brevity.

13. Some of the references providing good overviews and recent developments are Brass (1990), Manor (1994), and Yadav (1996).

14. We tried several specifications to test whether results changed significantly after 1989, when multi-party competition at the national level became more vigorous, and find no evidence of this—that is, the effect of partisanship is the same before and after 1989.

15. There are two communist parties in India that have dominated state elections in two states, Kerala and West Bengal, and have a distinguishable economic policy platform. But the platforms of these parties are different along specific dimensions such as labor regulations and land redistribution, rather than in broad terms such as size of government, and are therefore unlike the left-right distinctions in OECD countries.

16. An example from the state of Andhra Pradesh is illustrative in this context. The Congress party lost control of the state government in Andhra Pradesh in the 1983 state elections to a new regional party, the Telegu Desam. In the next national elections in 1984, even though it won an overwhelming majority of seats in the national legislature, the Congress lost most seats from Andhra Pradesh to the Telegu Desam despite the latter's novice status in national politics.

References

Alesina, A., N. Roubini, and G. Cohen. 1997. *Political Cycles and the Macroeconomy*. Cambridge: MIT Press.

Alesina, A., and R. Perotti. 1995. "The political economy of budget deficits." *IMF Staff Papers* (March): 1–31.

Alt, J., and R. Lowry. 1994. Divided government, fiscal institutions, and budget deficits: Evidence from the state. *American Political Science Review* 88(4): 811–28.

Anand, M., A. Bagchi, and T. Sen. 2001. Fiscal discipline at the state level: Perverse incentives and paths to reform. Paper presented at conference on India: Fiscal Policies to Accelerate Economic Growth. New Delhi, May 21–22.

Arellano, M., and S. Bond. 1991. Some tests of specification for panel data: Monte Carlo evidence and an application to employment equations. *Review of Economic Studies* 58, 277–97.

Blanchard, O., and A. Shleifer. 2001. Federalism with and without political centralization: China versus Russia. *IMF Staff Papers* 48 (Special Issue): 171–79.

Blinder, A. 1997. Is government too political? *Foreign Affairs* 76(6): 115–26.

Brass, P. 1990. *The Politics of India since Independence*. New York: Cambridge University Press.

Butler, D., A. Lahiri, and P. Roy. 1995. India decides: Elections 1952–1995. New Delhi: Books and Things Publishers.

Case, A. 2001. Election goals and income redistribution: Recent evidence from Albania. *European Economic Review* 45: 405–23.

Chhibber, P. 1995. Political parties, electoral competition, government expenditures and economic reform in India. *Journal of Development Studies* 32(1): 74–96.

Cox, G., and M. McCubbins. 1986. Electoral politics as a redistributive game. *Journal of Politics* 48: 370–89.

Dillinger, W., and S. Webb. 1999. Fiscal management in federal democracies: Argentina and Brazil. Policy Research Working Paper 2121. World Bank, Washington, DC.

Dixit, A., and J. Londregan. 1998. Fiscal federalism and redistributive politics. *Journal of Public Economics* 68: 153–80.

Eichengreen, B., R. Hausmann, and J. von Hagen. 1999. Reforming budgetary institutions in Latin America: The case for a National Fiscal Council. *Open Economies Review* 10: 415–42.

Frankel, F. 1987. Politics: The failure to re-build consensus. In M. Bouton, ed., *India Briefing*. Boulder, CO: Westview, pp. 25–48.

Frankel, F. 1978. *India's Political Economy, 1947–1977: The Gradual Revolution*. Princeton: Princeton University Press.

von Hagen, J. 1991. A note on the empirical effectiveness of formal fiscal restraints. *Journal of Public Economics* 44: 199–210.

Hallerberg, M., and J. von Hagen. 1999. Electoral institutions, cabinet negotiations, and budget deficits in the European Union. In J. Poterba and J. von Hagen, eds., *Fiscal Institutions and Fiscal Performance*. Chicago: University of Chicago Press.

Johansson, E. 2003. Intergovernmental grants as a tactical instrument: Empirical evidence from Swedish municipalities. *Journal of Public Economics* 87: 883–915.

Jones, M., P. Sanguinetti, and M. Tommasi. 2000. Politics, institutions, and fiscal performance in a federal system: An analysis of the Argentine provinces. *Journal of Development Economics* 61: 305–33.

Khemani, S. 2003. Partisan politics and intergovernmental transfers in India. Policy Research Working Paper 3016. World Bank, Development Research Group, Washington, DC.

Khemani, S. 2004. Political cycles in a developing economy: Effect of elections in the Indian states. *Journal of Development Economics* 73(1): 125–54.

Kochanek, S. 1976. Mrs. Gandhi's pyramid: The new congress. In H. C. Hart, ed., *Indira Gandhi's India*. Boulder, CO: Westview, pp. 93–124.

Kochanek, S. 1968. *The Congress Party of India: The Dynamics of One-Party Democracy*. Princeton: Princeton University Press.

Kornai, J. 1980. *Economics of Shortage*. Amsterdam: North Holland.

Kornai, J. 1986. The soft budget constraint. *Kyklos* 39(1): 3–30.

Manor, J., ed. 1994. *Nehru to the Nineties: The Changing Office of the Prime Minister in India.* Vancouver: University of British Columbia Press.

Manor, J. 1988. Parties and the party system. In A. Kohli, ed., *India's Democracy: An Analysis of Changing State-Society Relations.* Princeton: Princeton University Press, pp. 62–99.

McCarten, W. 2001. The challenge of fiscal discipline in the Indian states. In J. Rodden, G. Eskeland, and J. Litvack, eds., *Decentralization and Hard Budget Constraints.* Cambridge: MIT Press.

Miguel, E., and F. Zaidi. 2003. Do politicians reward their supporters? Public spending and incumbency advantage in Ghana. Mimeo. Department of Economics, University of California, Berkeley.

Ordeshook, P. 1996. Russia's party system: Is Russian federalism viable? *Post-Soviet Affairs* 12: 195–217.

Ozler, B., G. Datt, and M. Ravallion. 1996. A database on poverty and growth in India. Development Research Group, World Bank, Washington, DC. [Retrieved April 18, 2002 from *http://www.worldbank.org/poverty/data/indiapaper.htm*].

Perotti, R., and Y. Kontopoulos. 2002. Fragmented fiscal policy. *Journal of Public Economics* 86: 191–222.

Persson, T., and G. Tabellini. 2000. *Political Economics: Explaining Economic Policy.* Cambridge: MIT Press.

Poterba, J. 1994. State responses to fiscal crises: The effects of budgetary institutions and politics. *Journal of Political Economy* 102: 799–821.

Poterba, J., and J. von Hagen. 1999. *Fiscal Institutions and Fiscal Performance.* Chicago: University of Chicago Press.

Qian, Y., and G. Roland. 1998. Federalism and the soft budget constraint. *American Economic Review* 88(5): 1150–62.

Qian, Y., and B. Weingast. 1997. Federalism as a commitment to preserving market incentives. *Journal of Economic Perspectives* 11: 83–92.

Rao, G. 1998. India: Intergovernmental fiscal relations in a planned economy. In R. M. Bird and F. Vaillancourt, eds., *Fiscal Decentralization in Developing Countries.* Cambridge: Cambridge University Press.

Rao, G., and R. Chelliah. 1991. *Survey of Research on Fiscal Federalism in India.* New Delhi: National Institute of Public Finance and Policy.

Rao, G., and N. Singh. 2000. The political economy of center-state fiscal transfers in India. Paper presented at the Columbia University-World Bank Conference on Institutional Elements of Tax Design and Reform, February 18–19, 2000.

Reserve Bank of India. *Reserve Bank of India Bulletin,* 1972–1999.

Riker, W. 1964. *Federalism: Origin, Operation, Significance.* Boston: Little, Brown.

Rodden, J. 2002. The dilemma of fiscal federalism: Intergovernmental grants and fiscal performance around the world. *American Journal of Political Science* 46(3): 670–87.

Rodden, J., and E. Wibbels. 2002. Beyond the fiction of federalism: Macroeconomic management in multitiered systems. *World Politics* 54(4): 494–531.

Rodden, J., G. Eskeland, and J. Litvack, eds. 2001. *Decentralization and Hard Budget Constraints*. Cambridge: MIT Press.

Roubini, N., and J. Sachs. 1989. Political and economic determinants of budget deficits in the industrialized countries. *European Economic Review* 33: 903–38.

Rudolph, L., and S. Rudolph. 1987. *In Pursuit of Lakshmi: The Political Economy of the Indian State*. Chicago: University of Chicago Press.

Samuels, D. 2000. Concurrent elections, discordant results: Presidentialism, federalism, and governance in Brazil. *Comparative Politics* 33: 1–20.

Schady, N. 2000. The political economy of expenditures by the Peruvian Social Fund (FONCODES), 1991–95. *American Political Science Review* 94(2): 289–304.

Snyder, J. 1989. Election goals and the allocation of campaign resources. *Econometrica* 57: 637–60.

Stepan, A. 2000. Brazil's decentralized federalism: Bringing government closer to the citizens? *Deadalus* 129: 145–70.

Tanzi, V. 1993. Budget deficit in transition: A cautionary note. *IMF Staff Papers* 40: 697–707.

Varshney, A. 1995. *Democracy, Development and the Countryside: Urban-Rural Struggles in India*. Cambridge: Cambridge University Press.

Velasco, A. 1999. A model of endogenous fiscal deficits and delayed fiscal reforms. In J. Poterba and J. von Hagen, eds., *Fiscal Institutions and Fiscal Performance*. Chicago: University of Chicago Press.

Weiner, M. 1987. Rajiv Gandhi: A mid-term assessment. In M. Bouton, ed., *India Briefing, 1987*. Boulder, CO: Westview.

Weiner, M., and J. Field, eds. 1974. *Studies in Electoral Politics in the Indian States*. Delhi: Manohar Book Service.

Weingast, B. 1995. The economic role of political institutions: Market-preserving federalism and economic growth. *Journal of Law, Economics, and Organization* 11: 1–31.

Weingast, B., K. Shepsle, and C. Johnsen. 1981. The political economy of benefits and costs: A neoclassical approach to distributive politics. *Journal of Political Economy* 89: 642–64.

Wibbels, E. 2003. Bailouts, budget constraints, and Leviathans: Comparative federalism and lessons from the early United States. *Comparative Political Studies* 36(5): 475–508.

Wyplosz, C. 2002. Fiscal discipline in emerging market countries: How to go about it? Paper prepared for conference on Financial Stability and Development in Emerging Economies: Steps Forward for Bankers and Financial Authorities, organized by the Forum on Debt and Development (FONDAD) in Amsterdam, June 3–4, 2002.

Yadav, Y. 1996. Reconfiguration in Indian politics: State assembly elections, 1993–95. *Economic and Political Weekly* 31(January): 95–104.

4

The Political Economy of Education in Kenya

Michael Kremer

4.1 Introduction

Education and other social services are centralized in much of the developing world. Many now advocate decentralization and community participation, and reforms along these lines are increasingly being adopted.

This chapter examines the experience of Kenya. Kenya adopted elements of decentralization and community participation in its educational system long before these ideas became fashionable. Kenya's system of financing local public goods, including education, has great ideological importance in the country and is a key component of its political economy. The word *harambee* is emblazoned on the national crest of Kenya and on its currency. Literally translated as "let's pull together," harambee refers to the system adopted under Kenya's first president, in which local communities raise funds for schools and other local public goods. Under the educational system Kenya established after independence, local harambee fund-raisers typically cover initial capital costs for new schools. School fees set by local school committees and collected by headmasters cover most nonteacher recurrent costs, such as chalk, classroom maintenance, and teachers' textbooks. People who live within walking distance of more than one school—a considerable portion of the population—are in practice free to choose which school their children attend. Once local communities establish schools, the central government assigns teachers to schools and pays their salaries.[1] The government also sets the curriculum and administers national tests at the end of primary and secondary school. Outside donors supplement Kenyan finance, sometimes providing additional resources that are targeted to poor or poorly performing schools.

The harambee system funds not only schools, but also other small-scale local projects like local clinics, churches, and agricultural facilities. Barkan and Holmquist (1986) report that 90 percent of residents are or have been involved in the harambee process. Seventy-three percent of people participate in primary school projects and 63 percent participate in secondary school projects (Barkan and Holmquist, 1986). Wilson (1992) finds that most projects are funded from catchment areas of less than a 5 kilometer radius.

Although the harambee system can be traced to pre-colonial era institutions, it dovetails with much contemporary thinking about decentralization, community participation, and school choice. The system utilizes local knowledge about which projects are most needed and about each individual's capacity to pay for these projects. Relative to a system of centralized tax collection and expenditure determination, the more decentralized harambee system gives local officials greater incentives to collect funds from the population, and the local population more incentive to monitor the use of these funds.

In this chapter I argue that interactions among the various elements of the school finance system Kenya adopted at independence create perverse incentives. By financing teachers at the central level but allowing local communities to start schools, the system led to the construction of too many small schools; to excessive spending on teachers relative to nonteacher inputs; and to the setting of school fees and other school attendance requirements at a level that deters some from attending school and that exceeds the level preferred by the median voter. Moreover the school finance system renders the incentives for headmasters created by competition under school choice counterproductive and undermines tendencies for pupils to move to schools with the best headmasters. I also argue that the decision to adopt the system set Kenya on a path that led to growing fiscal costs and inefficiencies, the squeezing out of nonteacher expenditures, and the eventual abandonment of the commitment to assign teachers to any school created by a local community, freezing in place an inefficient and unequal distribution of schools.

The chapter draws on the work of several authors who have previously examined the harambee system. Wilson (1992) seeks to explain the puzzle of why people voluntarily contribute to public goods through harambee, arguing that voluntary provision can succeed in a repeated game in which participants know each other well and contributions are publicized. In contrast, our analysis suggests that widespread participation in the harambee system is due at least in part to massive subsidies from the central government. Ngau (1987) documents and decries efforts by the central government to control and regulate the harambee system, for example by imposing construction standards and trying to shift the harambee movement from local to districtwide or national projects. He sees this as disempowerment at the grassroots level. I interpret increased central regulation as an effort to correct inherent distortions in the Kenyan school finance system.

My analysis is closest to those prepared not simply as academic pieces, but rather as policy documents. Cohen and Hook (1986) discuss the recurrent cost implications of the harambee system for the central government. I go beyond this to argue that the system distorts the composition of educational expenditure and to document this empirically. Deolalikar (1999) examines educational spending in Kenya as a whole, rather than focusing on the harambee system. He shows that Kenya's pupil–teacher ratios are low for a country of its income level, that education budgets are concentrated on teacher salaries, and that fewer children participate in school than would be expected given Kenya's relatively high public expenditure on education. I show that these all can be seen as consequences of Kenya's school finance system, and present empirical evidence that this pattern of expenditure is not only out of line with international norms, but inefficient.

The remainder of the chapter is organized as follows. Section 4.2 provides background on the Kenyan political and educational system at independence and discusses the adoption of the harambee system by Kenya's first president, Jomo Kenyatta. Section 4.3 models the distortions created by the Kenyan school finance system and discusses empirical evidence. Section 4.4 discusses how the distortionary incentives created by the school finance system eventually led to the breakdown of the system. Section 4.5 concludes by arguing that Kenya could finance the inputs provided by the program through much smaller increases in class size than those associated with the program.

4.2 Jomo Kenyatta and the Adoption of the Harambee System

A number of reasons have been set forth for Kenyatta's adoption of the harambee system: the fiscal weakness of the state, a belief in decentralization and local control, and historical traditions dating to the precolonial period (Ngau 1987; Thomas 1987). In our view a key factor lay in the political economy of Kenya at independence.

Prior to colonization, the region that became Kenya was inhabited by a variety of different groups, some settled agriculturalists, others nomadic pastoralists, speaking different languages, each with its own political system. Britain imposed a centralized government on the country, allocated the most densely settled regions of the country to the local indigenous groups, and took other more sparsely populated land, used by pastoralists, for colonial settlement. Colonial settlers brought in farm laborers from other regions of the country.

During the colonial period various Christian denominations competed to proselytize, and these groups often established schools. Graduates could obtain jobs in the lower ranks of the civil service. Schools were opened most rapidly in the agricultural area around the capital the British established at Nairobi. However, by 1960 only 20 percent of the adult population was literate (Deolalikar 1999).

The British did not allow much local elected self-government in the colonial period. Although they sometimes relied on local chiefs, these chiefs often had little legitimacy. In many areas there had not been any chiefs prior to the colonial period. Hence at independence there were not strong independent elected institutions at the local level that could serve as a counterweight to the national government.

One of the key issues at independence was whether to adopt a federal system, with elected bodies at the provincial level, or a unitary centralized state. Two main political parties formed on opposing sides of this issue: KANU, which had strong constituencies among Kenya's two largest, most highly educated, and most politically mobilized ethnic groups, backed a unitary state. KANU's main rival KADU, which had a constituency among smaller, less politically influential groups, advocated a federal or *majimbo* system. KANU won power and in 1964 KADU was merged into the ranks of KANU. In 1966 Kenyatta appointed Daniel arap Moi, the former chairman of KADU, as vice president.

A reason why some of the groups that supported KANU opposed federalism was fear that it could lead to the emergence of local ethnic movements or parties that might discriminate against members of other ethnic groups who had moved to these regions to set up businesses, work for the government, or farm in areas where land was not as scarce. During the colonial period some people had moved out of the densely settled Central Province into areas used by nomadic groups where the British had set up colonial farms. (In fact, in another more recent debate over federalism in Kenya, many opponents saw *majimbo* or federalism as a code word for expulsion of certain groups from places outside their home area.) It seems likely that if local elected bodies were established and given authority to hire and fire teachers, some might discriminate against members of ethnic groups from other regions of the country. At independence, the members of the relatively educated groups that backed KANU were better off under a system in which civil service positions were allocated according to educational qualifications than they would have been if local elected bodies were in charge of hiring.

The adoption of a centralized system also increased the power of the national leadership and reduced the chance that alternative leaders could develop a local power base. To the extent that the allocation of funds was not totally rule based and that hiring was not totally meritocratic, the system helped incumbent politicians in the national government build patronage networks. Local candidates for parliament competed in large part on the basis of their ability to organize and finance harambee projects and to obtain support for them from the center. Well-connected local politicians could get the central government to start assigning teachers to the school more rapidly.

At the same time Kenya's leaders believed in local input, and wanted community participation. They chose a system that did not allow for elections at the provincial or district levels or give power over teachers to local governments, but did allow for community participation through school committees.

The government implicitly committed that if local communities raised funds, built schools, and kept them functioning for a short period, the central government would supply teachers. Teachers would be allocated so that there would be at least one teacher for each grade; if there were more than a certain number of students in a grade (currently 55), then another teacher would be added. (In practice, there are sometimes long delays before new teachers are assigned.) Initially the central government also had programs to provide some non-teacher inputs, such as textbooks, to schools. As discussed below, these programs providing nonteacher inputs eroded over time due to the increasing budget commitments for teachers implicit in the harambee system.

Relative to a system in which funds were allocated in proportion to population, the system provided more school funding to the prosperous and politically well-organized regions, which at the time of independence formed the heart of the KANU coalition. The harambee system was formally equal, but since it allocated central funding in proportion to the installed base of schools and in proportion to the funds that communities raised locally to establish new schools, it automatically allocated expenditure on education to politically organized communities. Areas that were educationally more advanced could continue to benefit from the system even after they had saturated their communities with primary schools by conducting harambees to build secondary schools. Ngau (1987) found that harambee contributions per capita varied widely by region. In 1979, contributions in Central Province were six times higher than in the impoverished North Eastern Province, and three times higher than in Nyanza Province. Thomas (1987) estimates that the Central Province received a third of the total national harambee contributions (as of 1989 it accounted for 14 percent of Kenya's population). Note also that the system is more flexible than a system that simply distributes resources among ethnic groups according to a fixed formula, since it automatically adjusts to provide more resources to communities that become more politically organized. This makes the system more able to survive changes in underlying political power.

The system harnessed local energies and allowed groups that were willing to partially finance new schools to obtain them, but because control over hiring, firing, and assignment of teachers was done centrally on the basis of formal educational credentials by the national Teachers' Service Commission, there was little scope for local school bodies to discriminate against teachers from other ethnic groups; this would have been detrimental to the relatively well-educated groups that held disproportionate political power at independence.

The system allowed the rapid expansion in education that Kenya certainly needed at independence. At independence, Kenya had 6,056 primary schools with a total enrollment of 891,600 students. Fifteen years later, there were nearly 3 million students in primary school. By 1990, there were 14,690 primary schools with an enrollment of slightly over 5 million. In 1963, there were only 151 secondary schools, with a total enrolment of 30,120 students. Fifteen years later, there were 362,000 students in secondary school. By 2001, there were nearly 3,000 secondary schools with a total enrollment of 620,000 students. (www .kenyaweb.com/educ/primary.html and Killick 1981). In 1960, the adult literacy rate was 20 percent. By 1995, it had increased to 77 percent (Deolalikar 1999).

4.3 Incentive Effects of the Kenyan School Finance System

The system of school finance Kenya adopted at independence created incentives for construction of too many small schools, at least in those communities that were able to solve collective action problems; for excessive spending on teachers relative to nonteacher inputs; and for the setting of school fees and other costs of attending school above the level that would be preferred by the median voter. Moreover the system distorted potentially useful incentives for teachers and head-masters generated by school choice. However, the system adopted at independence was probably not that distortionary initially, but it set Kenya on a path that entailed ever higher per pupil costs, and the squeezing out of nonteacher expenditures, and the eventual abandon-ment of the commitment to provide teachers to schools established by communities, which froze in place an inequitable and inefficient distri-bution of schools.

The model helps explain why people voluntarily contribute with such apparent generosity to harambees, and why these harambees focus on construction, rather than other inputs, such as textbooks. It can also help account for many of the responses of people outside the local area to the system, including donations to harambees from neigh-boring communities and the central government's efforts to insist on construction standards and to regulate harambees. Finally, it helps ac-count for the differing positions of the central government and local school committees on school fees.

4.3.1 Incentives for Excessive School Construction

Some prima facie evidence that the system led to the construction of too many small schools with low pupil–teacher levels is provided by comparing Kenya to other countries at its income level. In 1997, the average pupil–teacher ratio in Kenyan primary schools was 29, while in secondary school it was only 16 (Deolalikar 1999).[2] In con-trast, the average primary pupil–teacher ratio in low-income countries is 50 (World Development Indicators 2001). A regression of primary pupil–teacher ratio against real per capita GDP for selected African countries in 1995 shows that Kenya's current pupil–teacher ratios would be expected in countries with two to four times more GDP per capita (Deolalikar 1999).[3] Of course, the existence of a gap between pupil–teacher ratios in Kenya and other poor countries is consistent not only with the possibility that Kenya's pupil–teacher ratios are too low but also with the possibility that other poor countries' ratios are too high or that all countries are choosing optimally given their unique circumstances.

Further micro evidence comes two regions of Kenya, the Busia and Teso districts. Kremer et al. (2003) report that in 1995, 34 percent of schools in the region had an eighth grade enrollment of 15 or fewer, 11.46 percent of schools had seventh grade enrollment of 15 students or less, and 26.43 percent of schools had seventh grade enrollment of 20 students or fewer. More than 25 percent of sixth grades enrolled 21 students or fewer. Classes in lower grades tend to be larger, and the youngest grades are overcrowded. Concentrated but scattered population densities is not the underlying cause, as the median distance from a school to the nearest neighboring school in this region is only 1.4 kilometer. In fact, in some cases, two closely neighboring schools each have very small enrollment in particular grades. For example, two schools with eighth grade enrollments of five and nine students respectively were only 1.5 kilometer away from each other. If the two classes were merged, and the savings on teacher salaries were distributed among those 14 students, each would receive $139, or 40 percent of Kenyan per capita income. To put matters in perspective, the corresponding figure for the United States would be $14,000. It seems unlikely that students are better off with the small class size than they would be with the cash or increased expenditures on nonteacher inputs, such as textbooks, given that expenditures on teachers are large relative to nonteacher educational expenditures.

To explain incentives for excessive school construction, consider a small community that does not have its own school but can send its children to a nearby existing school. If the community builds its own school, its children will walk shorter distances to school, and will likely enjoy smaller class sizes. The new school will be under the control of the local clan/tribe and of the religious denomination that establishes the school. People from the community who become teachers will be able to obtain jobs near their homes, and prominent local citizens can lead the school rather than simply playing a secondary role at another school. The local community will bear only the construction costs of the new school, while the central government will pay the (much greater) recurrent costs.

To more formally identify the conditions under which incentives to build new schools will be too great, suppose there is an existing school in village 1 with school-age population x_1 and that the inhabitants of village 2 with school-age population x_2 are considering whether to build a school on their own. Denote the discounted value of learning per pupil that takes place in a school with population x as $L(x)$. The present discounted cost of building and staffing a new school is S, but the inhabitants of village 2 bear only the cost μS. It is efficient to create a second school if

$$x_1 L(x_1) + x_2 L(x_2) - S > (x_1 + x_2)L(x_1 + x_2) - x_2 w,$$

where w is the discounted per pupil extra cost of walking to the existing school. The inhabitants of village 2 will be willing to pay the cost of a harambee if $x_2 L(x_2) - \mu S > x_2 L(x_1 + x_2) - x_2 w$. Local incentives to build a school are therefore too great if $(1 - \mu)S > x_1[L(x_1) - L(x_1 + x_2)]$. The local community has too much of an incentive to create a school to the extent that they pay only part of the present discounted costs of operating the school, and too little incentive to create a school to the extent that they ignore the positive externalities of reducing class size in neighboring schools by drawing off pupils.

Building a school may create positive externalities for neighboring schools, but neighboring communities may interact in a way that internalizes these externalities. For example, a community may discriminate against outsiders (see Miguel 2000), or it may contribute to harambees held by neighboring communities that are seeking to build their own facilities. The proportion of the present discounted cost of establishing a school borne by the local community, μ, is likely less than 10 percent given that, as in most school systems, teacher compensation accounts for the vast bulk of education expenses. In the Kenyan case, teacher compensation accounts for more than 90 percent of expenses. Salaries are typically high relative to per capita GDP in developing countries, as teachers are highly educated relative to the rest of the population. Moreover teachers in Kenya have a strong union. Per capita GDP is about US$340, while we estimate that teacher compensation, including benefits, is approximately US$2,000 a year. The annualized cost of building a high-quality classroom might be on the order of US$130.[4] The central government therefore pays more than 90 percent of the cost of a new school.

While the school finance system creates excessive incentives for local communities to build schools, it does not necessarily create excessive incentives for *individuals* to build schools, since the free-rider problem within the local community must be set against the excessive incentives for school building at the community level. In theory, these two forces should offset each other in a way that produces optimal incentives for school building. In fact it seems that some communities are able to make considerable progress in solving the collective action problem while others are not. Thus, for example, in Wilson's model of harambee as a repeated game, there are many Nash equilibria, and some communities get in an equilibrium with excessive investment while others get stuck with people contributing privately optimal amounts in a single round game. Perhaps more important, some communities develop political methods for resolving this problem, and others do not. For example, although harambee is theoretically supposed to be voluntary, local government officials sometimes use the power of the state to extract harambee contributions. A local politician who does this successfully will raise the welfare of the area and will therefore be more likely to be elected. Other politicians may enter an implicit deal with the electorate under which they personally fund harambee projects and then repay themselves from rents they can extract from their public position. However, at any given moment, some areas will be able to organize around a political entrepreneur who can successfully undertake these activities, and others will not.

Thus, rather than immediately causing the construction of too many schools all over Kenya, the system set in motion a process that led to the construction of more and more schools over time, but still left significant areas where school construction lagged behind.

4.3.2   Incentives for Excessive Spending on Teachers Relative to Nonteacher Inputs

The model above suggests incentives for excessive spending on teachers. While local school committees bear only a small fraction of the cost of reducing class size by building additional schools and reducing the number of pupils per teacher, they bear the full cost of nonteacher inputs, such as textbooks. Thus it seems likely that outcomes could be improved by shifting funding from teachers to nonconstruction, nonteacher inputs.[5]

Prima facie evidence for excessive spending on teachers comes from the fact that teacher salaries account for 95 to 97 percent of Kenyan public recurrent expenditures on primary education (Deolalikar 1999).[6]

Further a Ministry of Education survey found a pupil–textbook ratio of 17 in primary schools in 1990. According to the 1995 Primary School Census, on average, 27 percent of the desks and 36 percent of chairs required in primary schools were not available (Deolalikar 1999).

4.3.3 Incentives for Excessive School Fees and Other Attendance Requirements

School fees are set by local school committees made up of the head-master, parents elected to represent families of children in each grade, local officials, and a representative of the religious denomination that is sponsoring the school. In some schools the committee is inactive, and the headmaster has almost complete de facto authority, while in other schools the school committee is active, independent, and influential. In any case, headmasters have a great deal of discretion about how strictly to collect school fees, and headmasters often wind up waiving most of the fees for households that are unable or unwilling to pay it.

Once schools have been established, both headmasters and parent representatives on school committees have incentives to set fees and other attendance requirements, such as uniform requirements, at levels that deter the poorest households from participating in school and that are greater than the median voter would prefer. Headmasters have little incentive to set low school fees and attendance requirements, since this will attract more students to a school, increasing the workload for the headmaster and teachers. Typically an increase of enrollment will not attract additional resources to a school, given that, at least in the upper grades, most schools are far from the 55 pupils required for another teacher to be assigned. (This in turn is due to the high density of schools relative to population induced by the excessive incentives for school construction discussed above.) Moreover, even if enrollment in a grade exceeds 55 students, the central government may be sluggish in assigning another teacher. Further, evidence from a NGO project discussed in detail in Kremer et al. (2003) suggests that increases in enrollment spur much less than proportional increases in the number of teachers assigned to a school. The ratio of enrollment in program schools to enrollment in comparison schools increased by 51 percent; the ratio of the number of classes offered in program and comparison schools increased by 16 percent.

Another reason headmasters may be reluctant to lower school fees and other attendance requirements is that while there are generally few incentives for headmasters, they are sometimes transferred to more or less desirable locations based on their school's performance, which is judged largely by the average score on the primary school leaving exam (KCPE). Pupils at the margin of dropping out may perform worse than average on exams. Also larger class size may decrease test scores. Incentives for headmasters to keep class size small are especially strong in the upper grades, since only students who make it through grade 8 take the KCPE. Finally, setting high school fees and other attendance requirements allows the school to provide more inputs, which may help it raise test scores and improve learning, and in any case, help make the school a more comfortable place to work, for example, by financing repair of leaky roofs.

Parents' committees are also likely to be biased toward setting school fees and other attendance requirements at levels above those that would be preferred by the median voter in Kenya and may prevent some children from attending school. Since only those parents who have children in school are represented on the school committee, parents whose children do not attend school because they have been deterred by the fees and other requirements, such as uniform purchase, do not have a say in setting fees. Parents who care more than average about education are more likely to take the time to participate in the school committee. Moreover, since the school committee has one representative from the parents of students in each grade, and since upper grade classes are typically much smaller than other classes, parents who have children in the upper grades, who are more likely to come from relatively advantaged backgrounds, are overrepresented.

Some suggestive evidence that fees set by school committees are higher than would be preferred by the typical household comes from the conflict between the central government and schools over school fees. In 1974, the central government declared the abolition of school fees. Fees then crept back in again through the back door as school "activity" fees, "building" fees, "parent-teacher association" fees, and so on. During the presidential election campaign in 1997, the president announced that schools should not charge fees and canceled the practice exams that students take and with them the fee for taking these exams. After the election, schools resumed charging fees. The government again announced the abolition of fees during the 2002 election campaign. The timing of these moves suggests that fees are greater than would be preferred by the median voter.[7]

Aside from school fees, uniforms are a key school attendance requirement. Pupils in Kenyan schools are required to purchase uniforms, which cost about $6, a substantial sum relative to per capita GDP, which is $340.

4.3.4 Distortions of Incentives under School Choice

There is considerable school choice in the region we examine, with Miguel and Gugerty (2002) reporting that one out of four families has a pupil in a school that is not the closest to their house. School choice can potentially benefit students, both by creating incentives for headmasters and teachers to improve school performance and by creating incentives for students to switch to schools with better headmasters and teachers. Unfortunately, Kenya's education finance system renders the incentives for headmasters and teachers counterproductive. Moreover one side effect of outside assistance is that it can weaken incentives for pupils to move to schools with better headmasters.

Suppose that headmasters maximize some function of the total resources available to the school, their effort, and the welfare of people in the area. As discussed above, typical class size is usually low enough that the integer constraint on the number of teachers is binding, and most schools will not be able to obtain more teachers by attracting a few additional pupils, at least in the upper grades. Headmasters who exert extra effort to raise the quality of their school will therefore simply attract more pupils but will not obtain corresponding increases in resources to serve those pupils, because the additional school fees paid by the students are very small compared with the funding from the central government. School choice produces limited incentive for headmasters unless money follows pupils.[8] (With fewer schools, more schools would be close to the margin of being able to hire additional teachers, and incentives would be stronger.) One piece of prima facie evidence that headmasters and teachers face weak incentives lies in their high absenteeism rates. Glewwe, Ilias, and Kremer (2002) find that teachers were absent from school 20 percent of the time on surprise visits. Glewwe, Kremer, and Moulin (2001) found that when surprise visits were made to fifty schools in Busia, teachers were absent from the classroom 31 to 38 percent of the time.

Aside from any desirable incentive effects on headmasters, school choice can create desirable incentives for selection of schools by students in the presence of exogenous variation in headmaster quality. If headmaster quality varies among schools, then it is likely to be efficient for the best headmaster to operate the largest school, and school choice can lead to this. To see this, suppose that learning in school i is

$$Y_i = Q_i^\alpha R_i^\beta N_i^{1-\alpha-\beta},$$

where Y is total learning, Q is the quality of the headmaster, R is the resources available in the school, and N is the number of pupils. Dividing by N gives learning per pupil, which declines with class size, holding other inputs fixed. Q is defined so that a headmaster of skill MQ can supervise a school with M times as many students and resources with no diminution of per pupil learning. The assumption that resources are complementary with headmaster quality seems reasonable, since good headmasters are likely to be able to supervise and motivate more teachers and bad headmasters are more likely to misuse or even steal school funds.[9] Under this complementarity assumption it is optimal to allocate resources and students in proportion to headmaster quality. Under a school choice system (with no locational constraints), in which resources are allocated in proportion to enrollment, optimizing households will choose schools in proportion to headmaster quality. Thus under a system in which resources follow students, school choice will lead to optimal allocation of both students and resources. A planner who allocates resources, but not students, could mimic the optimal allocation by allocating resources in proportion to headmaster quality, in which case students will also sort themselves in proportion to headmaster quality. In the actual Kenyan system, it is not clear whether the central government allocates resources in proportion to headmaster quality, but better headmasters, on average, do get more resources because they are assigned to larger schools.

Unfortunately, one side effect of external assistance is that it may weaken the tendencies for school choice to match more children and resources to strong headmasters. Assistance from external donors is a much smaller portion of school finance than government support or local finances, but it often focuses on particular schools. Even if the schools were randomly chosen, the correlation between headmaster quality and resources would be reduced by external assistance. In fact external donors are particularly likely to support poor or poorly performing schools. External donors also often provide more assistance per student in small schools, and this can create a negative correlation between external assistance and headmaster quality. For example, the CSP program we examine provided large amounts of resources to schools that were selected on the basis of having poor facilities initially. Similarly the Jomo Kenyatta Foundation/World Bank textbook program targeted poor schools. A UK-financed program provides teacher training and financial support for anti-AIDS clubs in schools with low test scores in neighboring Nyanza province. Poor schools are more likely to have bad headmasters because bad headmasters are generally less able to raise and manage money, and because the government often promotes good headmasters to bigger, more developed schools and assigns bad headmasters to poor schools as punishment.

Moreover much of the externally financed support for schools is on a per teacher or per school basis, and therefore provides more support per student to small schools. For example, this is the case for training for headmasters under the PRISM program or for teachers under the AIDS education program. However, since good headmasters attract pupils, providing more assistance per pupil in small schools may cause more students to switch into schools with bad headmasters.

Finally, external assistance to the weakest schools decreases the one significant incentive for headmasters in the Kenyan school system. Headmasters have less reason to fear transfer to poor schools if these schools are disproportionately likely to be assisted by external donors, particularly because it may be easier for headmasters to capture part of the funds raised by external donors than it is for them to capture locally raised funds.

External assistance is a small enough proportion of Kenyan school finance that it is only a secondary determinant of incentives for school choice and teacher and headmaster effort. By focusing on areas that are relatively neglected like textbook provision, external donors fill important gaps in the Kenyan school finance system, and are almost certainly beneficial overall. However, although this analysis suggests that external assistance should be targeted to poor areas, it should not necessarily be to the poor schools within those areas, especially given the dense networks of schools in the area, the willingness of families to send children to schools other than the closest school, and the fairly homogeneous poverty of rural Busia and Teso. Urban areas, in contrast, may be more likely to have dramatic income variation within small geographic areas. If outside organizations must target individual schools, they should explicitly consider the quality of the school leadership, as well as the physical resources of the school.

4.3.5 Evidence from a Child Sponsorship Program

Kremer et al. (2003) provide evidence on the trade-off between pupil–teacher ratios, nonteacher inputs, and the cost of attending school. They evaluate the Child Sponsorship Program (CSP), conducted by International Christelijk Steunfonds (ICS), a Dutch nongovernmental organization working in Kenya. The program took place in Kenya's Busia and Teso districts. In 1994, ICS selected fourteen particularly poor schools as candidates for the CSP program based on recommendations from the district education office, teachers and headmasters in the area, and site visits by ICS staff. The fourteen schools were then randomly divided into program and comparison groups.

The program provided uniforms, textbooks, and classroom construction to the seven treatment schools beginning in 1995. All children in treatment schools were provided with uniforms in the first three years of the program. In the fourth and fifth years, half of the grades were provided uniforms in each year (students that received uniforms in year 4 did not receive uniforms in year 5.) Ordinarily Kenyan parents are required to purchase uniforms for their children; these cost approximately $6, and might be used for two years, so the program substantially reduced the cost of attending school.[10]

The program led to a sharp reduction in dropout rates and a large inflow of students from nearby schools into program schools, thus increasing the class size in program schools by approximately nine students. Importantly they find no significant effect of the combination of higher pupil–teacher ratios and more nonteacher inputs on test scores. Evidence from transfers suggests that overall, parents preferred the combination of lower fees, more nonteacher inputs, and sharply higher pupil–teacher ratios associated with the program.

If fewer schools offered certain grades, higher ones especially tended to be very small. Kremer et al. (2003) show that the Kenyan government could finance the textbooks, classrooms, and reductions in cost of school to parents provided through the program without external funds, by a much smaller increase in class size. Such a policy would increase years of schooling by 17 percent.

The program also sheds light on the debate over user fees in education that is active generally in development, but particularly active now in Kenya, given the new government's decision to abolish fees. While user fees have been widely advocated as a way to relieve fiscal pressure on central governments and increase accountability of schools to local communities, they have also been criticized for keeping children out of school. The results from the randomized evaluation suggest that reducing the cost of attending school can greatly increase school participation.

4.4 The Transformation of the System

The post–Independence education system in Kenya contained the seeds of its own destruction. While in the beginning the system allowed many schools to be built at relatively low cost to the central government and low cost in distortion of incentives, the recurrent cost implications for the central government were unsustainable. The incentives for widespread school construction and low pupil–teacher ratios led to very high spending on education. Recurrent Ministry of Education expenditure as a percentage of net government recurrent expenditures, net of interest payments, rose from 15 percent in the 1960s to 40 percent in 1997–98: public spending on education was 7.4 percent of GDP in the late 1990s while health and agriculture spending constituted only 1.5 percent of GDP. Indeed, Kenya spends a higher share of its GDP on public education expenditures than any other low-income African country (Utz 2002). A comparison of public education expenditure and gross primary enrollment rates in African countries shows that Kenya has relatively low enrollment rates given the amount of money it spends (Deolalikar 1999).

Several shocks exacerbated the imbalance between schools and pupils and the financial burden on the state. First, Kenya's economy has stagnated in recent decades, reducing demand for education. The number of candidates taking the Kenya Certificate of Primary Education exam, which comes at the end of primary school, declined from 298,280 in 1985 to 249,080 in 1996 (Deolalikar 1999). Second, in 1984, the government increased the number of grades in primary school from seven to eight. Since children drop out between grades, grade eight classes are particularly small.

The move toward multiparty democracy in the 1980s increased the bargaining power of KNUT, the Kenya National Union of Teachers, which held a strike during the election year of 1997, winning promised pay increases of 27 percent for the first year, with smaller increases stipulated for the following years (Deolalikar 1999). The government later reneged on the out-year pay increases, and KNUT recently conducted another strike, which led to an agreement to reinstate the pay increases.

Faced with rising teacher costs, the government discontinued programs to provide schools with textbooks and other nonteacher inputs, raising costs for households. Despite high government expenditures on education, attending school therefore is a major expense for households, and as argued below, this expense deters many from attending school. Only 68.9 percent of children between the ages of 6 and 13 now attend school (Deolalikar 1999).

The rising inefficiencies and fiscal costs led the government to rein in the system. This is our interpretation of the central government's efforts, decried by Ngau (1987), to change the focus of the harambee movement from local projects to districtwide projects, such as district hospitals, and to insist on high construction standards for harambee schools. Shifting the focus of the harambee movement to district-level projects reduces tendencies toward excessive facility construction, since there can only be one district hospital per district. Mandating higher quality construction than the local community prefers may seem inefficient, given that local people may know more about the appropriate way to build in their area, the availability of different construction materials, and local weather conditions. However, imposing higher standards can mitigate the tendencies for excessive school construction. Regulation proved inadequate, since it was often left to local officials, who were happy to bring funding to their districts at the expense of future national budgets.

Eventually the open-ended commitment to provide teachers to harambee schools had to be abandoned. This was done in a way that froze in place an inefficient and inequitable distribution of resources. It is difficult to affix a precise date to the erosion of the system, but by the 1980s the government was no longer simply providing teachers to all new harambee secondary schools. In 1998, as fiscal pressures became more severe following the raise in teacher's pay, the government simply instituted a hiring freeze, rather than systematically close down classes that were below a particular size. This locked in rents for current teachers, as well as the existing distribution of schools. Presumably there would have been strong political opposition to closing down small schools and reallocating the teachers, both from communities that would lose their local schools and from teachers who would lose their jobs or have to relocate. (It is not clear why politicians seem much more willing to allocate new facilities based on political pork barrel considerations than to shut down old facilities based on these considerations, but this seems to be a general phenomenon worldwide.)

Because up to that point different regions had had varying success at solving the free-rider problem of soliciting harambee contributions, the resulting system simultaneously contained areas where pupil–teacher ratios were high and areas where they were low. While the national average pupil–teacher ratio was 29.1 in 1997, the pupil–teacher ratios across districts range from 14 to 45, with the 10th and 90th percentiles being 21 and 34. The variation in pupil–teacher ratios from one primary school to the next is much larger, ranging from 10 to 60. As teachers retire and die in different proportions at different schools, the hiring freeze has led to increasing misallocation of teachers across schools over time. The AIDS epidemic has exacerbated the problem.

It is worth noting that the erosion of the system coincided not only with rising costs but also with the transfer of power from Kenyatta to Moi. To the extent that Moi represented ethnic groups with less ability to conduct local fund-raising on their own, his constituency might have preferred central government direction of investment rather than an open-ended commitment to match local fund-raising.

Under pressure from international donors, Moi introduced multiparty democracy and term limits. For awhile, Moi and KANU were able to hold onto power, but in the most recent elections, KANU lost power. It is too early to tell whether there has been a fundamental change in the system, but it seems possible that there has been. The most recent elections pitted two Kikuyu candidates against each other, raising the possibility of a politics based on something other than ethnicity. Moreover, in a democratic system, appealing to the poor, rather than just elites, becomes more important. In this environment both parties promised free primary education. While similar promises had been made before, this time the promise has, until now, been fulfilled. In part, this is because of the new, more competitive political climate in Kenya, and in part it is because support has been made available from international donors, the World Bank in particular, to provide Kenyan primary schools with funds to purchase the inputs previously financed with school fees. However, the imbalances in teacher assignments have not been rectified. It is not clear how Kenya will respond if and when international donors no longer are willing to support the expenses traditionally covered by school fees. Perhaps the Kenyan government will reallocate expenditure from teacher to nonteacher inputs, but perhaps it will simply revert to the historic pattern of treating nonteacher inputs as a luxury to be funded in good times.

It seems possible that free primary education is fundamentally changing the political economy of Kenyan education, however. Class sizes have grown, particularly in the lower grades. The powers of teachers and elites are sufficient to prevent teachers from being reassigned from upper grades to lower grades to accommodate the influx of students from poor households. Hence class size in the lower grades in many areas are enormous. The combination of an influx of poor pupils, many of whom have had limited exposure to school, together with an increase in class size, has caused better-off parents to desert the public school system and turn to private schools, at least in cities and in towns of moderate size. This may create a type of hysteresis. As time goes by, school committees may represent elites less and less. It may be difficult politically to restore school fees. Local schools may no longer have local elites pulling for them politically, the way they did under the harambee system.

4.5   Conclusion

In this section I discuss ways of correcting the distortions inherent in Kenya's school finance system and policy implications of my finding that the choices of whether to attend school, and which schools to attend, are very responsive to the cost of education.

Neither the model nor the empirical evidence sheds light on whether more or fewer total resources should be invested in education. Rather, both the model and the data suggest that resources currently being devoted to education could be more efficiently allocated. Thus the level of nonteacher inputs may be optimal for the local community given the number of teachers, credit constraints, potential externalities, and so forth. However, given the government subsidies to education, it would be better to switch resources from teachers to nonteacher inputs. Of course, if credit constraints are not a big factor, and if there are no externalities to education, it might be even better to simply reduce the central resources going into teacher salaries and use the savings to fund health programs or cut taxes rather than finance other educational inputs.

The distortions in the Kenyan school finance system are not a necessary consequence of decentralization itself. Instead, they arise out of a mismatch between the decision-making power of local authorities and their financial responsibilities. The mismatch could be eliminated in a variety of ways, ranging from giving central authorities full responsibility for both school finance and school construction decisions to requiring local communities to pay for teacher salaries as well as school construction, perhaps out of a capitation grant provided by the central government. Providing schools with a fixed budget per student and allowing them to spend it as they wish would not only increase efficiency, it would also be more equitable. Under the current system the most-experienced and best-educated teachers are more likely to be able to arrange transfers to prosperous areas. Since the central government pays teacher salaries, rich areas in effect have greater per pupil teacher spending. There may be other combinations of shared authority and finance that would work as well.

As demonstrated by the CSP program (Kremer et al. 2003) and the surge of new pupils following the abolition of school fees in January 2003, school participation is sensitive to cost. User fees for education in Africa have been advocated as a way to increase financing as well as to provide more local oversight and control. Opponents of user fees have cited time series evidence to indicate that they have a large impact on school attendance, but this may be difficult to interpret, due to the presence of other, contemporaneous, shocks like financial or economic crises. The randomized evaluation suggests that lowering the cost of education can dramatically increase school participation. Widespread school choice also implies that programs like CSP, which provide large assistance to a few targeted schools, may lead to dissipation of program benefits as people walk from distant areas to take advantage of the program. Targeting larger geographic areas may not lead to much costly movement, but targeting individual schools apparently can, at least in rural Kenya.

The high mobility between schools induced by the program suggests a great deal of school choice, even in a rural area. This means there may be potential for vouchers or other school-choice programs in rural areas if funding could be better tied to enrollment.

The history of Kenya's school finance system offers an interesting example of how countries can wind up with counterproductive institutions. The institutions put in place at independence led to a rapid expansion of education, served the interests of politically cohesive communities, and did not severely distort education expenditures. Later, however, they created benefits for some at a tremendous financial cost for Kenya as a whole.

Much of the literature on institutions in developing countries focuses on corruption and incentives for private investment. Such factors no doubt play a critical role, and indeed they have been important in Kenya. Yet other features of the institutional environment are likely of comparable importance. Kenya's education system is a case in point. This study suggests that initial imbalances in political power led to the creation of a system of public service provision that, while formally equal and perfectly legal, helped sustain inequities and led to an education system in which one-third of eighth-grade classes in the region I examine have fewer than 15 pupils, teachers are absent from their classrooms more than a third of the time, and the costs of schooling to households cause pupils to stay in school 15 percent less than they would under an alternative allocation of spending. The damage to economic development caused by institutions that distort public investment may be as great as that caused by institutions that distort private investment.

Notes

1. Immediately after schools are established, parents may have to pay costs to cover teachers' salaries as well, but the central government takes this over quickly.

2. As discussed below, the ratio increased after this point as the government imposed a hiring freeze.

3. Lakdawalla (2001) argues that when countries have a relatively low-skill workforce, teachers' relative salaries will be high because teaching requires people fairly high up the skill distribution. As the skill level in the population as a whole increases, teachers relative skill and relative wage falls. When most of the population is unskilled, and teacher salaries are relatively high, countries adopt high pupil–teacher ratios, but as relative teacher skill levels and salaries fall, societies substitute quantity for quality, and pupil–teacher ratios fall. Although Lakdawalla focuses on time series comparisons within currently developed countries, a similar relationship holds in the cross section comparing countries with different levels of education.

4. Author's calculations.

5. Pritchett and Filmer (1999) note that OLS estimates in a variety of countries typically suggest that the marginal product per dollar of inputs like books is often 10 to 100 times higher than that of inputs like teacher salary. Of course, these estimates may be subject to a variety of biases.

6. While teachers' salaries are a large share of expenditures in most developing countries, they are particularly high in Kenya. In Kenya not only are teacher salaries high, but pupil–teacher ratios are low due to the incentives to set up many schools.

7. Note that while the model suggests that using funds from teachers to reduce school fees or to fund nonteacher inputs would be useful, it is silent on the trade-off between school fees and nonteacher inputs.

8. On the other hand, headmasters who exert effort and thereby increase the quality of their schools may be able to charge pupils more money.

9. Note that if headmaster quality and resources were substitutes, then it would make sense to provide more resources to weak headmasters.

10. The uniforms ICS provided were of higher quality than normal uniforms and cost somewhat more.

References

Barkan, J., and F. Holmquist. 1986. Politics and peasantry in Kenya: The lessons of harambee. Working Paper 440. Institute for Development Studies, University of Nairobi, Nairobi, Kenya.

Cohen, J. M., and R. M. Hook. 1986. District development and planning in Kenya. Development Discussion Paper 229. Harvard Institute for International Development, Cambridge, April.

Deolalikar, A. B. 1999. Primary and secondary education in Kenya: A sector review. Unpublished.

Glewwe, P., M. Kremer, and S. Moulin. 2001. Textbooks and test scores: Evidence from a prospective evaluation in Kenya. Unpublished.

Jamison, D., B. Searle, K. Galda, and S. Heyneman. 1981. Improving elementary mathematics education in Nicaragua: An experimental study of the impact of textbooks and radio on achievement. *Journal of Educational Psychology* 73(4): 556–67.

Lakdawalla, D. 2001. The declining relative quality of teachers. Working Paper 8263. National Bureau of Economic Research, Cambridge, MA.

Levin, H., and M. Lockheed. 1993. *Effective Schools in Developing Countries*. Washington, DC: Falmer Press.

Lockheed, M., and A. Verspoor. 1991. *Improving Primary Education in Developing Countries*. New York: Oxford University Press.

Miguel, E., and M. K. Gugerty. 2002. Ethnic diversity and social sanctions and public goods in Kenya. Working Paper. Department of Economics, University of California, Berkeley.

Miguel, E., and M. Kremer. 2001. Worms: Education and health externalities in Kenya. Mimeo.

Newman, J., L. Rawlings, and P. Gertler. 1994. Using randomized control designs in evaluating social sector programs in developing counties. *World Bank Research Observer* (July): 181–202.

Ngau, P. M. 1987. Tensions in empowerment: The experience of the harambee (self-help) movement in Kenya. *Economic Development and Cultural Change* 35(3): 523–38.

Olsen, R. J., and G. Farkas. 1990. The effect of economic opportunity and family background on adolescent cohabitation and childbearing among low-income blacks. *Journal of Labor Economics* 8(3): 341–62.

Pritchett, L., and D. Filmer. 1999. What education production functions *really* show: A positive theory of education expenditures. *Economics of Education Review* 18: 223–39.

Thomas, B. P. 1987. Development through harambee: Who wins and who loses? Rural self-help projects in Kenya. *World Development* 15(4): 463–81.

UNDP. 1990. *Human Development Report.* New York: Oxford University Press.

UNESCO. 1999. *Statistical Yearbook.* Paris: UNESCO. France.

Utz, R. J. 2002. Education sector reform to preserve past achievements and to ensure the sustainable development of education in Kenya. Unpublished.

Wilson, L. 1992. The harambee movement and efficient public good provision in Kenya. *Journal of Public Economics* 48: 1–19.

World Bank. 1989. Sub-Saharan Africa: From crisis to sustainable growth. World Bank, Washington, DC.

World Bank. 2001. *World Development Indicators.* Washington, DC: World Bank.

World Bank. 1990. *World Development Report.* New York: Oxford University Press.

III

Institutional Quality, Property Rights, and Appropriation

5   A Theory of Corruption, Political Exclusion, and Windfalls

Pedro C. Vicente

We have to begin at the top.
—Festus Mogae, President of the Republic of Botswana

5.1   Introduction

Public-sector windfalls, such as natural resource discoveries, have long been at the center of the development debate. This interest has been motivated by the widespread notion that natural resources represent a "curse" for less developed countries.[1] This idea was first introduced into the wider empirical growth literature by Sachs and Warner (1995) in an influential paper based on the observation that natural resource abundant economies have tended to grow slower than economies without substantial resources. More recently Mehlum, Moene, and Torvik (2002) helped develop the idea by arguing that the diverging experiences of resource-rich countries (in terms of growth) can be attributed to differences in the quality of institutions.[2]

At the same time corruption has received much attention within the development debate as a potential impediment to economic growth.[3] This increased focus has led to a marked expansion in the literature studying corruption and has been accompanied by the production of several important empirical works on cross-country measures of corruption (Transparency International, World Bank[4]).

An improved understanding of the relationship between public-sector windfalls and level of corruption may enable us to better comprehend the fundamentals determining growth and economic development. Earlier empirical work within this area has highlighted its potential importance. Ades and Di Tella (1999) as well as Leite and

Weidmann (1999) have clearly demonstrated that natural resource abundance across countries is an important factor in determining the level of corruption.[5] In this chapter I aim to provide a better understanding of the underlying mechanisms that may explain these empirical findings.

Within the existing literature there is a range of different initial-condition arguments for efficiency outcomes from windfalls that are compatible with Mehlum et al. (2002). For instance, Baland and Francois (2000) claim that in a multiple equilibrium model, resource booms in a primary good bias the economy toward rent-seeking through exogenous import quotas on manufactured goods and away from entrepreneurship. This is in case the economy begins from a position of high rent-seeking; then an import quota will already be of higher value than productive endeavors.[6] Robinson, Torvik, and Verdier (2002), in contrast, focus on political incentives. They argue that natural resource discoveries increase resource misallocation by raising the value of having political power when clientelistic institutions are in place.

We are interested in modelling the effects of a windfall on a simple economy with an endogeneized allocation of political power. This may be seen as a very rudimentary representation of a political regime as measured in franchise-extension terms. However, its simplicity allows us to incorporate political incentives—as in Robinson et al. (2002)—without assuming specific political systems. It also allows us to account for the occurrence of corruption, which has an intersection with the rent-seeking inefficiency concept. In doing so, we aim to integrate both approaches from the current literature. Our main focus, however, will be on the corruption concept, for which better empirical measurements exist.

Corrupt behavior, in this chapter, is treated as the allocation of "permits" to politicians. This is consistent with the traditional definition of corruption as the "use of public office for private gain."[7] The allocation of permits, in turn, is seen to be the outcome of arrangements between agents to exchange favors. Specifically, it is the result of the dynamic interaction of a bureaucrat and a politician. This is the broadest possible treatment of the corruption process. Most of the existing literature, for instance, does not take into account the dynamic features central to this relationship. In parallel, this generality enables one to better understand the allocation of political power. This understanding is dependent on the assumption of a fully structured hierarchy of public-sector allocations.

In the first half of the chapter, I construct a political economy game-theoretic model with a (repeated) hierarchic structure of allocations[8] of "jobs" and "permits." Political incentives[9] are included in the analysis by having an agent who represents the population and who has the ability to react to the other agents' actions through an insurrection. This represents the last political instrument available to the "people," and it implies a heavy penalty to the ruling politicians.[10] This setup then allows us to endogeneize corruption, the nature of the control of the model's allocations (allowing for the possible formation of a political elite, i.e., state capture), and the level of social unrest. The level of social unrest is parameterized by the distribution of relative "power" among the agents[11] and by a corruption technology.

From this setup, two equilibrium patterns can be derived. First, there is a "bad" pattern in which the population is weak, corruption is pervasive, the control of the state is captured by a few, and insurrections are initiated (provided the political elite faces a fragile insurrection threat). Second, a "good" pattern is characterized by a powerful population and no corruption. In this pattern, allocations may be controlled by any agent and social stability is ensured. We can depart from the basic equilibrium outline and extend the main model by adding an efficiency of allocations qualifier within a heterogeneous agent framework. This way we can explore the inefficiency associated with corruption when market incompleteness is stronger.[12]

A positive shock in the corruption technology is analogous to a natural resource boom. A positive effect on corruption occurs only in the "bad" equilibrium pattern. We can therefore argue that the resource curse is conditional on the population having a low relative power and thus associated with political capture. An anticipated shock thus can have a positive effect on corruption (under the "bad" equilibrium pattern) provided the politicians want to increase their probability of staying in power and provided increasing corruption is a way to repress the population (decrease the threat of insurrection).

In the second half of the chapter, I take this windfall shock to the data through the analysis of corruption and political outcomes in countries facing recent natural resource booms. The respective cases of Azerbaijan and Kazakhstan in the Caucasus, Angola, Republic of Congo, and Equatorial Guinea in sub-Saharan Africa all seem to be clear-cut examples of the "bad" equilibrium. I use newly available data on oil and gas discoveries in connection with perceptions of corruption over recent years, as a simple, but preliminary, test of my theoretical implications.

I argue that this evidence is generally consistent with the conceptual model presented.

Section 5.2 presents the basic repeated game model, characterizes equilibria and analyzes an anticipated shock in the corruption technology. Section 5.3 provides the basic evidence that supports my main theoretical findings. Section 5.4 concludes.

5.2   The Model

5.2.1   Setup

Consider an infinitely repeated game with observable actions and complete information with four agents assumed to interact at each period. Each of these players has exogenously given levels of constant ability and initial "strength." Assume, for simplicity, that initial strengths v^i_{-1} are equal for any player i.

Further assume that in the economy, at every period, there is one high-ranking job and one low-ranking job. At the beginning of each period two auctions take place sequentially: first, for the high-ranking job (layer 1) and, second, for the low-ranking job (layer 2). Suppose that the high-ranking job is a *politician* position, and the low-ranking job a *bureaucratic* position. The auctioneer of these two auctions—what we call the initial politician—is assumed to be defined; this means that the initial politician's identity is given as an initial condition. All politicians following the first are defined to be the winners of the previous period high-ranking job auction. The low-ranking job does not confer any rights onto its winner in the next period; instead it gives a right to sell a permit (a consumption good) in the same period (layer 3) after the job allocations.

Generalized versions of bids are submitted (by candidates) in the first two layers; a take-it-or-leave-it-offer is presented (by the bureaucrat) in the third layer. Generalized bids are assumed to be contract offers, corresponding to conditional (on allocations) payment patterns over time. Only one contract between two agents can be in place at a time, and repeated auctions imply contracts can be renegotiated. Figure 5.1 illustrates the described structure of allocations.

Assume that all agents except the current politician can bid at the auction in layer 1, and that all agents except the politician and the next period politician can bid at the auction in layer 2. This implies that the

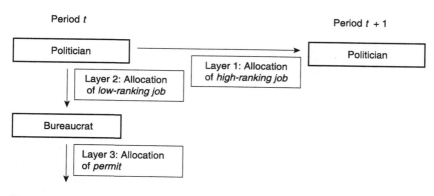

Figure 5.1
Structure of allocation in the model

current period politician, the next period politician, and the bureaucrat need to be different players. Concerning the allocation at layer 3, assume that only the current period politician and the fourth player—the one without any job allocated to her—can accept the bureaucrat's offer for the implied good. However, for the current politician to be able to accept the bureaucrat's offer, she has to previously incur a cost $k \geq 0$. This cost determines the probability $p \in [0, 1]$ that she is able to "attend" the allocation. Without "attending" the allocation, she will not be able to accept the offer:

$$p(k) = Af(k), \tag{5.1}$$

where $A \in \Re^+$ is a parameter (assumed to be sufficiently high) and $f'(.) > 0$, $f''(.) < 0$, $f(0) = 0$, $\lim_{k \to \infty} f(k) = 1/A$; we will refer to this function $p(.)$ as the *corruption technology*.

We assume that the gain from winning any allocation corresponds to the winner's ability. This does not hold for the politician position as it implies that the politicians win the ability amount twice, once in the period when the job is allocated and once in the period when the job is performed.

In this setting, again, we define corruption as the allocation of the permit to the current politician. We view state capture as the situation where only three agents can become the politicians/bureaucrat. An illustration of corruption together with state capture (which corresponds to an outcome that will become prominent in the equilibrium of this game analyzed in the next section) is provided in figure 5.2.

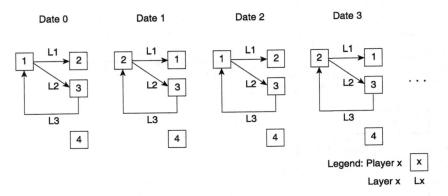

Figure 5.2
An illustration of corruption with state capture in the model

Note that agents 1 and 2 switch politician jobs every period, and 3 becomes a "grateful" bureaucrat, allocating the permit to the politician in place.[13] This pattern implies that there is exchange of "favors" (i.e., influence).

The loser of the auctions at layers 1 and 2 is demoted to a *plebeian* agent. After the allocations have taken place, suppose that the plebeian starts an *insurrection*. (This term refers broadly to any reaction.) This insurrection will be successful with probability λ. Assume $\lambda(.)$ to be a nondecreasing function of its argument; the plebeian share of strength (in period t) α_t is the plebeian's production (value added, or ability if used to produce) in the current and previous periods. Therefore $\alpha_t \equiv (v_{t-1}^{pl} + v_t^{pl})$, where t denotes period t, and pl denotes the plebeian agent. This provides us with an approximation of the relative power of the plebeian in the event of a conflict. In the first period of the game the $t-1$ value is given by the plebeian's initial value of strength. The probability λ is equal to 1 if the referred argument is higher or equal to a given threshold $\bar{\alpha}$. Otherwise, the probability of a successful insurrection will be low enough and constant (for the results below).[14] If an insurrection succeeds all agents with a job are eliminated and substituted by "newly born" agents who possess the same characteristics; the plebeian agent becomes the new active politician.

The sequence of play in the stage game is presented in figure 5.3. Values for the current job/permit takers are realized at the end of the period (i.e., production happens at the end of the period). Consumption by all players takes place after the end of the period and is a fixed

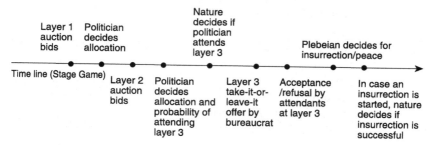

Figure 5.3
Sequence of play in the stage game

proportion $(1 - s)$ (with $s \in]0, 1[$) of the end-of-period wealth $w_t^{e,i}$ (where e denotes end of period, and i denotes the player).

We can assume that contracts are enforced. An exogenous entity is available to enforce contracts and therefore acts as a profitless intermediary (agents can credibly commit to future conditional transfers when "bidding/offering"). However, we assume that a rigidity (contract incompleteness) is in place, in the sense that only before production is realized can transfers be done to and from the entity. This means that the proportion $(1 - s)$ of a periods production cannot be negotiated ex ante because it has to be consumed.

The end of period wealth is given by

- $w_t^{b,i} + \tau^i + a^i + -k_t$ ($+a^i$, in case i wins the permit) for i as the politician,
- $w_t^{b,i} + \tau^i + a^i$ for i as the next period politician,
- $w_t^{b,i} + \tau^i + a^i$ for i as the bureaucrat,
- $w_t^{b,i}$ ($+\tau^i + a^i$, in case this agent wins the permit) for i as the plebeian,

where $w_t^{b,i}$ is the beginning-of-period t wealth of the player i, τ^i is the net transfer from the intermediary entity to agent i, a^i is the ability of the player i. We assume for simplicity $w_0^{b,i} = 0$ $\forall i$. The game payoff for player i is

$$\sum_{t=0}^{\infty} [\delta^t u^i] = \sum_{t=0}^{\infty} [\delta^t (1 - s) w_t^{e,i}], \tag{5.2}$$

where $\delta \in]0, 1[$ is the discount factor for high enough δ, as we assume in our analysis here.

5.2.2   Equilibrium Characterization

Our equilibrium analysis focuses on the best (from the initial politicians point of view) symmetric (in the sense that players in the same position who possess the same ability will have equal strategies) subgame perfect equilibrium.[15] This may be interpreted as a type of first-mover advantage on behalf of the first active politician.

We begin with the case of a trivial distribution of ability, which implies there is homogeneous (or constant) ability among all agents in the model. We start with a simple result.

LEMMA 2.1 (Characterizing the best constrained equilibrium for the first politician without the possibility of insurrections)

The highest equilibrium payoff the initial politician can make with no successful insurrections corresponds to:

• Making an agreement with two other agents to exchange allocations every period—the initial politician switches with another player in power over time and a "permanent" bureaucrat allocates the permits to the politician in power at layer 3 auctions whenever possible (corruption may then arise);

• Allowing politicians to decide on the probability of attendance of layer 3 allocations by maximizing at each period the net gain from this allocation subject to the corruption technology.

Proof   See the appendix at the end of this chapter.   ■

Figure 5.2 provides the possible pattern of allocations described in the lemma whereby two politicians rotate forever, having made an agreement with a bureaucrat for the allocation of the permit whenever possible. We are now in a position to derive a complete equilibrium characterization of this economy.

PROPOSITION 2.1 (Equilibrium characterization)

Assume $\bar{\alpha} = a$.

1. If the initial strength, v_{-1}, is sufficiently low ($<a$), then:

• The pattern of allocations described in lemma 2.1 arises here (a political/bureaucratic elite is formed with the initial politician achieving a close enough payoff to the one described in the lemma): expected corruption (as given by a probability $\rho > 0$) and state capture emerge;

• Insurrections are started but are unsuccessful most of the time (almost stable equilibrium pattern).

2. If the initial strength, v_{-1}, is sufficiently high ($\geq a$), then:

• Neither expected corruption nor state capture emerge;

• No insurrections are started—the economy stays in this equilibrium pattern with probability 1 (stable equilibrium pattern).

Proof Part 1. We know that under the described strength condition the plebeian is powerless to threaten or amass a successful insurrection with a probability of 1 in the first period (α_0 is not high enough). Let us assume that this is the case forever. This means that the initial politician is almost (given the sufficiently low probability of success in the insurrection) not restricted in her actions by the other agents, so the outcome described in lemma 2.1 is valid (in terms of the pattern of arrangements between agents) with one qualification: the full equilibrium probability for attending layer 3 auctions, p^{equil}, will be higher than the level identified in the lemma. This is provided by the additional gain from increasing the probability p on decreasing the likelihood of successes in insurrections, which is not considered in the net gain from attending a layer 3 allocation described in the lemma. We can write the corresponding problem as

$$\max_k\ p(k)[P(a) + \delta E] - k,$$

where E is the expected one-period-ahead payoff for the initial politician. The same logic applies to the second politician's decision.[16] The FOC is

$$p'(k)[P(a) + \delta E] = 1, \tag{5.4}$$

which defines a higher k than the condition at the lemma above—this is the level of k corresponding to p^{equil}.

In this context (provided that A is sufficiently high, so that p^{equil} will, in turn, be sufficiently high) the gain from a successful insurrection for the plebeian is higher than that of winning the remaining permits, which have not been allocated to the elite. As a result insurrections are started every period as a best response.[17]

Finally, we can verify that the threat of insurrection with probability 1 remains sufficiently low in the equilibrium path. In this equilibrium case, the plebeian has very low probability of showing strength a in the two subsequent periods (provided A is sufficiently high, so that p^{equil} will, in turn, be sufficiently high). This makes this equilibrium pattern almost stable (i.e., there may be successful insurrections).

Part 2. We know that under a sufficiently high initial share of strength α_0, the threat of a successful insurrection with probability 1 restricts the initial politician's behavior.

This means that the initial politician has to meet the plebeian's minimum payoff for her not to initiate insurrections. The politician is not interested in being replaced as an agent since δ is high enough. Note that the plebeian always has the chance of initiating a successful insurrection at $t = 0$ and getting to be the new initial politician at $t = 1$ (therefore winning $2a$ as allocated value in these two periods). In terms of our symmetry assumption in the equilibrium concept (which applies to the new agents strategies in case of insurrection), this implies that the plebeian has to get at least a at every period of the equilibrium path. All other agents have to get at least a, since otherwise they will prefer to become insurrecting plebeian agents. This leads us to conclude that $k = 0$ under these parameters. In addition, as offers will be 0 in this equilibrium, if any bidder bids higher, this agent will see herself in a worse situation (provided that she wins the good for sure and has the same gain from it). If the bureaucrat offers a higher payout, the plebeian's best response is to start an insurrection. This is worse for the bureaucrat. So we can conclude that no profitable deviations for any player at any subgame exist.

For this reason the aggregate surplus after the first period must be equally divided among the four agents, and no corruption arises in this equilibrium pattern. Each agent will be indifferent about getting any of the possible four allocations during any period. The payoff of the initial politician will be

$$\sum_{t=0}^{\infty} \left[\delta^t a(1-s) \sum_{i=0}^{t} s^i \right],$$

provided that the plebeian is always indifferent between initiating or not initiating an insurrection, and that we are focusing on the best equilibrium for the initial politician. In addition, since the plebeian's strength stays constant over time after the second period ($2a$) and is never below $2a$ (provided the initial condition), this equilibrium pattern is stable. ∎

Note that the difference between ρ^* and ρ^{equil} in part 1 of the proposition may be interpreted as *repression* because it corresponds to the elite incurring on a cost to decrease the power of her opponent. In such a model that endogeneizes corruption and the allocation of political power, two equilibrium patterns emerge as a function of an initial parameter embedding a notion of power in the population. The emergence of corruption, of a political elite that captures the state, and of repression is a distinctive feature of economies with disempowered populations.

We now extend this model to allow for heterogeneous ability, in order to derive the efficiency of allocations considerations. We find that inefficiency may be associated with corruption when contract incompleteness is strong. Later we also analyze the effect of a positive shock on the corruption technology.

Extension to Heterogeneous Ability Agents: An Efficiency Qualification

Suppose that the distribution of ability is such that there is positive probability of high, a^h, and low, a^l, ability (with $a^h > a^l$). More precisely there are two high-ability agents and two low-ability agents.

LEMMA 2.2 (Lemma 2.1 revisited: Heterogeneous agents with differing abilities)

The highest payoff the initial politician can make corresponds to an equivalent of the one presented at lemma 2.1 modified where suitable by two considerations.

1. If the first politician is of high ability, the two initial politicians rotate in power, with the second politician being the other high-ability agent.

2. If the first politician is of low ability, and the savings rate s is high enough, the two high-ability agents share political power after the first period, with the first politician extracting the full transferable surplus. Otherwise, when the savings rate s is low enough, the two initial politicians rotate in power, with both politicians being low-ability agents.

Proof Part 1. If the initial politician is a high-ability agent, the surplus of the first politician is maximized by rotation in power forever (as in lemma 2.1) with another high-ability agent. High-ability politicians always prefer to match up with high-ability counterparts as this type of agent raises a higher surplus (since that agent, being a politician, will get permits).

Part 2. If the initial politician has low ability, then no deals can be made in the first period with high-ability agents to capture the political power forever. If future surpluses can be extracted to a sufficiently high extent (s, δ are high enough), the best payoff the initial politician can make corresponds to extracting the expected (provided that there is uncertainty in layer 3 corruption) surplus of a game where the pair of high-ability players rotate in power from the second period on. If future surpluses cannot be extracted at a sufficiently high extent (s is low enough), as high-ability bidders are highly contract-constrained—and therefore cannot offer a high enough part of their surplus—the initial low-ability politician will always prefer to keep political power. This means she will rotate in power instead of relinquishing it forever after the initial period. Note that a high-ability agent will always deviate from an agreement with the other high-ability agent. Despite the fact that she will pay the initial politician consistently with the first period maximum bidding, she will profit from the higher surplus of the other high-ability agent in the politician role. This the reason why under these conditions low-ability politicians stay in power. ∎

This facilitates the derivation of the next result regarding efficiency of allocations in this heterogeneous-agent model extension.

PROPOSITION 2.2 (Efficiency)

1. If s is sufficiently high (low contract constraints), the aggregate surplus, S, raised by the economy at a period after the first, has the following composition:

• For a low initial strength (part 1 of proposition 2.1), a^h at layer 1, a^l at layer 2, and $-k$ plus almost always a^h at layer 3 (we define this value for the aggregate surplus as S_1);

• For a high initial strength (part 2 of proposition 2.1), indifference between layers; that is, there will be two a^h and two a^l (we define this value for the aggregate surplus as S_2).

2. If s is sufficiently low (severely contract-constrained environment), then part 1 of this proposition emerges, except for when a low-ability politician begins the game with low initial plebeian's strength. Then the aggregate surplus is composed of a^l at layer 1, a^h at layer 2, and $-k$ plus almost always a^l at layer 3 (we define this value for the aggregate surplus as S_3).

3. Assume a^h and a^l are such that $S_1 = S_2 = S^{\max}$. Then the inefficiency arises with sufficiently strong contract incompleteness and low initial strength (and also corruption, as we saw in proposition 2.1).

Proof The proof of proposition 2.1 together with the proof of lemma 2.2 allow us to derive the results. ∎

Proposition 2.2 conservatively assumes that the technological cost of corruption is equivalent to its efficiency gain (implied in having more allocations to high-ability agents). So we have a foundation for the idea that corruption may be associated with inefficiency when contract incompleteness is higher, when a low-ability agent has initial political power.

Generally, we can interpret this result as an efficiency qualifier for the allocations in the model. Note that we address explicitly the notion of efficiency gains due to corruption.[18] To this extent our contract-constraint hypothesis proves to be effective in determining allocative inefficiency of corruption.

A Shock in the Corruption Technology

We now analyze the impact of an announcement of an increase in parameter A of the corruption technology, namely a windfall. This will be interpreted below as a natural resource boom because it has the property of decreasing the politician's cost of attending the auction of permits (which is an improvement in the corruption technology).[19]

PROPOSITION 2.3 (Positive shock in the corruption technology)

1. For the economy with the parameter set of part 1 in proposition 2.1 (low initial plebeian share of strength), an increase in A will increase p (probability of attending the permit auction for the politician at a certain period) and therefore increase the extent of expected corruption. Moreover, if the shock is announced before it happens, an increase in p will take place from the moment of the announcement.

2. For the economy with the parameter set of part 2 in proposition 2.1 (high initial plebeian share of strength), a decrease in A does not have an impact in p. It makes no difference whether or not an announcement is made before the shock happens.

Proof Part 1. From the proof of proposition 2.1, part 1 (more precisely from observing equation 5.4), we can see that an increase in A leads to an increase in p^{equil}.

Since the announcement of a future increase in A makes the future politician's position more attractive, the optimal p increases right after the announcement and before the shock takes place (given that an additional reason for repression arises).

Part 2. Provided that, as in proposition 2.1, part 2, the corruption technology does not have a role in characterizing the equilibrium, no changes will arise in the equilibrium of this parameter set from the shock on A. ∎

Therefore under certain conditions, windfalls, or more specifically, natural resource booms, can increase corruption/repression. In line with the work by Mehlum, Torvik, and Verdier (2002) on growth, who emphasize the importance of the quality of institutions in determining the effects of natural resource booms, we conclude that these conditions relate to the strength/voice of the population.

5.3 Discussion

We saw above the possibility that windfalls such as natural resource discoveries can cause a generalized increase in corruption. We saw that this change depends on the initial conditions regarding the threatening power/voice of the population. In this section we consider some recent cases where such conditions have clearly matched these modeled facts.

The model of the last section communicates that increases in corruption and increases in repression are related; both are a response to natural resource booms. With this simple observation we now focus our exercise on countries that have witnessed major booms over the last fifteen years. Some examples are clear-cut and from diverse world regions—Central Asia, sub-Saharan Africa. To these we add some less obvious examples from Latin America, where the pressures present are consistent with the model above, and consider the "no-corruption-increase equilibrium" empirical counterpart (for which Norway is the cleanest example, though Australia or Denmark could also feature prominently). We then examine the preliminary (where the major constraint is the limited data on corruption over time) empirical data and results. We find that as a response to natural resource booms, there do seem to be two distinct corruption equilibrium patterns as predicted by our model.

We begin with one of the new Caucasian oil-producing countries, which provides a good example of the resource shock over the "bad" equilibrium pattern of our model. On Azerbaijan, *The Economist* (July 11, 1998) writes:

It is only a ragged shirt, but Azerbaijan is putting it all on oil. The government has already done ten lucrative deals with foreign oil companies.... Local businessmen trying to get going in the post-communist era are hamstrung by corruption and red tape. Despite its boomtown tag, Baku still has only two passable hotels. It boasts just one foreign bank. Large foreign firms, including accountants such as Arthur Andersen and KPMG, wait months to get licences. All this should be bad news for the country's president, Heidar Aliev. Yet he remains the overwhelming favourite to keep his job after the presidential election due in October, largely because no real challenger could run freely against him. Last month, a former deputy interior minister under the country's first post-Soviet president, Albufaz Elchibey, whom Mr Aliev ousted five years ago, was arrested after a grenade was allegedly found in his car.

Azerbaijan continues to date on the same trend: Heidar Aliev was substituted by his son Ilham as president, amid highly controversial elections and reports of violence. Nevertheless, the US Department of Energy currently predicts that the opening of the under-construction Baku–T'bilisi–Ceyhan pipeline (linking the Caspian sea, where the natural gas and oil fields are, to the Mediterranean sea) will contribute to a doubling of the economy by 2008. This may explain world tolerance of the continued trend.

The neighboring country Kazakhstan, also far from being a free-speech, free-election democracy (although President Nazarbayev, in power since 1989, claims that "he advocates democracy as a long-term goal, he also warns that stability could be at risk if change is too swift"[20]) seems to be moving in the same direction. *The Financial Times* (December 11, 2000) writes:

Kazakhstan's Prime Minister Kasymzhomart Tokayev smiles broadly when speaking of the country's Kashagan offshore oil structure—a discovery that could catapult his country into becoming one of the world's leading petroleum producers.... For the moment, then, the former Soviet republic seems to be sitting pretty.... An anti-corruption commission has been set up under the president. New tax legislation has been passed and the banking sector is being strengthened. But some say the combination of current buoyant oil prices and the prospect of big production increases has already caused the government to slow, if not reverse altogether, the momentum for structural change. Others doubt the government's sincerity in tackling corruption and point to the fact that [president] Nazarbayev's daughter and two sons-in-law occupy senior government positions. "They seem intent on fighting corruption on the lower and medium levels, but not up top," says an EU official.

Indeed, in September 2003 a former senior Mobil executive was sentenced to prison in New York on tax evasion charges linked to a government investigation into bribery schemes in oil deals in Kazakh-stan.[21] This was the largest ever foreign corruption investigation in US legal history.[22]

In a different part of the world, but not less illustrative of the repres-sive (corrupt) response in our model, is Angola, a country divided by a long-lasting (1975–2002) civil war funded on natural resources[23] (oil on the side of the MPLA government, diamonds on the side of the in-the-end-defeated UNITA). Angola has seen oil production rising steadily throughout much of the last fifteen years. As *The Financial Times* (Octo-ber 1, 2003) puts it:

Angola is experiencing one of the world's biggest oil booms, and the crude gushing from wells...earns about $4bn a year for one of the world's poorest countries....But the oil money, like the drilling, stays largely offshore....The IMF, in a leaked un-published report written last year, said Angola's govern-ment could not account for more than $4.3bn of inflows. NGOs claim President Jose Eduardo Dos Santos's administration has spirited much of the money abroad. Swiss criminal authorities recently froze $56m of funds held in the Cayman Islands branch of a Geneva bank, which investigators believe belong to the Angolan president....Campaigners have tried to promote financial transparency in oil-rich countries like Angola by pressing oil companies through Publish What You Pay.[24] ... The campaign started after BP Explora-tion in 2000 revealed payment of a $111m signature bonus for Angola's block 31 in its 1999 accounts, and committed in future to publish annual production and payments data. Sonangol, the state-owned oil company, accused BP of breach of contract and threatened to expel it from Angola....None of the other oil majors has followed suit.

At the same time, with a weakened internal opposition, President Dos Santos, included in the 2000 list of the ten worst enemies of the press (published by the US-based Committee for the Protection of Journalists), continues to delay the long-ago promised elections. As the BBC writes, "if they do happen, the MPLA will win: the ruling party has money, it is organised and it keeps a tight grip on the administration."[25]

The case of the conflict-ridden Republic of Congo (Brazzaville) shares a similar story. As the British Foreign and Commonwealth Office[26] writes:

Successive post-independence governments have not been able to translate the oil dividend into improvements in living conditions for the population. The opaque workings of the national oil company, Société Nationale des Pétroles du Congo–SNPC, were recently exposed in an independent audit carried out by KPMG. SNPC's virtual control of the country's finances and the lack of transparency in its operations were highlighted as major problems.

The Global Witness adds that "the national oil company SNPC makes a multi-million dollar profit but, according to the IMF, does not pay a single penny of this money into the government's coffers."

A problematic country in terms of human-rights violations, Congo has nevertheless been sending mixed signals to the international community. It has pledged to adhere to the Extractive Industries Transparency Initiative (EITI), a voluntary scheme designed to increase transparency in the oil and mining sectors.[27] This is most probably caused by its high debt dependence.

Equatorial Guinea is probably the most extreme illustration of our main proposition. This country's fierce and violent (with a long history of allegations of human-rights violations from Amnesty International) dictatorship has been in place since the current president Obiang Nguema gained power in a 1979 coup in which he overthrew and killed his uncle (for a personally witnessed description of this regime in the 1980s; see Klitgaard 1990). Equatorial Guinea, not an oil producer in the 1980s, has seen a major boom in oil production from mid-1990s. At the same time President Obiang has been re-elected twice amid allegations from opponents of electoral fraud. Despite calls for improved oil governance, President Obiang has maintained that "oil revenues are a state secret."[28] As the IMF (May 6, 2005) cautiously puts it:

Since oil production began in 1995, hydrocarbon production has increased from 6,000 barrels of oil equivalent per day (boe/day) to 282,000 boe/day in 2003, supporting an average annual growth of 31 percent. In 2004, real GDP grew by 34 percent, reflecting a sharp increase in oil production.... Unfortunately, the country's oil and gas wealth has not yet let to a measurable improvement in living conditions for the majority of the population.[29]

However, even countries with higher living standards and/or higher free-speech standards (more democratic political regimes), seem to be facing similar pressures in the face of natural resource booms.[30] Trinidad and Tobago, a Caribbean country whose democratic politics are divided along racial lines, and where crime and violence have risen steeply in the last years, was described by *The Economist* (October 6, 2003), as follows:

Basdeo Panday, the prime minister, was rousing his supporters on the evening of October 2nd.... But not far away, at a rival rally on the same night, three of Mr Panday's ministers were denouncing what they claimed was his government's corruption. One of the dissidents, Ramesh Maharaj, had been sacked as attorney-general by Mr Panday on October 1st; the other two resigned in protest.... Critics accuse the government of a host of irregularities.... Last month, Mr Maharaj sent files on alleged malpractice at three state enterprises and an insurance company to the director of public prosecutions.... Trinidad is enjoying a natural-gas boom, with $4 billion invested over the past four years.... Though it provides few direct jobs, the energy industry enriches the state. Yet in health and education Trinidad struggles to meet standards reached a generation ago by neighbouring Barbados. For years, demands for the investigation of corruption have been ignored. There are now worrying hints of more serious trouble. Mr Maharaj says his life has been threatened.

Among the Latin American countries, the interesting case of Bolivia is worth mentioning. It is one of the region's poorest countries and, though democratic, is politically unstable. There an activist population seems to have taken the initiative on decisions over natural resources in an effort to counteract an inevitable fate. *The New York Times* (May 23, 2005) puts it as:

The struggle over globalization and who controls natural resources is being waged across Latin America, but the battle lines are no sharper anywhere than here in Bolivia, where a potent confederation of protesters plans a march on Monday to demand more state control of energy resources.... Last week, Bolivia's Congress, under pressure from protesters, signed into law a new tax-and-royalty scheme so tough that energy experts say oil and gas multinationals will curtail investments.... Political analysts say the divisive crisis could lead to violence or, in time, the disintegration of a country whose state has little presence or control over its far-flung provinces. The discovery of large gas deposits in the late 1990's was supposed to have brought Bolivia more stability and wealth.... But the masses of poor indigenous people have never forgotten how the Spanish and a series of corrupt governments plundered the country's silver, tin and gold, leaving them more poverty-stricken than before.

Finally, and diametrically opposed to the other cases cited is Norway. Norway, a country with one of the highest living-standards (according to the United Nations' Human Development Index) and one of the most competitive economies (following the World Economic Forum's Global Competitiveness Report), has always led a general welfare approach to natural resource booms. In the context of our model this coincides with equilibrium under high population surveillance/ threatening power. Indeed in the 1990s the Norwegian government created a Petroleum Fund. A portion of annual oil and gas revenues flow each year into that fund, which serves the dual purpose of buffering the short-term variations in oil revenues and providing a mechanism to transfer current wealth to future generations. The fund holds a combination of cash, bonds, and shares in both domestic and foreign companies, amounting to some $179 billion in June 2005.[31]

5.3.1 *Some Basic Empirical Evidence—Oil and Gas Discoveries*

Using a newly available database of sizable oil and gas fields from Horn (2005; published by the American Association of Petroleum Geologists[32]), we now attempt to provide an empirical counterpart to our main result. We look specifically at proposition 2.3 for the impact of positive shocks on the corruption technology, which we now interpret as oil and gas discoveries. As oil is undoubtedly the most important of the natural resources, this appears to be a sensible simplification.

We graph total discoveries per capita (using World Bank–SIMA for population data) in the period 1990 to 2003 (in millions of barrels) on perceived changes in corruption from Kaufmann, Kraay, and Mastruzzi (2005), which measure the difference between the symmetric value of their indicator of Control of Corruption from 1996 and 2004.[33] We should expect a positive relation in the positive corruption change quadrant for low initial strength (depicted below), and a vertical distribution of countries around zero change in corruption for high initial strength. We have simply interpreted initial strength as initial income per capita (using World Bank Development Indicators, for 1989, where available, or closest available year). We graph the highest and lowest income countries in different formats—the middle cases cannot be reasonably expected to yield precise predictions, so a light color (and smaller font) is used for these countries. The anticipated patterns (no clear variation in corruption for highest income countries; positive correlation of corruption/discoveries for lowest income countries) can easily be observed in figure 5.4.

Taking a simple regression equivalent to our main proposition allows us to investigate whether corruption increased more in lower income countries when larger oil and gas discoveries took place. Table 5.1 presents our results. We first treated income as a binary variable (using the classification of lowest income countries of the graph) and then incorporated this variable in continuous terms. We can see that the interaction term (income per capita times oil and gas discoveries) is closest to, or indeed significant, where no other coefficient is or comes as close to being significant. Note that we can rule out that the coefficient for oil and gas discoveries and the interaction term are statistically equal, so we can conclude that increases in corruption are more likely to happen in low initial income countries.

This is not to say that this is a solid test of the model. Data on corruption perceptions only started in 1995–96, so not much data are

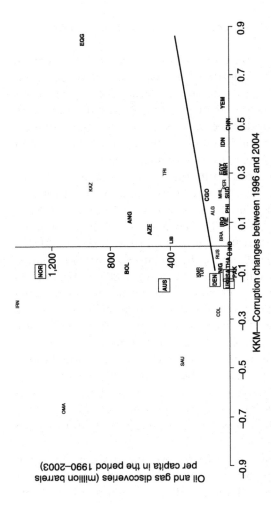

Figure 5.4

Oil and gas discoveries and corruption changes. Sources: Oil and gas discoveries per capita from Horn (2005) and World Bank SIMA; corruption from Kaufmann et al. (2005)—this indicator goes from −2.5 to +2.5. Dark bold represents lowest GDP per capita countries (with trendline), dark bold with squares is used for highest income countries, and light gray is applied to middle income countries (data on GDP per capita PPP comes from World Development Indicators 2005, and concerns 1989 or closest available year at constant prices—rankings for Libya, Myanmar, and Iraq are found by using closest ten countries from 2004 CIA data rescaled to World Bank SIMA).

Table 5.1
OLS regressions of differences in corruption, 1996 to 2004

	(1)	(2)
logoil	−0.111	0.660
	0.080	0.402
dummygdp	−0.101	
	0.216	
logoil ∗ dummygdp	0.175	
	0.107	
loggdp		0.023
		0.221
logoil ∗ loggdp		−0.189
		0.111*
Constant	0.201	0.050
	0.175	0.785
Observations	41	41
Adjusted R^2	0.236	0.327

Notes: * significant at 10 percent; logoil is log of total oil discoveries in 1990 to 2003; dummygdp takes value 1 for lowest income countries consistently with figure 5.4.

readily available to undertake a definite test. My hope is that this will inspire further empirical work on the relationship between windfalls and corruption.

5.4 Concluding Remarks

This chapter has addressed an increasingly important question in the development literature: What are the impacts of windfalls, such as natural resource discoveries, on the level of corruption in a country?

I have presented an original theoretical framework that endogeneizes political incentives/system and corruption. I have used a dynamic setting that allowed us to look at long-term agreements. This enabled me to derive two equilibrium patterns that are dependent on a broad notion of the power to insurrect successfully by the population. I was able to conclude that contract incompleteness can be associated with inefficient corruption—although, of course, exclusion of the population agent from allocations may be taken as inefficiency in itself. This model was found to imply that there are different responses to a shock in the corruption technology parameter, with increases in corruption appearing when corruption is due to rule by a few and when social unrest is already common.

These results should help shed some light on the connections among corruption, political exclusion of large portions of the population, and the existence of natural resources. The fact that corruption is strongly associated with inefficiency may explain the low growth that is associated with a natural resource boom.

In terms of policy implications, many developing countries that experience windfalls have a public sector that when left alone, is ill-prepared to share and safeguard their future resources. It is important that international institutions and the world community become aware of the predictability of the windfall problem. The use of monitoring and conditionality in the international playground may be the only way to prevent lost opportunities for economic growth. I strongly believe that the best way to implement such policy is by strengthening the empirical measurement of the main public-sector infirmity: corruption.

Appendix: Proof of Lemma 2.1

No successful insurrections imply that all agents live forever, and therefore are not constrained by the insurrection threat.

Provided that there is a contract incompleteness, the initial politician always prefers to occupy the position of a politician for as long as possible (every other period). Being a politician is better than being the bureaucrat or the plebeian provided that the opportunity to hold the permit in a contract constrained environment (provided that A is high enough so that the cost k is low enough).

From competition by the bidding agents, the second politician bids her full transferable surplus from rotating in political power with the first politician. This stems from the fact that the conditionality of payments (done by the second politician), in the event that the first politician sticks to the agreement, will make the second politician indifferent between deviating or not (as she is constrained to give any transferable surplus to the intermediary entity). On the other hand, if the first politician deviates, the second auctioneer would prefer to make a slightly higher payoff with a third agent (she would not be constrained by the initial agreement).

The allocation of the bureaucrat position follows the same logic: no profitable deviations exist for the bureaucrat (constrained by a contract conditional on allocations), who competes with the plebeian, thereby raising the winning offers at this layer to the maximum transferable amounts. Note also that the exchange of favors at all layers emerges in equilibrium, provided that corruption in the permit allocations (best for the initial politician) is sustained by having a deal between current politicians and bureaucrats whose future payoff depends on the good-will of the next politician.

Finally, at the permit layer, the plebeian is indifferent between pay-ing δsa (since initial wealth is 0; δsa is the full transferable amount from getting a permit) or refusing the bureaucrat's offer for that amount.[34] Politicians optimize attendance at layer 3 auctions subject to the cor-ruption technology.

This proves that the above described strategies constitute the equilib-rium under the conditions of this lemma (implying the capture of the full transferable surplus of the economy by the initial politician; the best equilibrium for that agent). Note that this way the second politi-cian and the bureaucrat get to "eat" the nontransferable part of what they raise, and the plebeian gets zero surplus.

For precision, we quantitatively characterize the payoff of the initial politician in this equilibrium.

The best-constrained equilibrium for the initial politician (assuming no insurrections) implies that she stays in the political power forever, getting from her own job,

$$[a(1-s)] + \delta[as(1-s) + a(1-s)] + \cdots = \sum_{t=0}^{\infty} \left[\delta^t a(1-s) \sum_{i=0}^{t} s^i \right].$$

Fully transferable amounts from holding the second politician's job and from holding the bureaucrat's job (through the second politician, when this agent is in power) tote up to

$$\delta(2sa - k_2) + \delta^2 2sa + \cdots = X,$$

where k_2 is the k amount chosen by the second politician (provided that it is borne before production, which implies that it is taken from her transferable surplus). This adds to the payoff of the initial politician in the total

$$P(X) = \delta(2sa - k_2)(1-s) + \delta^2[s(2sa - k_2)(1-s) + 2sa(1-s)] + \cdots.$$

Regarding the ex post surplus for the politicians from layer 3 alloca-tions, this is composed of discounted $(a - k)$ for all times a politician gets to bid at those auctions or discounted $(\delta sa - k)$ for every period the plebeian wins the permit. However, the politicians have to decide ex ante the probability of attendance at layer 3 auctions. We define this chosen probability as ρ^*; this is the ρ value corresponding to the solution of the following problem:

$$\max_k \rho(k)[P(a) - P(\delta sa)] - k,$$

where ρ is given by (5.1) and $[a - \delta sa]$ is the net gain from attending the layer 3 allocation. So as FOC we have

$$Af'(k^*)[P(a) - P(\delta sa)] = 1. \tag{5.5}$$

This expression defines the optimal level k^*, and therefore ρ^*. Ex ante we will then have as the expected surplus from layer 3 auctions for politicians

$$(\rho^* a - k^*) + \delta[\rho^* a + (1 - \rho^*)sa] + \cdots = Y,$$

which implies addition

$$P(Y) = \rho^* a(1 - s) - k^* + \delta[\rho^* a(1 - s) + \rho^* as(1 - s)$$
$$+ (1 - \rho^*)s^2 a(1 - s)] + \cdots$$

to the payoff of the initial politician. Note that we assume $s \neq 0$ and contract incompleteness because we want to assume an advantage for the politician in being allocated the permit directly. ∎

Notes

I wish to thank primarily Roger Myerson for invaluable advice and encouragement. I am also grateful for suggestions to Cátia Batista, Gary Becker, Sven Feldmann, Daniel Kaufmann, Luis Rayo, Philip Reny, Hugo Sonnenschein, and Christopher Udry. I thank participants in seminars at the University of Chicago (Micro Lunch, Political Economy Workshop), VIII Conference in Econometric Modeling for Africa, and II Nordic Conference in Development Economics for comments. I gratefully acknowledge financial support from the (Portuguese Government) Fundação para a Ciência e a Tecnologia (BD1215/2000), Fundação Calouste Gulbenkian, Department of Economics at the University of Chicago, and the Henry Morgenthau Jr. Memorial Fund.

1. Collier (2005) argues that unconditional public-sector aid (e.g., public debt relief) can sometimes also be a "cursed" windfall.

2. Other interesting recent states of affairs that coincide with the presence of natural resources are explored by Bannon and Collier (2003), civil wars, and Lam and Wantchekon (2002), dictatorships.

3. See, for instance, Mauro (1995), Gupta, Davoodi, and Alonso-Terme (1998), and Kaufmann and Kraay (2002).

4. Kaufmann, Kraay, and Mastruzzi (2005).

5. Vicente (2006) analyzes the corruption effects of a West African oil discovery. Knack (2000) uses cross-country evidence to show that aid (which can be regarded as a kind of windfall) contributes to corruption.

6. Other foundations for the resource curse in rent-seeking models are Tornell and Lane (1999), who argue that resource booms, while enabling increasing returns to capital in the formal sector (which is mined by rent-seekers unlike the informal sector), can lower income; Torvik (2002) obtains similar results on assuming a demand externality.

7. Bardhan (1997) presents a comprehensive look at the economic literature on corruption, including its usual definition. See Becker and Stigler (1974), Rose-Ackerman (1978), Cadot (1987), Klitgaard (1988), and Myerson (1993) for early studies on the economics of corruption.

8. Corruption concepts in allocation games have previously been explored by other authors: Bernheim and Whinston (1986), who introduce influence in the context of first-price auctions, and Banerjee (1997), who analyzes mechanisms with red tape and asymmetric information.

9. See Grossman and Helpman (1994) for a classic political economy model on endogenous lobbying that is related to this model in its structure, and Damania and Frederiksson (2000) for a repeated games version aimed at studying the formation of lobbying groups.

10. Such an insurrection could be an overthrow of government (see Lohmann 2000 for an explicit economic treatment of social movements), although many real life coups have not resulted in high penalties for the ruling elite; rather, they correspond simply to transfers of political power among the elite in reaction to signs of social unrest. The threat of insurrection as a threat of revolution is explored by Acemoglu and Robinson (2000, 2001) in historical studies of political transitions (e.g., democratization) in Western Europe and Latin America.

11. See Kaufmann and Vicente (2005) for specific empirical counterparts to this parameter, and for a cross-country analysis of a closely related version of this model.

12. A different explanation—not related to corruption—for the association of inequality with inefficiency is presented by Esteban and Ray (2004). They find that even a benevolent government may be confounded by lobbies whose pressure is due to both merit and wealth.

13. Note that the figure depicts the case where the politician attends the permit allocation in the first four consecutive periods (which could be the consequence of a high investment in k).

14. Therefore the function λ is discontinuous at $\bar{a}$.

15. In our game, using the general notation of repeated games in Myerson (1991), we can define N as the set of four players at each period, Θ as the set of states of nature (relative to the random variables of the game: ability, initial strength, politician's attendance at permit allocation, insurrection success), $\bar{D}$ as the general set of moves for player i at each round of the game—ex ante equal for all players provided any player can take any role in the stage game (described above, and illustrated in figure 5.2)—$\bar{S}$ as the set of signals that player i may receive at each round of the game (equal for all players). Take $D = \times_{i \in N} \bar{D}$ and $S = \times_{i \in N} \bar{S}$. Then an initial distribution q in $\triangle(S \times \Theta)$ (which gives

the identity of the initial politician and values of strength), a transition function $t : D \times \Theta \rightarrow \triangle(S \times \Theta)$ (which provides the evolution of signals and states of nature), a payoff function $u_i : D \times \Theta \rightarrow \Re$ (implicitly defined when reaching (5.2)), complete the definition of the game Γ.

However, because we have a game with complete state information, $\forall i \in N$, $\forall s_i \in S$, $\exists \omega(s_i) \in \Theta$ such that for $\forall \theta$, $\hat{\theta} \in \Theta$, $d \in D$, $s_{-i} \in \times_{j \in N_{-i}} S_j$, then $t(s, \hat{\theta}|d, \theta) = 0$ if $\hat{\theta} \neq \omega(s_i)$. In this setting we define the set of behavioral strategies of player i as

$$B_i = \{\sigma_i = (\sigma_i^k)_{k=1}^{\infty} \mid \sigma_i^k : (S_i)^k \rightarrow \triangle(D_i), \forall k\}.$$

Moreover, if we restrict our attention to symmetric strategies in the sense of $\forall i \in N$, the set of considered strategies for player i is

$$C_i = \{\sigma_i \mid \sigma_i = \sigma_j; \sigma_i \in B_i, \sigma_j \in B_j, \forall j \in N_{-i}\}.$$

A behavioral strategy profile $\sigma \in \times_{i \in N} C_i$ is an equilibrium of Γ iff $\forall i$, $\hat{\sigma}$

$$\sum_{k=0}^{\infty} \sum_{d \in D} \sum_{\theta \in \Theta} T^k(d, \theta|\sigma, q, t) \delta^k u^i(d, \theta) \geq \sum_{k=0}^{\infty} \sum_{d \in D} \sum_{\theta \in \Theta} T^k(d, \theta|\hat{\sigma}_i, \sigma_{-i}, q, t) \delta^k u^i(d, \theta), \tag{5.3}$$

where $T^k(d, \theta|\sigma, q, t)$ is the probability that at round k, θ is the current state of nature and d is the profile of moves chosen by the players, if every player i uses her behavioral strategy σ_i at all rounds, and where transitions are given by functions q and t.

The notion of equilibrium we will look at is defined by the solution to the following problem:

$$\max_{\sigma} \sum_{k=0}^{\infty} \sum_{d \in D} \sum_{\theta \in \Theta} T^k(d, \theta|\sigma) \delta^k u^{inpol}(d, \theta)$$

subject to σ being an equilibrium as defined in (5.1) such that if restricted to any subgame of Γ, it is still an equilibrium of that subgame (*inpol* denotes the initial politician).

This focus—on the best equilibria from the point of view of the initial politician—is equivalent (in terms of outcome of corruption) to assuming the best equilibrium for the three initial job owners: this could be decentralized by a noncooperative notion of equilibrium proposed by Myerson (1989).

16. This is the optimal amount from the perspective of the first politician during the corresponding period.

17. Note that a no-insurrections-started agreement (for a lower ρ) is not an equilibrium, since the population will want to start a successful insurrection.

18. This goes back to Becker and Stigler (1974).

19. We can think of this improvement, in the context of a natural resource boom, as the emergence of a new oil sector under the control of the state, meaning expanded possibilities of corruption.

20. BBC Country Profile, November 2005.

21. Reuters, September 19th 2003.

22. According to the independent *Global Witness*:

The scheme was based around President Nazarbayev and Oil Minister Nurlan Balgimbayev demanding that international oil companies such as Chevron (now Chevron-Texaco) and Mobil (now ExxonMobil) pay a series of unusual fees to [a] middleman . . . on behalf of the Republic of Kazakhstan. This arrangement, the indictment alleges, helped ... send some US$78 million in kickbacks to President Nazarbayev and others through dozens of overseas bank accounts in Switzerland, Liechtenstein and the British Virgin Islands.... Another US$1 billion of Kazakh oil money has also been uncovered off-shore and out-of-sight under Nazarbayev's direct control in a secret fund in Switzerland. Ironically, the only reason that such information has emerged is because president Nazarbayev inadvertently revealed the true state of affairs whilst trying to discredit a presidential rival.

23. Note that this may be seen as an extreme case of repression through the lens of our model.

24. The Publish What You Pay ⟨www.publishwhatyoupay.org⟩ campaign led by a coalition of over 280 NGOs worldwide calls for the mandatory disclosure of the payments made by oil, gas, and mining companies' to all governments for the extraction of natural resources.

25. November 11, 2005.

26. November 2005.

27. Tony Blair, the UK prime minister, announced the initiative at the World Summit on Sustainable Development in Johannesburg, September 2002 ⟨http://www.eitransparency .org/⟩. The present endorsing countries are Azerbaijan, Republic of Congo, Ghana, Kyrgyz Republic, Nigeria, Sao Tome and Principe, Timor Leste, and Trinidad and Tobago.

28. BBC Country Profile, November 2005.

29. According to the *Global Witness*, journalists (from *The Los Angeles Times*) have recently uncovered evidence that major US oil companies are paying revenues directly into an account under the president's control at Riggs Bank in downtown Washington, DC.

30. For the interesting case of Sao Tome and Principe, a neighboring democratic country of Equatorial Guinea with late-1990s oil discoveries, see Vicente (2006).

31. US Department of Energy, November 2005.

32. Although not comprehensive (smaller oil and gas fields are not included), this database is considerably more reliable than publicly available data from the US Department of Energy, which relies on politically motivated reserve reports from a number of countries (e.g., as is clear from lack of variation in reserves, after years of production without known notable discoveries).

33. For Equatorial Guinea, this indicator is only available from 1998, so it is the difference to this year that is used here (the best proxy for the value appears to be in 1996).

34. This may be seen as the kind of petty bribery (instantaneous, not lagged in time, "sale" of a permit).

References

Acemoglu, D., and J. A. Robinson. 2000. Why did the west extend the franchise? Growth, inequality and democracy in historical perspective. *Quarterly Journal of Economics* 115: 1167–99.

Acemoglu, D., and J. A. Robinson. 2001. A theory of political transitions. *American Economic Review* 91: 938–63.

Ades, A., and R. Di Tella. 1999. Rents, competition, and corruption. *American Economic Review* 89(4): 982–93.

Baland, J.-M., and P. Francois. 2000. Rent-seeking and resource booms. *Journal of Development Economics* 61: 527–42.

Banerjee, A. V. 1997. A theory of misgovernance. *Quarterly Journal of Economics* 62: 1289–1332.

Bannon, I., and P. Collier, eds. 2003. *Natural Resources and Violent Conflict: Options and Actions*. Washington, DC: World Bank.

Bardhan, P. 1997. Corruption and development: A review of issues. *Journal of Economic Literature* 35: 1320–46.

Becker, G. S., and G. J. Stigler. 1974. Law enforcement, malfeasance, and compensation of enforcers. *Journal of Legal Studies* 3(1): 1–18.

Bernheim, B. D., and M. D. Whinston. 1986. Menu auctions, resource allocation, and economic influence. *Quarterly Journal of Economics* 101(1): 1–32.

Cadot, O. 1987. Corruption as a gamble. *Journal of Public Economics* 33: 223–44.

Collier, P. 2005. Is aid oil? An analysis of whether Africa can absorb more aid. Mimeo. University of Oxford.

Damania, R., and P. G. Fredriksson. 2000. On the formation of industry lobby groups. *Journal of Economic Behavior and Organization* 41: 315–35.

Esteban, J., and D. Ray. 2004. Inequality, lobbying and resource allocation. *American Economic Review* 96(1): 257–79.

Grossman, G. M., and E. Helpman. 1994. Protection for sale. *American Economic Review* 84(4): 833–50.

Gupta, S., H. Davoodi, and R. Alonso-Terme. 1998. Does corruption affect income inequality and poverty? IMF Working Paper 76.

Horn, M. K. 2005. *Giant Oil and Gas Fields 1868–2004*. Tulsa, OK: American Association of Petroleum Geologists.

Kaufmann, D., A. Kraay, and M. Mastruzzi. 2005. Governance matters IV: Governance indicators for 1996–2004. Mimeo. World Bank.

Kaufmann, D., and A. Kraay. 2002. Growth without governance. *Economia* 3: 169–229.

Kaufmann, D., and P. C. Vicente. 2005. Legal corruption. Mimeo. World Bank.

Klitgaard, R. 1988. *Controlling Corruption*. Berkeley: University of California Press.

Klitgaard, R. 1990. *Tropical Gangsters: One Man's Experience with Development and Decadence in Deepest Africa*. New York: Basic Books.

Knack, S. 2000. Aid dependence and the quality of governance: A cross-country empirical analysis. Mimeo. World Bank.

Lam, R., and L. Wantchekon. 2002. Political dutch disease. Mimeo. New York University.

Leite, C., and J. Weidmann. 1999. Does Mother Nature corrupt? Natural resources, corruption, and economic growth. IMF Working Paper 85.

Lohmann, S. 2000. Collective action cascades: An informational rationale for the power in numbers. *Journal of Economic Surveys* 14(5): 655–84.

Mauro, P. 1995. Corruption and growth. *Quarterly Journal of Economics* 110(3): 681–712.

Mehlum, H., K. Moene, and R. Torvik. 2002. Institutions and the resource curse. *Economic Journal* 116(508): 1–20.

Myerson, R. B. 1989. Credible negotiation statements and coherent plans. *Journal of Economic Theory* 48: 264–303.

Myerson, R. B. 1991. *Game Theory: Analysis of Conflict.* Cambridge: Harvard University Press.

Myerson, R. B. 1993. Effectiveness of electoral systems for reducing government corruption: A game-theoretic analysis. *Games and Economics Behavior* 5: 118–32.

Robinson, J. A., R. Torvik, and T. Verdier. 2002. Political foundations of the resource curse. *Journal of Development Economics* 79: 447–68.

Rose-Ackerman, S. 1978. *Corruption: A Study in Political Economy.* San Diego: Academic Press.

Sachs, J. D., and A. M. Warner. 1995. Natural resource abundance and economic growth. NBER Working Paper 5398.

Tornell, A., and P. R. Lane. 1999. The voracity effect. *American Economic Review* 89: 22–46.

Torvik, R. 2002. Natural resources, rent seeking and welfare. *Journal of Development Economics* 67: 455–70.

Vicente, P. C. 2006. Does oil corrupt? Evidence from a natural experiment in West Africa. Mimeo. University of Oxford.

6   Explaining Conflict in Low-Income Countries: Incomplete Contracting in the Shadow of the Future

Michael McBride and Stergios Skaperdas

6.1   Introduction

Since the end of World War II civil wars have taken place in at least 73 countries. The millions of casualties and economic costs have greatly contributed to these countries' slow, or negative, growth.[1] From a traditional economic perspective it is difficult to understand such a record of apparent inefficiency. Besides the cost of arming, the puzzle is why different parties don't just settle their differences peacefully under the threat of conflict. Given that war is destructive, breaks the various complementarities in production and trade, and has a number of other external and indirect effects both in space and time (see Collier et al. 2003), a peaceful settlement in the shadow of conflict would appear perfectly feasible. Such a peace would by no means necessitate disarmament. A cold war or the traditional balance of power that periodically takes place for decades at a time could conceivably take place within countries between contending ethnic, class, or religious groups. Of course, such settlements do occur, but the question, posed from an economic perspective, remains why don't settlements take place in every case?

One possible explanation involves asymmetric information. The contending parties within a country might not know one another's strengths and weaknesses, preferences, capabilities, or any other attributes of the environment within which they are operating. It has been known for some time in economics that asymmetric information in any one dimension can prevent parties from attaining mutually beneficial trades. Models specifically addressing the possibility of conflict in the presence of mutually beneficial settlement when there is asymmetric information include Brito and Intriligator (1985) and Bester and Wärneryd (1998). Especially when secrecy is important, as in the case of coups, asymmetric information appears to be a reason why peaceful settlements might not occur (although asymmetric information is not necessary for coups; see McBride 2004).[2] On the other hand, many civil wars and low-level conflicts last for many years, even decades. The contending parties involved in such conflicts seem to have learned over time the principal aspects of one another's capabilities and preferences, and therefore continuing conflict is difficult to explain by means of asymmetric information. For example, the inability of the FARC and the various Colombian governments over the long civil war not to settle, and likewise the government of Angola and UNITA, can hardly be considered an outcome of informational asymmetries.

In this chapter we argue for a possible explanation of conflict that has received much less attention than it deserves. There are two components in the explanation we discuss: (1) Adversaries are unable to enforce long-term contracts on arming, although short-term contracts, under the threat of conflict, can be written. (2) Open conflict changes the future strategic positions of the adversaries in different ways than does a peaceful contract under the threat of conflict.

The first component has become familiar to economists over the past two decades, especially for dynamic settings.[3] If there are difficulties in writing or enforcing long-term contracts on items like the job-specific training of an employee in a high-income country with a modern government and functioning institutions, it should not be surprising that enforcing long-term disarmament in a country with weak governance and institutions can be difficult. For arming is not just any item of job-specific training; in the presence of weak institutions it is the ultimate source that contending parties have at their disposal for enforcing other contracts. If contracts on arms cannot be written or enforced, arming can be expected to take place. Warfare, however, can be avoided since short-term contracts on everything else can be enforced given the arsenal possessed by each party. That is, condition (1) alone is not sufficient to generate open conflict.

What is also needed is time dependence as described in condition (2). Open conflict results in winners and losers not just in terms of immediate rewards but also in changing the strategic positions of the adversaries well into the future. Typically the winners have a higher chance of success and losers a lower one if they seek to continue their confrontations into the future. A peaceable short-term contract does not dramatically change the future relative positions of the adversaries the way open conflict does. There might be secular trends that favor one party over another, but such a trend would be different from the change in strategic positions that comes about through open conflict. As long as open conflict and short-term settlements have different implications for the parties' future strategic positions, one or more parties might decide to forgo the short-term advantages of peace for the uncertain but higher expected future benefits that can come from open conflict.

A discussion of the ideas that we explore in this chapter can be found in Fearon (1995). Skaperdas and Syropoulos (1996) showed how making the "shadow of the future" longer increases arming, but they did not distinguish between open conflict and settlement under the threat of conflict. Garfinkel and Skaperdas (2000) developed a finite-horizon model that actually demonstrates how open conflict occurs. Related in spirit is Acemoglu and Robinson's (2000) finding that there might not exist short-term transfers that can prevent a revolt. Powell (2006) also discusses the main issues and presents an illustrative model. Bester and Konrad (2004, 2005) examine the decisions of rivals on whether to attack or not to capture territory over finite or infinite horizons and show how large asymmetries in power or expectations of future equality can induce warfare. Mehlum and Moene (2006), although they do not distinguish between open conflict and settlement under the threat of conflict, concentrate on the role of the incumbency advantage that control of the state confers and how it stimulates arming.

In this chapter we examine an infinite-horizon model that shows how open conflict occurs within the context of low-income countries, where political institutions are weak and condition (1) above is more likely to be satisfied. Open conflict leads to destruction and therefore there is a short-run incentive to settle and peacefully divide the disputed output. War, though, eliminates one of the adversaries or increases the chance of winning a future war for the winner and increases the chance of future losses for the loser. Thus the possible current losses due to war are weighed against the possible future benefits of weakening or eliminating one's opponent. In our model, the benefits to the winner come from the reduction or elimination of future arming, but there are many other benefits that exist and we discuss them briefly.

The explanation for war that we advance is not meant to apply to the post–World War II period only. Organized warfare has been central to the experience of humanity since the agricultural revolution of prehistoric times. And, in particular, the place in which modern governance evolved—Western Europe—has had more than its share of civil and inter-state warfare. For example, most late medieval Italian cities were wracked by clan warfare for centuries before their governments developed ways of limiting arming through checks and balances, representative politics, or through autocracy. But what followed was inter-state warfare at a higher level in the whole Italian peninsula, between city-states, ecclesiastical states, and absolutist monarchs (that was the world that Machiavelli lived in; see McNeill 1982, ch. 3, or Tilly 1992, chs 2 and 3, for overviews). It was only in the second half of the nineteenth century that Italy was unified. It would be hard to argue that all this warfare was caused by asymmetric information, or to some systematic misperceptions and miscalculations. The combination of incomplete contracting and the fundamental nonstationarity or time-dependence of the future should be seriously considered as an explanation of open warfare that is complementary to existing ones.

6.2   The Basic Setting: War or Armed Peace

Consider two groups, A and B, that compete for power and interact over an indefinite horizon. They compete for output of value Y. Because the two groups cannot write contracts on the ultimate source of enforcement, arms, they have to expend resources r_A and r_B to maintain their positions. These expenditures are necessary regardless of whether War or "Armed Peace" ultimately prevails.[4] In the event of War, arms affect the probabilities of winning for each side; we denote these probabilities by p_A and p_B. (How these probabilities depend on arms is examined in the next section.) In the case of Peace, r_A and r_B— through their effect on the probabilities of winning in the event of War—influence each group's bargaining position in arriving at a particular settlement.

If War takes place, only a fraction $\phi \in (0, 1)$ of Y can be consumed; the rest, $(1 - \phi)Y$, is destroyed in the conflict. Because of lower production complementarities in low-income countries compared to high-income countries, we expect a lower level of destruction under War in low-income countries. In each period the expected single-period payoff of group $i = A, B$ in the event of War is

$$U_i^w = p_i \phi Y - r_i. \tag{6.1}$$

Since War is destructive, in each period both sides will prefer to divide Y in shares that equal their winning probabilities, with the resulting payoff of $p_i Y - r_i > p_i \phi Y - r_i = U_i^w$. The range of other possible divisions of Y is also Pareto superior to the payoffs under War. Under an indefinite repetition of such single-period simple interactions, there should never be an incentive to go to War provided that the two groups costlessly communicate and output Y is divisible.

However, if War does occur, we can reasonably expect interactions between the two groups to be different in the future. Given that the winner of the War will receive ϕY and the loser nothing, the resources that the winning side will command in the future can be expected to be higher than those of the loser. This outcome should bias future wars even further in favor of today's winner. The winner might even gain possession of the state, something that can provide greater resources than can be obtained otherwise, as well as greater ability to withstand challenges from the loser group in the future. Such induced asymmetries can well make War an attractive possibility, since a lower expected payoff for today can be traded off for more in the future.

For now we allow a stark and simple form of dependence of future power on today's war. We suppose that the loser of a war in any period is unable to raise the resources necessary to challenge the winner in future periods, and thus the winner is able to enjoy the output Y in all future periods while the loser receives nothing. (In section 6.4 we illustrate how our findings extend to the less well delineated setting whereby a group drops completely out of contention after a series of battles, and not just one, are lost.)

Consider then the negotiations that could result in either Peace or War in any particular period if no War has occurred in the past and each group has already invested its resources in guns (i.e., r_i is a sunk investment). Further, and without loss of generality, suppose that group A is the one that takes the initiative in making a proposal (e.g., by reining in a weaker government). In case of Peace, group A will receive the whole value of Y and will make an offer of subsidy S to group B, which can either accept or reject A's offer. If the offer is rejected, War will ensue. The resources that either party has invested in arms is considered sunk, so they abandon their current negotiations.

Assuming a discount factor $\delta \in (0, 1)$, the discounted expected payoff for group i in the event of War is the following:

$$V_i^W = p_i\phi Y + p_i \sum_{t=1}^{\infty} \delta^t Y + (1 - p_i) \sum_{t=1}^{\infty} \delta^t 0 = p_i\left(\phi + \frac{\delta}{1 - \delta}\right)Y. \qquad (6.2)$$

Note how in the event of war, because one group can be eliminated from contention, it will devote no future resources to arming. Group B can accept any offer S from group A that satisfies the following inequality:

$$S + \delta V_B(S) \geq V_B^W, \qquad (6.3)$$

where $V_B(S)$ denotes the continuation payoff of group B when it is out of power given the subsidy S. As part of any Markov perfect equilibrium in which a positive subsidy is given, group A would offer a subsidy S^* that satisfies (6.3) as an equality. Assuming that S^* is accepted in this period, it will be acceptable in all future periods and therefore $V_B(S^*) = (S^* - r_B)/(1 - \delta)$. Then, from (6.3) and (6.2), the subsidy will be

$$S^* = p_B[\phi(1 - \delta) + \delta]Y + \delta r_B. \qquad (6.4)$$

Note that this subsidy, which must be offered by group A to group B in order to prevent War, depends positively on the power of group B (as proxied by its probability of winning p_B), on the share of output that is not destroyed in the event of War, on the discount factor, as well as on the value of output Y. However, this minimally acceptable subsidy to group B might not be in group A's interest to offer. In particular, the resultant payoff of group A should be preferable to its expected payoff under War, or

$$Y - S^* + \delta V_A(S^*) \geq V_A^W, \qquad (6.5)$$

where $V_A(S^*) = (Y - S^* - r_A)/(1 - \delta)$ is the continuation payoff of group A if Peace prevails forever.

Supposing the probabilities of winning for the two sides to sum to one (i.e., $p_A + p_B = 1$), it is straightforward to show that the condition for Armed Peace (so that equations 6.3 and 6.5 are both satisfied) is as follows:

$$Y \geq \frac{\delta(r_A + r_B)}{(1 - \phi)(1 - \delta)}. \qquad (6.6)$$

When this inequality is reversed, there will not be a subsidy that is feasible, and War will ensue. Thus, based on (6.6), War is more likely and Armed Peace is less likely,

1. the lower is the contested output Y;

2. the higher are the resources devoted to arming $(r_A + r_B)$ by the two groups;

3. the higher is the discount factor δ; and

4. the less destructive War is (or, the higher is ϕ).

When contested output is low, as it presumably is in low-income countries, the current cost of going to War (controlling for ϕ) is low (as that cost equals $Y(1 - \phi)$), and therefore going to War becomes easier. On the one hand, greater arming increases the likelihood of War because War tilts the balance of power in favor of one side and reduces (and in our case, completely eliminates) the future costs of arming. Armed Peace, on the other hand, as its name suggests necessitates incurring the cost of arming forever.

Given the long conditioning of folk-theorem arguments, the effect of the discount factor on War appears to be counterintuitive. Note that folk-theorem arguments merely describe the possibility of cooperation by means of supergame strategies, typically in stationary settings. Nothing guarantees cooperation in such settings because the accompanying strategies and equilibria are rather fragile and not renegotiation proof. By contrast, we concentrate on regular strategies and equilibrium in a time-dependent setting. The more the future is valued, as indicated by a higher value of the discount factor δ, the greater the salience of the expected future rewards as compared to the current costs of War and therefore the higher is the likelihood of War.

Thus far the resources devoted to arms (r_A and r_B) have been treated as exogenous parameters. That might well be the case in many low-income countries if the groups involved face liquidity constraints and organizational disadvantages that prevent them from increasing their arming to levels that would be consistent with an unconstrained equilibrium. Arms embargoes and difficulties in accessing the international arms market can also play a role in restraining arming to levels that are considered as given. We next consider conditions where no such constraints exist.

6.3   Endogenous Arming

To allow for endogenous arming, we first need to specify how probabilities of winning depend on arming. We suppose that these probabilities depend on arming through the following additive contest success function (see Tullock 1980; Hirshleifer 1989):

$$p_i(r_A, r_B) = \frac{r_i^m}{r_A^m + r_B^m}, \tag{6.7}$$

where $i = A, B$ and $m \in (0, 1]$. The parameter m has been described as a measure of the effectiveness of conflict. A higher value of this parameter can be associated with more advanced forms of warfare that were traditionally less prevalent in many low-income countries but are now available there.

Assume that arming is available at constant marginal cost $\omega > 0$. Given that an integral part of the cost of arming is actually the cost of hiring soldiers, and since the cost of labor is lower in low-income countries, we expect a lower ω to be associated with lower incomes.

In each period the sequence of moves by the two sides is the following:

1. Levels of arming, r_A and r_B, are chosen simultaneously by the two groups.

2. The two groups bargain, with group A making an offer of dividing the period's surplus (denoted by the subsidy S to B). If the offer is accepted by B, group B receives S, group A receives $Y - S$, and the next period repeats the same two steps.[5] If the offer is not accepted by B, War takes place with the winning probabilities described in (6.7). The winner receives ϕY for the period and Y for every period thereafter, whereas the loser receives 0 for the period and thereafter.

Note that when group A contemplates whether to offer a subsidy to group B or go to War, the continuation payoff of group B is still the one described in (6.2). Conditional on Armed Peace, the subsidy that will just induce B not to go to War is the following variation of (6.4):

$$S^*(r_A, r_B) = p_B(r_A, r_B)[\phi(1 - \delta) + \delta]Y + \delta \omega r_B. \tag{6.8}$$

This subsidy is derived under the condition that the same level of arming, (r_A, r_B), is chosen in every future period as well as in the current period. Note how this subsidy to group B depends on its probability of winning, which is increasing in the arming of the group, as well as directly on the arming of the group. The reason is that under Armed Peace the group will have to incur the cost of arming in every period.

The payoffs of the two groups under Armed Peace can now be calculated. Group A will receive in every period the total surplus minus the subsidy, $Y - S^* = Y - p_B(r_A, r_B)[\phi(1 - \delta) + \delta]Y - \delta\omega r_B$, whereas in every period it will pay the cost of arming, ωr_A. We denote by (r_A^P, r_B^P) the future level of guns as part of a Markov perfect equilibrium, and denote the choices in the current period by (r_A, r_B). Then group A's payoff is as follows:

$$V_A^P(r_A, r_B) = \frac{1}{1 - \delta}\{Y - p_B(r_A, r_B)[\phi(1 - \delta) + \delta]Y - \delta\omega r_B^P - \delta\omega r_A^P\} - \omega r_A. \tag{6.9}$$

Group B receives the subsidy $S^* = p_B(r_A, r_B)[\phi(1 - \delta) + \delta]Y + \delta\omega r_B$ in every period and pays the cost of arming (ωr_B) in every period as well. Then group B's payoff reduces to the following:

$$V_B^P(r_A^P, r_B^P) = \frac{1}{1 - \delta}\{p_B(r_A, r_B)[\phi(1 - \delta) + \delta]Y\} - \omega r_B. \tag{6.10}$$

The payoffs are not symmetric because group A is always the proposer and the subsidy offered is just the one that equates the Armed Peace payoff of B to B's expected payoff under War.

The Markov perfect equilibrium strategies under Armed Peace are such that r_A^P maximizes $V_A^P(r_A, r_B^P)$ whereas r_B^P maximizes $V_B^P(r_A^P, r_B)$. To solve for these equilibrium strategies, first differentiate to obtain the first-order conditions $\partial V_A^P / \partial r_A = 0$ and $\partial V_B^P / \partial r_B = 0$. Next use

$$\frac{\partial p_B}{\partial r_A} = \frac{-mr_A^{m-1}r_B^m}{(r_A^m + r_B^m)^2}, \tag{6.11}$$

$$\frac{\partial p_B}{\partial r_B} = \frac{-mr_A^m r_B^{m-1}}{(r_A^m + r_B^m)^2}, \tag{6.12}$$

obtained from (6.7). The first-order conditions show that

$$r_A^P = r_B^P = \frac{m}{4\omega}\frac{\phi(1 - \delta) + \delta}{1 - \delta}Y. \tag{6.13}$$

Both sides choose the same level of arming despite the asymmetry of payoffs in (6.9) and (6.10) because the cost of arming is the same. What becomes effectively contestable is the discounted total surplus under War: $[(\phi(1 - \delta) + \delta)/(1 - \delta)]Y$.

The positive influence on arming of the effectiveness of conflict (as represented by the parameter m) and the negative effect of the cost of arming (ω) are intuitively very plausible. The negative dependence of arming on the destruction that conflict brings about (as represented by the parameter ϕ) is also plausible and intuitive.

Perhaps of greater significance, however, is the strong positive dependence on arming of the discount factor, through the effect of the discounted total surplus under War, $[(\phi(1-\delta)+\delta)/(1-\delta)]Y$. For example, if $\phi = 0.5$, an increase in the discount factor from 0.9 to 0.95 more than doubles the term $(\phi(1-\delta)+\delta)/(1-\delta)$ from 9.5 to 19.5. As we saw in the previous section (see equation 6.6), a higher discount factor, as well as higher levels of (fixed) arming, increases the likelihood of War. Since with endogenous arming a higher discount factor increases the equilibrium arming, the set of parameters for which War becomes an equilibrium must increase compared to the case with exogenous arming.

Before deriving such a set of parameters, we consider the case of War. The payoffs under War are the following:

$$V_i^W(r_A, r_B) = p_i(r_A, r_B)\frac{\phi(1-\delta)+\delta}{1-\delta}Y - \omega r_i, \qquad i = A, B. \tag{6.14}$$

It is straightforward to show that equilibrium arming is not just symmetric but the same as under Armed Peace:

$$r_A^W = r_B^W = \frac{m}{4\omega}\frac{\phi(1-\delta)+\delta}{1-\delta}Y = r_i^P, \qquad i \in A, B. \tag{6.15}$$

The reason for the identical levels of arming under both Armed Peace and War is that even under Armed Peace, the determinant of equilibrium arming is the payoff under War, and the latter determines the disagreement point in bargaining for the two sides. Under both Armed Peace and War the relevant portion of B's payoff that can be influenced by its choice of arming is $p_B(r_A, r_B) \times [(\phi(1-\delta)+\delta)/(1-\delta)]Y$, whereas for A it is either $-p_B(r_A, r_B) \times [(\phi(1-\delta)+\delta)/(1-\delta)]Y$ (for the case of Armed Peace) or $p_A(r_A, r_B) \times [(\phi(1-\delta)+\delta)/(1-\delta)]Y$ (for the case of War), which equals $[1 - p_B(r_A, r_B)] \times [(\phi(1-\delta)+\delta)/(1-\delta)]Y$. Both cases lead to the same marginal incentives for arming.

The set of parameters under which either Armed Peace or War prevail can be derived by susbstituting the cost of arming into (6.6) or, equivalently, by determining whether or not, conditional on this period's arming, the total discounted surplus under Armed Peace is higher or lower than the total discounted surplus under War. By the latter approach, War will occur if and only if

$$\frac{Y}{1-\delta} - \delta\omega r_A^P - \delta\omega r_B^P = \frac{Y}{1-\delta} - \frac{2\delta\omega m}{4\omega}\frac{\phi(1-\delta)+\delta}{1-\delta}Y < \frac{\phi(1-\delta)+\delta}{1-\delta}Y,$$

$$(6.16)$$

where the left-hand side of the inequality represents the total discounted surplus under Armed Peace and the right-hand side the total surplus under War. Note that the left-hand side represents the present discounted value of all the surplus Y minus the discounted value of arming, whereas the right-hand side represents the reduces surplus from War today (ϕY) plus the discounted value that accrues to the winner of War from next period, $(\delta/(1-\delta))Y$. War occurs if and only if the current loss from War, $(1-\phi)Y$, is lower than the discounted sum of total arming under Armed Peace. Then inequality (6.16) reduces to

$$\frac{\delta m(\phi(1-\delta)+\delta)}{2(1-\delta)^2(1-\phi)} < 1.$$

$$(6.17)$$

Note that the level of income (Y) in (6.17) does not change whether there is Armed Peace or War. This finding is contrary to that in (6.6), where arming is exogenous. The endogenous cost of arms is proportional to Y and cancels out in (6.16). Furthermore the marginal cost of arming (ω) does not have an effect either because any change in that cost is met by a change in the equilibrium level of arming that exactly cancels out the change in the cost.[6]

From (6.17) we can conclude that War is more likely and Armed Peace less likely when

1. the effectiveness of conflict as represented by m is high;

2. the discount factor δ is higher; and

3. the War is less destructive (or, ϕ is high).

Items 2 and 3 were identified in the previous section where arming is exogenous. The effect of the discount factor is, if anything, stronger under endogenous arming, since the higher discount factor not only increases the value of the future cost of arming but also increases the equilibrium level of arming. For even small discount factors, if the cost of arming (in equation 6.13 or 6.15) is large enough, we might expect the adversaries to face serious liquidity constraints so that War is averted in some cases. However, as Collier et al. (2003) have found, recently some rebel groups have raised funds by selling the advance rights to the extraction of minerals that they currently do not control, and thus are able to at least partly circumvent the severe liquidity constraints that War entails. If the liquidity constraints were to be binding for both adversaries, we would then revert to the analysis of the previous section or continue with the more complex one in terms of states in the next section.

6.4 Multiple Victories for Winning the War

Our analysis thus far assumes that one War determines the victor. However, completely eliminating one's opponent is often only achieved after a series of smaller victories. We extend here the basic model of section 6.2 into a repeated game in which more than one War, more appropriately called a battle in this context, must be won in order to achieve total victory.

In any given period t, A and B will again make the same War-or-Armed Peace decision as before, yet now their interaction will depend on the existing state of relative power, which can differ over time. To keep the analysis as simple as possible, we will suppose there are five states, $x = 0, 1, \ldots, 4$. Let x denote the relative strength of A and B so that if they are in state x at time t, then A wins the next armed conflict with probability $p_A = x/4$. Should conflict occur in this state and A wins, then the setting moves to state $x + 1$ in time $t + 1$, whereas if B wins, then the setting moves to state $x - 1$ in time $t + 1$. A achieves total victory by winning enough battles to reach state 4, since $p_A = 4/4 = 1$ in that state. Conversely, B achieves total victory by reaching state 0.

Further suppose that the last winner of an open conflict has temporary control over the resources not destroyed by the fighting, and so is the player in position to make a settlement offer. Specifically, let A be the proposer in state 3, let B be the proposer in state 1, and let either A or B be the proposer in state 2 depending on who won the prior War. The idea here is that if we start in the even strength state 2, then states 1 and 3 are only ever reached by a victory of B or A in the prior period.

Notice how winning a War brings the victor closer to Total Victory in two ways. First, winning today brings the state closer to the Total Victory state, and second, winning today increases the chances of winning the future Wars that are needed to achieve that Total Victory. Also note that the basic setting presented earlier in section 6.2 is a three state, $x = 0, 1, 2$, version of this model in which $p_A = x/2$.

This type of competition has been termed "tug-of-war" by earlier researchers because of the potential for each side to move from a position of strength to weakness, and because the contest occurs over many periods. For example, Harris and Vickers (1987) use a multi-state race with contest success functions to study an R&D race in which each organization achieves victory only after separating itself from its rival, and Budd, Harris, and Vickers (1993) examine duopoly firms that in a similar race achieve market dominance. That said, the nature of the tug-of-war in our model differs in one key respect. In addition to one side's victory today bringing them closer to total victory, victory today also confers an additional advantage by increasing the victor's relative strength today. That is, victory today increases the likelihood that the same group will win again in the next period. This changing of relative power acts to increase the benefits of victory today while also increasing the cost of losing today. Our work also differs in that we apply the tug-of-war model to a new setting of War and Armed Peace.

To examine which is optimal for each group, War or Armed Peace, requires multiple steps in the logic. First, we must find the value functions for the situation in which War always occurs in each of the contention states $x = 1, 2, 3$. Next, we calculate what settlements must be offered to avert War and sustain Armed Peace in each period. This procedure, which is detailed in the appendix, yields the following four conditions for a Markov perfect equilibrium:[7]

- In state 3, A will offer an accepted subsidy only if

$$Y \geq 3\delta \frac{(\delta^2 + 8\delta - \delta^3)r_A + (8 - \delta^2 + \delta^3)r_B}{8(4 - 3\delta - \delta^2)(1 - \phi)}. \tag{6.18}$$

- In state 2, if A is the proposer, an accepted subsidy will be made only if

$$Y \geq 3\delta^2 \frac{2(1 + \delta)r_A + (1 + \delta)r_B}{3 + (13 - 12\phi)(1 - \delta^2)}. \tag{6.19}$$

- In state 2, if B is the proposer, an accepted subsidy will be made only if

$$Y \geq 3\delta^2 \frac{2(1 + \delta)r_B + (1 + \delta)r_A}{3 + (13 - 12\phi)(1 - \delta^2)}. \tag{6.20}$$

• In state 1, B will offer an accepted subsidy only if

$$Y \geq 3\delta \frac{(\delta^2 + 8\delta - \delta^3)r_B + (8 - \delta^2 + \delta^3)r_A}{8(4 - 3\delta - \delta^2)(1 - \phi)}. \tag{6.21}$$

Equations (6.18) through (6.21) are directly related to condition (6.6) for Armed Peace in the basic setting examined in section 6.2. Again, War is more likely in any period and any state when

1. the contested output Y is lower;

2. the two groups' resources devoted to arming $(r_A + r_B)$ are higher;

3. the discount factor δ is higher; and

4. the War is less destructive (or, ϕ is higher).

Notice that the conditions for War in multi-stage conflict are qualitatively identical to those found using the basic model in section 6.2. Thus the basic model captures the primary strategic elements at work in the choice between War and Armed Peace.

Nevertheless, the conditions for War are not identical quantitatively, and we can ask whether Armed Peace is more likely when total victory requires more War victories. To find out, we check whether equation (6.6) is less likely to be met than equations (6.18) through (6.21). To simplify this comparison, let us suppose that $r_A = r_B = r$. The symmetry implied by this assumption means that we need only compare (6.6) with (6.18) and (6.19), since (6.20) and (6.21) will now be identical to (6.18) and (6.19), respectively.

With this additional symmetry, (6.6) becomes

$$Y \geq \frac{2\delta r}{(1 - \phi)(1 - \delta)}, \tag{6.22}$$

and (6.18) and (6.19), respectively, become

$$Y \geq \frac{3\delta(\delta + 1)r}{(4 - 3\delta - \delta^2)(1 - \phi)} \tag{6.23}$$

and

$$Y \geq \frac{9\delta^2(1 + \delta)r}{3 + (13 - 12\phi)(1 - \delta^2)}. \tag{6.24}$$

A little bit more algebra reveals that the right-hand side terms of (6.23) and (6.24) are both less than (6.22) (since δ and ϕ are both less than 1).

Thus more victories do increase the likelihood of Armed Peace. Requiring more victories lengthens the time it takes to achieve total victory, thereby increasing the cost of defeating one's opponent.

Although Armed Peace is more likely in this setting, it is not guaranteed. In technical terms, Armed Peace never becomes the only equilibrium for all parameter settings. This is true even if the model were extended to a larger number of states, whereby a larger number of Wars must be won for total victory to be achieved. The reason is that there is always an incentive to achieve total victory, since it is the only way to avoid costly arming. As long as this total victory incentive exists, there is an incentive to fight, and the question is whether or not the benefits of Armed Peace outweigh those of fighting. As our analysis shows, many conditions present in low-income countries are those that make Armed Peace less likely even if total victory requires winning a series of battles.

6.5 Concluding Remarks

Why does conflict occur, and disproportionately so in low-income countries? Our analysis examines two key factors, that adversaries cannot make long-term contracts to enforce disarmament, and that open conflict changes the strategic nature of future interaction. Our analysis also considers two key features of low-income countries, that adversaries can make short-run (as distinguished from long-term) contracts, and that achieving total victory prevents one from having to spend resources on arming. Even though total victory, once achieved, is in some sense efficient because it no longer requires costly arms buildup, the only way to achieve it is through open conflict. However, open conflict is not only inefficient because it requires the costly buildup of arms, but it also leads to the destruction of resources. Armed Peace is thus a possible middle ground.

Yet our analysis shows that Armed Peace is not inevitable because the incentives to fight are strong. Our basic model shows that conflict is more likely than Armed Peace when large resources are devoted to arming, the future is not highly discounted, and war is not very destructive. When opponents choose their arming levels, we find that conflict is more likely when the effectiveness is conflict is high. Prolonging the length of time necessary to achieve total victory can increase the chances of Armed Peace, although the same conditions as those above will still lead to conflict. The lure of total victory and its impact on future strategic positioning remains a strong incentive to engage in open conflict.

In short, the combination of incomplete contracting and the expectation of complete victory are inducements to conflict. If parties can make long-term contracts, then the destructive nature of War leads to settlement that makes each side better off than fighting. Moreover, even if parties are unable to make long-term contracts, there still might be the possibility of short-term contracts that can be enforced by each side's threat to fight; that is, these short-term contracts might be enough to enable Armed Peace. However, if conflict today alters the future positions of the adversaries, then one or more parties might forgo the short-term relative safety of Armed Peace and by open conflict opt for the chance of total victory and its associated high benefits.

We conclude that the shadow of the future looms large in low-income countries that exhibit the conditions conducive to War described herein. Achieving lasting peace requires the development of institutions necessary to enforce and foster peaceful resolutions to competition over scarce resource. Since these institutions are costly to implement (Gradstein 2004) and take time to develop (Genicot and Skaperdas 2002),[8] our findings suggest that low-income countries will remain in a vicious cycle of poverty and violent civil or political violence for prolonged periods.

Appendix

Let $V_i^t(x)$ denote i's present discounted value of being in state x. The value functions for the total victory states are thus $V_A^t(0) = 0$, $V_A^t(4) = Y/(1 - \delta)$, $V_B^t(0) = Y/(1 - \delta)$, and $V_B^t(4) = 0$. Note that in the total victory states there is no need to arm by expending r_A or r_B, since the opponent has been eliminated.

To examine which is optimal for the groups, War or Armed Peace, in the other states requires two steps in the logic. First, we find the value functions for the situation where War always occurs in each of the contention states $x = 1, 2, 3$. Next, we calculate what settlements must be offered to avert War and sustain Armed Peace in each period. In this manner we obtain the conditions for a Markov perfect equilibrium.

Value Functions under War in Each Period

War in a contested state yields the following value functions:

$$V_A^{W,t}(1) = \frac{1}{4}(\phi Y + \delta V_A^{t+1}(2) - \delta r_A), \tag{6.25}$$

$$V_A^{W,t}(2) = \frac{1}{2}(\phi Y + \delta V_A^{t+1}(3) - \delta r_A) + \frac{1}{2}(\delta V_A^{t+1}(1) - \delta r_A), \tag{6.26}$$

$$V_A^{W,t}(3) = \frac{3}{4}\left(\phi Y + \delta \frac{Y}{1-\delta} - \delta r_A\right) + \frac{1}{4}(\delta V_A^{t+1}(2) - \delta r_A), \tag{6.27}$$

$$V_B^{W,t}(1) = \frac{3}{4}\left(\phi Y + \delta \frac{Y}{1-\delta} - \delta r_B\right) + \frac{1}{4}(\delta V_B^{t+1}(2) - \delta r_B), \tag{6.28}$$

$$V_B^{W,t}(2) = \frac{1}{2}(\phi Y + \delta V_B^{t+1}(1) - \delta r_B) + \frac{1}{2}(\delta V_B^{t+1}(3) - \delta r_B), \tag{6.29}$$

$$V_B^{W,t}(3) = \frac{1}{4}(\phi Y + \delta V_B^{t+1}(2) - \delta r_B). \tag{6.30}$$

To find the present discounted values for group A if War occurs in every contested period, plug (6.25) and (6.27) into (6.26) to solve for $V_A^W(2)$, and then plug that back into (6.25) and (6.27). Do a similar procedure for group B. The results are

$$V_A^W(1) = \frac{(8\phi - 2\delta^2\phi - 4\delta\phi - 2\delta^3\phi + 3\delta^3)Y + (3\delta^4 + 5\delta^3 - 8\delta)r_A}{8(1-\delta)(4-\delta^2)}, \tag{6.31}$$

$$V_A^W(2) = \frac{(3\delta^2 - 4\delta^2\phi + 4\phi)Y + (5\delta^3 + 3\delta^2 - 8\delta)r_A}{2(1-\delta)(4-\delta^2)}, \tag{6.32}$$

$$V_A^W(3) = \frac{(24\phi - 20\delta\phi - 6\delta^2\phi + 2\delta^3\phi + 24\delta - 3\delta^3)Y}{8(1-\delta)(4-\delta^2)}$$
$$+ \frac{(11\delta^3 - 3\delta^4 - 32\delta + 24\delta^2)r_A}{8(1-\delta)(4-\delta^2)}, \tag{6.33}$$

$$V_B^W(1) = \frac{(24\phi - 20\delta\phi - 6\delta^2\phi + 2\delta^3\phi + 24\delta - 3\delta^3)Y}{8(1-\delta)(4-\delta^2)}$$
$$+ \frac{(11\delta^3 - 3\delta^4 - 32\delta + 24\delta^2)r_B}{8(1-\delta)(4-\delta^2)}, \tag{6.34}$$

$$V_B^W(2) = \frac{(3\delta^2 - 4\delta^2\phi + 4\phi)Y + (5\delta^3 + 3\delta^2 - 8\delta)r_B}{2(1-\delta)(4-\delta^2)}, \qquad (6.35)$$

$$V_B^W(3) = \frac{(8\phi - 2\delta^2\phi - 4\delta\phi - 2\delta^3\phi + 3\delta^3)Y + (3\delta^4 + 5\delta^3 - 8\delta)r_B}{8(1-\delta)(4-\delta^2)}. \qquad (6.36)$$

We will use these equations in a moment, after we determine when Armed Peace or open conflict will result from optimizing behavior.

When Armed Peace Is Optimal

Let $S_i(x)$ be the offer made by i in state x. Note that if i's offer is accepted by j in state x in period t, then that same offer will be accepted in period $t+1$ because both parties are still in state x. Thus, to determine what $S_i(x)$ will be accepted by j, we compare the infinite stream of $S_i(x)$'s that j will get with what j will get going to War from period t on. For state 3, this comparison is

$$S_A(3) + \frac{\delta}{1-\delta}(S_A(3) - r_B)$$

$$\geq \frac{(8\phi - 2\delta^2\phi - 4\delta\phi - 2\delta^3\phi + 3\delta^3)Y + (3\delta^4 + 5\delta^3 - 8\delta)r_B}{8(1-\delta)(4-\delta^2)},$$

where the RHS is from equation (6.36). Since A will make the smallest such offer that satisfies the inequality, setting this to equal yields

$$S_A^*(3) = \frac{(8\phi - 2\delta^2\phi - 4\delta\phi - 2\delta^3\phi + 3\delta^3)Y + (24\delta - 3\delta^3 + 3\delta^4)r_B}{8(4-\delta^2)}.$$

Similar calculations for the other states yield

$$S_A^*(2) = \frac{1}{2}\frac{(3\delta^2 - 4\delta^2\phi + 4\phi)Y + (3\delta^3 + 3\delta^2)r_B}{2(4-\delta^2)},$$

$$S_B^*(2) = \frac{1}{2}\frac{(3\delta^2 - 4\delta^2\phi + 4\phi)Y + (3\delta^3 + 3\delta^2)r_A}{2(4-\delta^2)},$$

$$S_B^*(3) = \frac{(8\phi - 2\delta^2\phi - 4\delta\phi - 2\delta^3\phi + 3\delta^3)Y + (24\delta - 3\delta^3 + 3\delta^4)r_A}{8(4-\delta^2)}.$$

We next ask which one of these offers is optimal for the proposer.

Group A will offer $S_A^*(3)$ in state 3 if doing so now and forever is better than fighting forever:

$$Y - S_A^*(3) + \frac{\delta}{1-\delta}(Y - S_A^*(3) - r_A)$$

$$\geq \frac{(24\phi - 20\delta\phi - 6\delta^2\phi + 2\delta^3\phi + 24\delta - 3\delta^3)Y}{8(1-\delta)(4-\delta^2)}$$

$$+ \frac{(11\delta^3 - 3\delta^4 - 32\delta + 24\delta^2)r_A}{8(1-\delta)(4-\delta^2)},$$

where the RHS is from equation (6.33). Some algebra reduces this condition to

$$Y \geq 3\delta \frac{(\delta^2 + 8\delta - \delta^3)r_A + (8 - \delta^2 + \delta^3)r_B}{8(4 - 3\delta - \delta^2)(1 - \phi)},$$

which is exactly equation (6.18). Doing the same comparison for an offer by group A in state 2 yields condition

$$Y \geq 3\delta^2 \frac{2(1+\delta)r_A + (1+\delta)r_B}{3 + (13 - 12\phi)(1 - \delta^2)},$$

which is equation (6.19).

Repeating the process for group B in states 2 and 1 yields

$$Y \geq 3\delta^2 \frac{2(1+\delta)r_B + (1+\delta)r_A}{3 + (13 - 12\phi)(1 - \delta^2)},$$

$$Y \geq 3\delta \frac{(\delta^2 + 8\delta - \delta^3)r_B + (8 - \delta^2 + \delta^3)r_A}{8(4 - 3\delta - \delta^2)(1 - \phi)},$$

respectively, which are equations (6.20) and (6.21).

Notes

We would like to thank Jim Fearon, Arye Hillman, Kai Konrad, Bob Powell, and seminar participants for valuable comments, and especially Roger Myerson for both comments and for discovering an error in section 6.3 of a previous version of the chapter.

1. An overview of the costs and other problems associated with conflict can be found in the World Bank report of Collier et al. (2003). The number of countries mentioned is quoted from Fearon and Laitin (2003). Hess (2003) provides estimates of the indirect costs of conflict in terms of reduced trading and welfare, which are about 8 percent of GDP on average for low-income countries and, of course, much higher for some countries while nonexistent for other countries. For an overview of the recent academic literature on civil wars, see Sambanis (2004).

2. McBride (2004) describes how coups can arise from incomplete contracting. When incumbent politicians cannot commit to efficient policies, they will resort to clientelist practices to gain popular support. If the incumbents are successful, political opponents' only way to gain political power is by attempting a coup.

3. Grossman and Hart (1986) introduced the main idea for the theory of the firm whereby parties cannot write long-term contracts on relationship-specific investments. Skaperdas (2003) discusses how incomplete contracting relates to civil wars.

4. The term "Armed Peace" is due to Jack Hirshleifer.

5. The results in this section on the level arming and the conditions under which War occurs do not depend on the particular sequence of moves. The same results will obtain with another bargaining protocol, an equal division of the surplus (which would correspond to any symmetric bargaining solution, including the Nash and Kalai-Somorodinsky solutions). The only difference is the payoffs obtained under Armed Peace, in which group A receives more than the War payoff.

6. We would like to thank Roger Myerson for discovering an error in an earlier version of our chapter in which ω was mistakenly shown to have a negative effect on the total cost of arming.

7. See Fudenberg and Tirole (1996) for a discussion of the Markov perfect equilibrium concept.

8. Of course, external shocks can help a country get started on a good path. McBride (2005), for example, shows how economic crises in low-income countries have led to economic reforms and declines in conflict.

References

Acemoglu, D., and J. Robinson. 2000. Why did the West extend the franchise? Democracy, inequality, and growth in historical perspective. *Quarterly Journal of Economics* 115: 1167–99.

Bester, H., and K. Konrad. 2004. Delay in contests. *European Economic Review* 48(5): 1169–78.

Bester, H., and K. Konrad. 2005. Easy targets and the timing of conflict. *Journal of Theoretical Politics* 17(2): 199–215.

Bester, H., and K. Wärneryd. 1998. Conflict resolution under asymmetric information. Unpublished manuscript.

Brito, D., and M. Intriligator. 1985. Conflict, war and redistribution. *American Political Science Review* 79(4): 943–57.

Budd, C., C. Harris, and J. Vickers. 1993. A model of the evolution of duopoly: Does the asymmetry between firms tend to increase or decrease? *Review of Economic Studies* 60: 543–73.

Collier, P., V. L. Elliott, H. Hegre, A. Hoeffler, M. Reynal-Querol, and N. Sambanis. 2003. *Breaking the Conflict Trap: Civil War and Development Policy*. New York: Oxford University Press.

Fearon, J. 1995. Rationalist explanations for war. *International Organization* 49(3): 379–414.

Fearon, J., and D. D. Laitin. 2003. Ethnicity, insurgency, and civil war. *American Political Science Review* 97(1): 75–90.

Fudenberg, D., and J. Tirole. 1996. *Game Theory*. Cambridge: MIT Press.

Garfinkel, M., and S. Skaperdas. 2000. Conflict without misperception or incomplete information: How the future matters. *Journal of Conflict Resolution* 44(6): 793–807.

Genicot, G., and S. Skaperdas. 2002. Investing in conflict management. *Journal of Conflict Resolution* 46: 154–70.

Gradstein, M. 2004. Governance and growth. *Journal of Development Economics* 73: 505–18.

Grossman, S., and O. Hart. 1986. The costs and benefits of ownership: A theory of vertical and lateral integration. *Journal of Political Economy* 84: 691–719.

Harris, C., and J. Vickers. 1987. Racing with uncertainty. *Review of Economics Studies* 54: 1–21.

Hess, G. 2003. The economic welfare cost of conflict: An empirical assessment. CESifo Working Paper 852.

Hirshleifer, J. 1989. Conflict and rent-seeking success functions: Ratio vs. difference models of relative success. *Public Choice* 63(2): 101–12.

McBride, M. 2004. Clientelism, Coups, and Commitment. Unpublished manuscript.

McBride, M. 2005. Crises, reforms, and regime persistence in sub-Saharan Africa. *European Journal of Political Economy* 21(3): 688–707.

McNeill, W. 1982. *The Pursuit of Power*. Chicago: University of Chicago Press.

Mehlum, H., and K. Moene. 2006. Fighting against the odds. *Economics of Governance* 7(1): 75–87.

Powell, R. 2006. War as a commitment problem. *International Organization* 60(1): 169–203.

Sambanis, N. 2004. Using case studies to expand economic models of civil war. *Perspectives on Politics* 2(2): 259–79.

Skaperdas, S. 2003. An economic approach to analyzing civil wars. UC Irvine Working Paper 02-03-18.

Skaperdas, S., and C. Syropoulos. 1996. Can the shadow of the future harm cooperation. *Journal of Economic Behavior and Organization* 29: 355–72.

Tilly, C. 1992. *Coercion, Capital and European States*. New York: Blackwell.

Tullock, G. 1980. Efficient rent seeking. In J. M. Buchanan, R. D. Tollison, and G. Tullock, eds., *Toward a Theory of the Rent Seeking Society*. College Station: Texas A&M University Press, pp. 3–15.

7

Information and Incomplete Investor Protection

Karl Wärneryd

7.1 Introduction

As reported by *USA Today* in 1999, Inkombank, established in 1988, was a Russian bank that seemed to hold a lot of promise. In 1993, it raised capital from a select group of foreign investors, including the New York–based Morgenthow & Latham holding company. No dividends were forthcoming, however, and the new shareholders soon began to suspect Inkombank of wrongdoing. In 1994, the legal representative of the shareholders wrote to Inkombank threatening a lawsuit. A response was sent to Michael Shick, the director of Morgenthow & Latham, inviting him to come to Moscow, meet officials of the bank, and discuss the issues. Shick traveled to Russia and was later found dead in the Moscow River, having been shot in the head. The circumstances of Shick's death were never settled, the shareholders' lawsuit was never tried, but in 1998 Inkombank's license to operate as a bank in Russia was finally revoked following allegations that it was involved with organized crime groups and engaged in money-laundering schemes.[1]

This story suggests that when investing in Russian businesses, at least occasionally it is a good idea to own a gun. There are, of course, many such stories of investment gone horribly wrong in transition and developing economies, where a formal framework for investor protection may be underdeveloped or missing entirely. If in a nation it is costly for an investor to have his rights enforced, this in turn naturally means that it may be difficult to attract investors. Accordingly a recent empirical literature on law and finance highlights the importance of formal legal investor protection in facilitating the funding of businesses (e.g., see La Porta et al. 1998; La Porta, López-de-Silanes, and Shleifer 1999; Shleifer and Vishny 1997.)

But even with formal legal institutions in place, the stockholder-management relation is at heart an archetypical incomplete contract. There is no guarantee whatsoever, even when buying stocks in a corporation in a Western nation, that the investor will receive anything at all in return. As German banker Carl Fürstenberg (1850–1933) is so memorably reported to have said,

Die Aktionäre sind dumm und frech; dumm, weil sie Aktien kaufen, und frech, weil sie auch noch Dividende erwarten.

That is, shareholders are stupid and impertinent. Stupid because they buy shares, meaning they invest in projects they will have no real control over, impertinent because they nevertheless demand dividends.

Because of the very nature of the corporation, the most legal protection can ensure is that the firm's internal activities are transparent to the outside investor, and that managers can be sued for violation of their fiduciary duty—the vaguely defined obligation of management to act in the interests of the owners. But this in no way means that enforcement of the interests of the investor becomes costless with such legal provisions in place. Just like the investor in Russia may have to buy a gun to protect himself, the investor in a nation with more well-developed formal investor protection must also expend resources on safeguarding his investment. If management misbehaves, this does not mean that they will automatically be punished. At the very least, the investor must initiate litigation procedures. Once in court, an investor who has not spent anything on lawyers and on preparing his case will lose with certainty, since the only information used by the court to reach a decision is that provided by the parties themselves.

Hence any set of legal institutions, incomplete or extensive, will necessarily still give rise to social costs associated with the enforcement of investor interests. To this should be added, of course, the resources expended by management in trying to retain funds within the firm. To the extent that the resources used up in the conflict between owners and management have alternative, productive uses, they represent a deadweight loss, since they are only used to effect a transfer of income. (As famously argued, in the context of what is now known as *rent-seeking* activities more generally, by Tullock 1967.)

These observations naturally give rise to the *constitutional* question of what the properties are of a legal system that minimizes such expenditure. There is an obvious initial answer to this question: The influence–

cost-minimizing system is a draconian one where decisions *cannot* be influenced by the activities of the parties involved. An example is a legal system in which managers who are sued by investors are *always* found guilty. But it should be apparent that such a system would have severely negative incentive effects. If the participation of entrepreneurs is necessary for cooperative projects to be undertaken and be of high quality, then there will be some trade-off between minimizing conflict expenditure and providing incentives for the entrepreneur to be active.

The rest of this chapter focuses on the implications for an optimal legal framework for investor protection of the distinction between

1. legal institutions that increase the transparency of the firm in the sense of making it easier for an outside investor to get an idea of what the actual realized value of the firm's project is, on the one hand, and

2. legal institutions that lower the cost to the investor of successfully suing management for violation of fiduciary duty, on the other.

In a model that explicitly takes into account the strategic nature of the conflict between the investor and management over the realized surplus, given the rules provided by the legal framework, I show that there may be complicated interaction between these two different types of legal protection of investors. In particular, I focus on the implications for development. Many studies (e.g., López-de-Silanes 2002) report a positive correlation between growth and various measures of investor protection. I show that increasing the ease with which managers can be sued in a legal setting where the firm's transparency is low can have the undesirable effect of leading managers to select low-quality projects.

I follow Müller and Wärneryd (2001) and Castillo and Skaperdas (2005) in modeling the relationship between investors and insiders in the firm as a costly *conflict*, but add informational asymmetry. Formally the model is then of a common-value contest with asymmetric information, as studied more generally in Wärneryd (2003). That is, unlike what is common in other contributions to the corporate governance literature, such as that of Shleifer and Wolfenzon (2002), who assume there is an exogenously given probability of managerial diversion being detected and punished, I let the share that the manager can retain of the generated value of the firm be a function of costly safeguarding or appropriative efforts on the parts of both manager and investor.

There is by now a substantial literature on equilibrium behavior in conflict, with applications ranging from the study of outright armed conflict in situations of imperfectly defined property rights (as in McBride and Skaperdas 2005) to the analysis of rent-seeking and lobbying. It is less common to note the conflictual aspects of enforcement of corporate governance regimes—although one would expect them to be especially pronounced in developing and transition economies.[2]

In showing that enforcing fiduciary duty more strictly in a situation with low transparency may lead the manager to select poor projects, in the sense of projects that are stochastically dominated by other feasible projects, my perspective is somewhat related to that of Burkart, Gromb, and Panunzi (1997), for example, who have noted that too much monitoring, such as by a large blockholder, dulls the incentives of managers to exert effort or make relation-specific investments that increase the value of the firm. Here I show that even if the entrepreneur can costlessly select a high probability of success, if there is informational asymmetry and he can expect to keep too little of the returns, he will prefer to select a low probability of success. This is because a low probability of success increases the informational advantage of the entrepreneur vis-à-vis the investor.

7.2   Managerial Diversion and Fiduciary Duty

Consider a risk-neutral entrepreneur, E, who can, if he obtains funds $k > 0$, undertake a project that yields a value of the firm of $y > 0$ with probability π and zero with probability $1 - \pi$. The value of the firm y and investment cost k are assumed to be exogenously given, but the entrepreneur can select the probability π of success freely.

A risk-neutral investor, I, supplies the capital. If the project is a success, what the entrepreneur manages to retain is determined by the *safeguarding expenditures* (a term borrowed from Williamson 1985) of both parties and the degree of investor protection enforced by the law.

Under any corporate governance system, what an investor can get out of a project necessarily depends on costly activities undertaken by both investor and management. To see this, suppose that an investor is told by management that the project has been a failure and nothing can be paid back. If the investor suspects mismanagement or outright management diversion of funds, yet does nothing, he will certainly be left with nothing. The investor must at the very least initiate litigation against management. Once the case goes to court, the investor must expend further resources. Since the court is not omniscient and does no investigation on its own, its decision depends on the evidence presented by the respective parties. A party who presents no evidence is unlikely to prevail. And evidence, of course, is costly to produce.

In developing countries, where legal institutions may be informal, unreliable, and susceptible to corruption, evidence production may be even costlier than in industrialized nations. In extreme cases, such as the circumstances suggested by the Russian Inkombank story discussed at the start of this chapter, safeguarding may involve buying guns and hiring thugs to enforce your interests in case of conflict.

Specifically, assume that I spends x_I on safeguarding, and E spends x_E. Then the share of the generated value of the firm that I will be able to extract from the firm is

$$p_I(x_I, x_E) := \begin{cases} \theta x_I / (\theta x_I + (1 - \theta)x_E) & \text{if } \theta x_I + (1 - \theta)x_E > 0, \\ 0 & \text{otherwise,} \end{cases}$$

where $0 < \theta < 1$ is a parameter that measures the advantage given the investor by the degree of effectiveness of legal protection. That is, if $\theta > 0.5$, the entrepreneur is disadvantaged relative to the investor, and if $\theta < 0.5$, the investor is disadvantaged.[3] If the investor spends nothing, assume the entire value of the firm remains with the entrepreneur. As it turns out, this can never happen in equilibrium.

In line with the earlier discussion one may think of p_I as the probability of the investor prevailing in court.[4] Since the parties are assumed to be risk neutral, no meaningful distinction can be made between a probability of the investor gaining the entire value of the firm and a deterministic share awarded with certainty. The parameter θ may then be thought of as measuring the strength of a legal presumption in favor of the investor, should the investor decide to take the entrepreneur to court. Note, however, that given that both parties know the probability of the investor prevailing in court, no court proceedings need to actually take place—the parties can simply share the value of the firm in such a fashion that the investor ends up with his expected value.

The safeguarding expenditures of the entrepreneur should be thought of as effort spent on hiding managerial self-dealing, outright theft, and other diversions of company funds in violation of fiduciary duty—but not attempts to hide the value of the firm through accounting and other measures, specifically. The corresponding safeguarding expenditure of the investor could be thought of, for example, as legal expenses incurred in trying to hold the entrepreneur to his duty of loyalty—but not efforts to uncover specifically the generated value. The parameter θ then measures the relative costliness to the investor of getting a court to uphold the fiduciary duty of the manager.

I make the distinction between appropriation effort and efforts directed at revealing the value of the firm because I want to separate the effects of legal protection in the sense of enforcement of ficuciary duty, on the one hand, and those of informational asymmetry, on the other. The degree of informational asymmetry is, of course, also to some extent a function of legal provisions, and ultimately I want to distinguish legal measures that allow shareholders to sue managers for misconduct from those that increase the transparency of the firm.

The time line of the game is as follows:

1. E selects the observable probability π of project success, and offers the project to I.

2. I accepts or rejects the project. If I has accepted, he pays k.

3. If I has accepted, the value of the firm is realized and observed by E. In one scenario I will consider the value is also observed by I, and E knows if this has happened.

4. The parties make their safeguarding expenditures and receive payoffs according to the contest success function p_I.

7.3 Litigation Equilibrium

I solve the game backward from the end, focusing first on equilibrium at the contest stage. That is, I assume that the value of the firm has been realized and litigation has been initiated, and consider the levels of safeguarding expenditure the parties would rationally select at this point. I first study the case of symmetric information, where both parties are informed about the realized value.

7.3.1 *Informed Investor*

Suppose the value of the firm is y, and both parties are informed about this. The entrepreneur then wishes to select $x_E^s(y)$ so as to maximize

$$v_E^s := (1 - p_I(x_I^s(y), x_E^s(y)))y - x_E^s(y),$$

given the safeguarding expenditure $x_I^s(y)$ of the investor.

Note that it cannot happen in equilibrium that one or both parties expend zero if the value of the firm is positive. For suppose one party expends zero. Then the other party will win with probability one in return for an arbitrarily small expenditure.

Since v_E^s is strictly concave in his strategic variable $x_E^s(y)$, the entrepreneur's best reply is therefore found by differentiating his objective function with respect to $x_E^s(y)$, and setting the derivative equal to zero. Hence it must be that

$$x_E^s(y) = \frac{\sqrt{\theta(1-\theta)x_I^s(y)y} - \theta x_I^s(y)}{1-\theta}.$$

Similarly the investor's best reply function is

$$x_I^s(y) = \frac{\sqrt{\theta(1-\theta)x_E^s(y)y} - (1-\theta)x_E^s(y)}{\theta}.$$

In equilibrium, both parties must be playing best replies. Hence there is a unique equilibrium where

$$x_E^s(y) = x_I^s(y) = \theta(1-\theta)y,$$

and naturally

$$x_E^s(0) = x_I^s(0) = 0.$$

The investor's expected equilibrium utility is therefore

$$u_I^s := \theta^2 \pi y$$

and that of the entrepreneur is

$$u_E^s := (1-\theta)^2 \pi y.$$

7.3.2 Uninformed Investor

Consider next the case where the investor is uninformed, and only the entrepreneur knows the realized value of the firm.

Since the entrepreneur knows whether the value is y or zero, he rationally spends zero on appropriative activities if the value is zero. Hence in this situation $x_E^a(0) = 0$. If the value is y, E wishes to select $x_E^a(y)$ so as to maximize

$$v_E^a := (1 - p_I)y - x_E^a(y).$$

Consider the first partial derivative of v_E^a with respect to $x_E^a(y)$,

$$\frac{\partial v_E^a}{\partial x_E^a} = \frac{\theta(1-\theta)x_I^a}{(\theta x_I^a + (1-\theta)x_E^a(y))^2} - 1.$$

This derivative is negative for all $x_E^a(y) > 0$ if we have $x_I^a > (1-\theta)y/\theta$, and hence the entrepreneur's best reply is $x_E^a(y) = 0$. Otherwise, the entrepreneur's best reply is

$$x_E^a(y) = \frac{\sqrt{\theta(1-\theta)x_I^a y} - \theta x_I^a}{1-\theta}.$$

I, knowing only the prior distribution of the value, wishes to select his appropriation expenditure x_I^a so as to maximize

$$v_I^a := (1-\pi) \cdot 0 + \pi p_I y - x_I^a,$$

for which the first-order condition, given a positive $x_E^a(y)$ is

$$\frac{\theta(1-\theta)x_E^a(y)}{(\theta x_I^a + (1-\theta)x_E^a(y))^2}\pi y = 1.$$

At an equilibrium where the entrepreneur expends a positive amount at y, equilibrium appropriation expenditures are therefore

$$x_E^a(0) = 0,$$

$$x_E^a(y) = \frac{\theta(1-\theta)\pi}{(1-(1-\pi)\theta)^2}y,$$

and

$$x_I^a = \frac{\theta(1-\theta)\pi^2}{(1-(1-\pi)\theta)^2}y.$$

Since $x_I^a < (1-\theta)y/\theta$, this is the only equilibrium that can exist.

Note that if both parties were uninformed about the value of the firm, they would each spend $\theta(1-\theta)\pi y$ in expectation in equilibrium. But because of the entrepreneur's informational advantage, the investor must try to avoid a phenomenon analogous to the winner's curse of auction theory. Instead of valuing the firm at its ex ante expectation, the investor must adjust his expenditure downward.

In equilibrium, the investor's ex ante utility is

$$u_I^a := v_I^a = \frac{\theta^2\pi^3}{(1-(1-\pi)\theta)^2}y.$$

The entrepreneur's ex ante utility is

$$u_E^a := \pi v_E^a = \frac{(1-\theta)^2 \pi}{(1-(1-\pi)\theta)^2} y.$$

From the point of view of efficiency, conflict expenditures should be as small as possible, since the contest itself concerns only the allocation of the expected value of πy among the two risk neutral participants. Note that both parties spend the same amount in expectation in equilibrium. Since $x_I^a < \theta(1-\theta)\pi y$ for $\pi < 1$, this means that asymmetric information increases efficiency relative to situations in which either both parties are informed or both are uninformed. Furthermore, giving either party an advantage by letting $\theta \neq 0.5$ also decreases equilibrium expenditure. Both of these effects are examples of how asymmetries of various kinds more generally lower conflict costs in contests.

7.4   Project Selection

Although on the face of it, so far the informational asymmetry between investor and entrepreneur seems to be beneficial from the point of view of efficiency, one still needs to take one more step back toward the beginning of the game and consider the selection of project by the entrepreneur. This turns out to complicate the picture.

Suppose that the entrepreneur is free to select projects with respect to the probability π of success, subject to the investor's participation constraint $u_I \geq k$. Which projects would the entrepreneur prefer to offer to investors, and how does this depend on the level of legal investor protection?

For simplicity assume that π can be set costlessly at any value in $[0,1]$. Assuming that higher values of π come at greater cost would simply serve to reinforce our conclusions about the effects of informational asymmetry.

7.4.1   Informed Investor

When the investor is informed, the entrepreneur's ex ante utility is

$$u_E^s = (1-\theta)^2 \pi y.$$

Since this payoff is strictly increasing in π, E would trivially select a project with $\pi = 1$, regardless of the value of θ.

Hence the efficient value of θ, from a constitutional perspective, is one that minimizes the conflict expenditures, which equal $2\theta(1 - \theta)$. If the entrepreneur's reservation utility is zero, a minimum is achieved by setting $\theta = 1$, corresponding to perfect investor protection.

7.4.2 Uninformed Investor

When the investor is uninformed, depending on the value of θ, the entrepreneur's expected utility u_E^a may be nonmonotonic in π, since

$$\frac{\partial u_E^a}{\partial \pi} = \frac{(1 - \theta)^2(1 - \theta - \pi\theta)y}{(1 - (1 - \pi)\theta)^3}.$$

Assuming an interior solution, and forgetting about the investor's participation constraint (which, of course, also depends on y and k), u_E^a is maximized with respect to π at

$$\pi = \frac{1 - \theta}{\theta},$$

which is strictly decreasing in θ. Hence, if the entrepreneur's choice of project were entirely unconstrained, he would choose poor projects, in the sense of projects unlikely to be successful, when the degree of investor protection is high. But if $\theta \leq 0.5$, so that the parties are evenly matched or the entrepreneur advantaged from a legal point of view, the entrepreneur optimally selects projects with $\pi = 1$. In this case the entrepreneur does not have to compensate a legal disadvantage by an informational advantage. Figure 7.1 illustrates the entrepreneur's optimal choice of probability of success.

The intuition for this is the following: The entrepreneur only expends something on appropriation when a positive value has in fact been realized. The investor in selecting his appropriative expenditure discounts for the informational advantage of the entrepreneur, which improves with π. Hence there is a trade-off from the point of view of the entrepreneur—a higher π increases the ex ante gross expectation of the project, but also the appropriative expenditure of the investor. Furthermore the higher is θ, the more costly it becomes for the entrepreneur to counter the appropriative expenditure of the investor.

One might object that I have neglected to take into account that there may be a market for investment opportunities, and that market com-

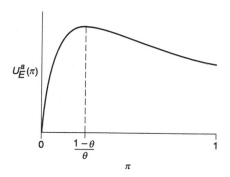

Figure 7.1
Entrepreneur's optimal choice of project

petition may therefore nevertheless force entrepreneurs to offer high-quality projects. But in the settings I have in mind, such as transition and developing economies, such well-functioning markets are frequently absent.

Consider now the constitutional question of what the optimal level of investor advantage in court is, taking into account the rational project choice of the entrepreneur. One might use as the measure of social welfare the expected sum of utilities

$$w := u_I^a + u_E^a = \frac{1 - 2\theta + (1 + \pi^2)\theta^2}{(1 - (1 - \pi)\theta)^2} \pi y.$$

If the entrepreneur sets

$$\pi = \begin{cases} 1 & \text{if } \theta < 1/2, \\ (1 - \theta)/\theta & \text{otherwise,} \end{cases}$$

the sum of utilities reduces to

$$w = \begin{cases} (1 - 2\theta + 2\theta^2)y & \text{if } \theta < 1/2, \\ (1 - \theta)y/(2\theta) & \text{otherwise.} \end{cases}$$

This function is everywhere strictly decreasing in θ. Hence from an efficiency point of view one would then want θ to be as low as possible, subject to the investor's participation constraint. That is, if the entrepreneur selects projects optimally, the optimal degree of enforcement of fiduciary duty is the lowest level compatible with the investor's participation.

7.5   Concluding Remarks

The model studied in this chapter is of an incomplete contract between
an investor and an entrepreneur. The investor must expend costly effort in order to get something out of the firm in a strategic contest with
the entrepreneur. If the success or failure of the project is the entrepreneur's private information, a high degree of investor protection, in the
sense of the ease of successfully suing the entrepreneur-manager for
misconduct, may give the entrepreneur an ex ante incentive to select a
project with a low probability of success. From a political economy
perspective, there is the constitutional issue of efficient institutions
for investor protection. This raises the question of a trade-off between
measures designed to increase the transparency of the firm, such as
disclosure rules, and enforcement of fiduciary duty ex post.

Djankov, La Porta, and Shleifer (2005) develop measures of the
transparency of transactions engaged in by the firm, the extent of management's liability for self-dealing, and the ease with which shareholders can sue management for misconduct. Some countries, such as
Belarus, Bolivia, Ecuador, Greece, Honduras, Hungary, Sweden, and
Switzerland, combine fair scores on the management liability indexes
with a low score on transparency. (A standout is the Maldives, which
scores very high on the management liability indexes but zero on
transparency.) The theory developed in the present chapter suggests
that the incentives for management to look for high-quality projects in
these countries may be poor, which in turn might impact the growth
prospects of these nations. At the very least, an implication of the analysis here is that the interrelation and potential negative interaction of
the transparency and liability indexes must be taken into account
when applying the findings of Djankov, La Porta, and Shleifer, rather
than simply taking the average of the indices as an indication of the
overall quality of investment opportunities across nations.

As a theoretical contribution, the model of this chapter introduces
endogenous uncertainty into a model of investor–entrepreneur conflict. I have here assumed that the information partition of the investor
is of a particularly simple structure—the investor either knows nothing
or knows with certainty the realized value of the firm. A natural extension would be to consider a situation where the investor has some
more general signal about the realization, with a continuously varying
precision. This would allow a further investigation of the exact nature

of the tradeoff between transparency and manager liability. I suggest this as a potentially fruitful topic for further research.

Notes

I thank Helmut Bester, Kai Konrad, Stergios Skaperdas, and Gisela Waisman for helpful remarks.

1. This brief synopsis cannot do full justice to all the intricate complications of this instructive case, which includes sexual harrassment charges and the involvement of the Bank of New York, to mention just a few things.

2. Konrad (2002) studies the problem of foreign direct investment in countries where the legal system is sufficiently unreliable that there is a risk of expropriation of a project by a nondemocratic government. In this chapter I analyze what may be considered a microlevel version of this problem, in that the threat of expropriation comes from the management of the project itself.

3. The symmetric version of this *contest success function*, where $\theta = 0.5$, is the contest model most commonly encountered in the literature (e.g., see Tullock 1980; Nitzan 1994; Hirshleifer 1989; Rajan and Zingales 2000). It has been axiomatized by Skaperdas (1996).

4. For an argument to the effect that the probability of the court deciding in favor of the investor based on Bayesian updating might indeed take on a reduced form such a this, see Skaperdas and Vaidya (2005).

References

Burkart, M., D. Gromb, and F. Panunzi. 1997. Large shareholders, monitoring, and the value of the firm. *Quarterly Journal of Economics* 112: 693–728.

Castillo, R., and S. Skaperdas. 2005. All in the family or public? Law and appropriative costs as determinants of ownership structure. *Economics of Governance* 6: 93–104.

Djankov, S., R. La Porta, and A. Shleifer. 2005. The law and economics of self-dealing. Working Paper. Harvard University.

Hirshleifer, J. 1989. Conflict and rent-seeking success functions: Ratio vs difference models of relative success. *Public Choice* 63: 101–12.

Konrad, K. A. 2002. Investment in the absence of property rights: The role of incumbency advantages. *European Economic Review* 46: 1521–37.

La Porta, R., F. López-de-Silanes, and A. Shleifer. 1999. Corporate ownership around the world. *Journal of Finance* 54: 471–517.

La Porta, R., F. López-de-Silanes, A. Shleifer, and R. Vishny. 1998. Law and finance. *Journal of Political Economy* 106: 1113–55.

López-de-Silanes, F. 2002. The politics of legal reform. UNCTAD Discussion Paper G-24.

Müller, H. M., and K. Wärneryd. 2001. Inside vs outside ownership: A political theory of the firm. *RAND Journal of Economics* 32: 527–41.

Nitzan, S. 1994. Modelling rent-seeking contests. *European Journal of Political Economy* 10: 41–60.

Rajan, R. G., and L. Zingales. 2000. The tyranny of inequality. *Journal of Public Economics* 76: 521–58.

Shleifer, A., and R. W. Vishny. 1997. A survey of corporate governance. *Journal of Finance* 52: 737–83.

Shleifer, A., and D. Wolfenzon. 2002. Investor protection and equity markets. *Journal of Financial Economics* 66: 3–27.

Skaperdas, S. 1996. Contest success functions. *Economic Theory* 7: 283–90.

Skaperdas, S., and S. Vaidya. 2005. Persuasion as a contest. Working paper.

Tullock, G. 1967. The welfare costs of tariffs, monopolies, and theft. *Western Economic Journal* 5: 224–32.

Tullock, G. Efficient rent seeking. In J. M. Buchanan, R. D. Tollison, and G. Tullock, eds., *Toward a Theory of the Rent-Seeking Society*. College Station: Texas A&M University Press. 1980, pp. 269–82.

Wärneryd, K. 2003. Information in conflicts. *Journal of Economic Theory* 110: 121–36.

Williamson, O. E. 1985. *The Economic Institutions of Capitalism*. New York: Free Press.

IV

Norms and Culture

8 Islamic Resurgence and Social Violence during the Indonesian Financial Crisis

Daniel L. Chen

8.1 Introduction

One of the most influential views of our time attributes a large part of the failure of development in the postwar period to group conflicts. Recent research in development economics has identified a large collection of policy innovations that would help the poor. But these policies often do not get adopted because of conflicts between groups. Researchers have traditionally focused on the number of groups that are in conflict with each other (Easterly and Levine 1997; Alesina, Baqir, and Easterly 1999; Miguel and Gugerty 2005). This chapter focuses on the intensity with which people identify with their groups. Violence is a negative externality with enormous social costs (e.g., Alesina, Baqir, and Easterly 1999; Abadie and Gardeazabal 2003), so to the extent group identity and social violence (physical acts of destruction, killing, looting, attacks, burning, clashes, taking hostages, etc., by one group against another) are related, policies taking into account intensity of group identity need to be considered.

In this chapter I examine group identity and group conflict in the specific context of Islamic resurgence during the Indonesian financial crisis. Indonesia experienced a dramatic financial crisis between 1997 and 1998. The exchange rate fell dramatically from 2,400 Rupiah to the US dollar to 16,000 Rupiah to the US dollar, while the CPI index for food increased from 100 to 261. In one year, asset values dropped by 91 percent. In contrast, it took three years for asset values to drop 87 percent during the US Great Depression (Friend 2003). Millions of people lost jobs or shifted to the informal sector (Irawan, Iftikhar, and Iyanatul 2000). The crisis reached a peak in early 1998 and led to riots and lootings in every province but one. Between 1990 and 2001, social violence led to more than 6,208 deaths in Indonesia, increasing sharply after the financial crisis of 1997 (Tadjoeddin 2002).

The variety of evidence presented in this chapter indicates a strong relationship between religious intensity and social violence during the crisis. I use a unique dataset that tracks every incident of social violence in Indonesia reported by the national news agency and the national daily over a decade spanning the financial crisis. High religious intensity areas before the crisis have more social violence after the crisis. Stronger measures of religious intensity (potentially better at inculcating group identity) are more strongly associated with social violence. Social violence is negatively associated with other social activities. These results are unlikely to be driven by omitted environmental variables: social violence increases fastest where participation in Koran study also increases the fastest, and this is not true for state or industrial violence. Higher presence of faith-based groups is assocated with higher levels of conflict reported by village heads after the financial crisis (Barron, Kaiser and Pradhan 2004). As to why these relationships might be observed, see Chen (2005a, b) for theory and evidence of religious intensity as social insurance.

In the following sections, I present an analysis of data from the Database on Social Violence in Indonesia 1990–2001, collected by the UN Support Facility for Indonesian Recovery, and data from the Hundred Villages Survey, a panel of 8,140 households, conducted by the Indonesian census bureau. Section 8.2 describes the data.

Section 8.3 establishes that religious intensity and social violence are related during the financial crisis. OLS estimates indicate that in high religious intensity areas, violence is more likely to arise, where violence is measured by total number of incidents of social violence as well as number of incidents with minimum of one death. These results hold even after controlling for a large set of village and environmental characteristics. In addition stronger forms of religious intensity, such as religious schools and seminaries, are more strongly associated with violence than are weaker forms, such as Koran study and worship buildings. Multiplying the estimated coefficients by the mean of the religious intensity measures sums up to the mean of the violence incidents, suggesting religious intensity may explain practically all the violence that occurred if the vector of religious measures are taken as exogenous. The R^2 of the specifications suggest religious intensity may explain one-third of the variance of violence that occurred.

Section 8.4 discusses the possibility of reverse causality. Because most religious intensity measures are collected before the crisis and are relatively time-invariant and because villages are unlikely to build schools, seminaries, or religious buildings in anticipation of social violence that mostly occurred after the crisis, reverse causality is an unlikely confound. In fact the relationship between pre-crisis measures of religious intensity and social violence largely begins after the crisis. Section 8.5 finds that social violence is negative correlated with other social activities, suggesting that networks of engagement across groups may mitigate group conflict (Barron, Kaiser and Pradhan 2004). It also suggests that omitted variables associated with both Koran study groups and "placebo" social activities are not driving the relationship between religious intensity and social violence.

A fundamental issue in the interpretation of the OLS specification is the presence of fixed unobservable factors that are correlated with religious intensity and social violence across provinces. To address this potential source of bias, section 8.6 uses longitudinal data on Koran study that are tracked over time. Koran study remains associated with communal violence after controlling for province and time fixed effects but is unrelated to state or industrial violence. This last finding lessens the concern that omitted variables drive changes in both Koran study and violence, since there is something specific about communal violence rather than violence in general that is associated with Koran study during the financial crisis. Section 8.7 discusses some alternative explanations and section 8.8 concludes.

8.2   Data

The empirical analysis draws from the UNSFIR Database on Social Violence in Indonesia 1990–2001, which tracks violence before and during the financial crisis, and the Hundred Villages Survey, which tracks economic and religious aspects of over 8,000 households before and during the financial crisis. The analysis in subsequent sections examine the relationship between religious intensity recorded in the Hundred Villages Survey and violence recorded in the Database on Social Violence in Indonesia 1990–2001. (Chen 2005b examines how economic conditions recorded in the Hundred Villages Survey affects the relationship between religious intensity and social violence.)

8.2.1 Social Violence Data

The UNSFIR Database on Social Violence in Indonesia 1990–2001 (Tadjoeddin 2002) contains every incident of social violence reported by the national news agency, *Antara*, and the national daily, *Kompas*. The database tracks property damage as well as interpersonal violence. Social violence refers to of destruction, killing, looting, attacks, burning, clashes, taking of hostages, and other such physical acts by a group of people. Because press policies differ before and after the crisis, the analysis uses cross-sectional as well as longitudinal data to avoid relying solely on time series variation of media coverage.

A priori, there appears to be prima facie evidence of a rise in religion-based violence during and after the financial crisis. Even if violence began for nonreligious reasons, the lines of demarcation often became religious. Communal violence accounts for 77 percent of the total deaths due to social violence; the other categories are state-community and industrial violence. Communal violence is defined as violence between two groups of community, one group being attacked by the other. State-community violence is violence done by communities protesting against state institutions, such as the military, the administration, or security officials. Industrial violence is violence that arises from problems of industrial relations. Communal violence has the widest regional distribution. It is found in 116 of 295 district/cities and 22 of 26 provinces.

Ethnic, religious, and migration-related violence is the most severe type of communal violence, accounting for 68 percent of total deaths due to communal violence. While both ethnic and religious violence are coded together (ethnic groups are usually associated with a particular religion in Indonesia), at least some of these acts of communal violence are definitely religious in nature: descriptions in Tadjoeddin (2002) include killings by shamans invoking black magic (a form of voodoo), mass rage incited by someone who has recognized himself as God's messenger, churches and sacred locations desecrated, human hostage taking by so-called holy warriors of Islam, sacking of gambling and prostitution houses, and firebombing entertainment places. Violence as a result of differences in political views accounts for only 3.3 percent of deaths due to communal violence (table 8.2). This violence is so called because the conflicts arise between and within political parties and their supporters. Figure 8.1 shows the sharp increase of

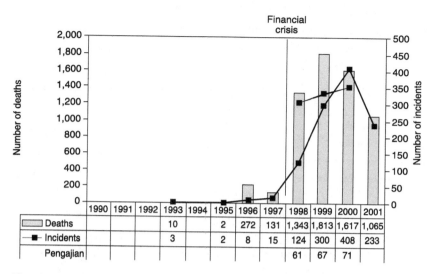

Figure 8.1
Social violence, 1990 to 2001

violence in 1998. Tables 8.1 and 8.2 and figure 8.1 are from Tadjoeddin (2002).

Because the national media often do not record localized conflicts, the data may underreport levels of conflict. UNSFIR captures 1,093 incidents of conflict and 6,208 deaths over 12 years. Under a broader definition of conflict, the PODES (Potensial Desa/Village Potential Statistics) data document nearly 5,000 villages as reporting conflicts in one year alone (Barron, Kaiser and Pradhan 2004).

8.2.2   Religion and Economic Data

Household religion and economic data come from the Hundred Villages Survey, collected by the Indonesian Central Statistics Office. The panel dataset follows 8,140 households from May 1997 to August 1999, beginning before the 1997 Indonesian financial crisis and continuing in four waves after the crisis (figure 8.2). Religious intensity at the household level was measured by the question "In the past 3 months, has your household increased, decreased, stayed the same, or not participated in the study of Koran (Pengajian)?" Responses to this question are coded as 1/0. In Chen (2005a) I verified the Pengajian participation

Table 8.1
Social violence by category, 1990 to 2001

Category	Number of incidents (1)	Number of incidents with min 1 death (2)	Number of deaths (minimum value) (3)	% Death to total death (4)
Communal violence[a]	465	262	4771	76.9
Separatist violence[b]	502	369	1370	22.1
State-community violence[c]	88	19	59	1.0
Industrial relations violence[d]	38	4	8	0.1
Total	1093	654	6208	100

Source: Social violence data from UN Support Facility for Indonesian Recovery, "Database on Social Violence in Indonesia 1990–2001."
Notes: An incident of social violence is recorded if the national news agency, *Antara*, or the national daily, *Kompas*, reported an incident with at least one victim, be it human (casualties or injuries) or material (e.g., houses, buildings, or vehicles damaged or burned). Ninety-six percent of the incidents occur between 1998 and 2001; most are communal violence, defined as social violence between two groups of community, one group being attacked by the other.
a. Communal violence: Social violence between two groups of community, one group being attacked by the other.
b. Separatist violence: Social violence between the state and the people of a certain area because of regional separatism.
c. State-community violence: Violence between the state and the community who are expressing protests against state institutions.
d. Industrial violence: Violence that arises from problems of industrial relations.

in activity of religious intensity by correlating the responses with other measures of religious intensity, such as Islamic school attendance, Koran ownership, and worshipping practices, and also with measures relating to belief such as choosing "It is up to God" in response to "What is your ideal number of sons?" and opposition to contraceptive use for religious reasons.

Village-level religiosity measures of per capita number of mosques, Islamic chapels, churches, Hindu temples, and Buddhist temples are taken from the 1997 PODES data (Potensial Desa/Village Potential Statistics). The religiosity measures of per capita number of Islamic boarding schools, religious schools, and seminaries are taken from 1998 PODES. Since it is unlikely that new religious institutions were built during the crisis, I interpret these as pre-crisis numbers and divide by the 1997 PODES population accordingly (1998 PODES population numbers would be affected by crisis-induced migration).

Table 8.2
Communal violence by subcategory, 1990 to 2001

Subcategory	Deaths		Incidents	
	Number (1)	% of total (2)	Number (3)	City/ district (4)
Ethnic, religion, and migration[a]	3230	67.7	233	39
The May 98 riots[b]	1202	25.2	6	10
Differences in political views[c]	156	3.3	79	54
Civil commotion (Tawuran)[d]	87	1.8	70	28
Issue of "Dukun Santet"[e]	65	1.4	28	17
Competing resources[f]	16	0.3	16	10
Food riots[g]	5	0.1	23	22
Other	10	0.2	10	9
Total	4771	100	465	116

Source: Social Violence data from UN Support Facility for Indonesian Recovery, "Database on Social Violence in Indonesia 1990–2001."
Notes: An incident of social violence is recorded if the national news agency, *Antara*, or the national daily, *Kompas*, reported an incident with at least one victim, be it human (casualties or injuries) or material (e.g., houses, buildings, or vehicles damaged or burned). Ninety-six percent of the incidents occur between 1998 and 2001; most are communal violence, defined as social violence between two groups of community, one group being attacked by the other.
a. Ethnic, religion, and migration: Religion propagation related to particular regions and ethnic groups.
b. The May 98 riots: Riots in big cities preceding fall of President Suharto in May 1998.
c. Differences in political views: Conflicts between and within political parties and their supporters.
d. Civil commotion (Tawuran): Clashes between villages, neighborhoods, or groups.
e. Issue of "Dukun Santet": Killings of people accused of evil magic and witchcraft.
f. Competing resources: Disputes between community groups competing for economic resources.
g. Food riots: Mass riots and lootings for staple foods between January to March 1998.

Since the Hundred Villages Survey does not cover separatist areas such as Aceh, no incident of separatist violence is included in the following analysis. The Hundred Villages Survey and the Database on Social Violence overlap for the following eight provinces: Bali, Jawa Barat, Jawa Timur, Kalimantan Timur, Lampung, Nusa Tenggara Timur, Riau, and Sulawesi Tenggara. Since violence data are recorded at the province level, province-level clusters are included in the specifications where religious intensity is measured at the village level.

Figure 8.2
Timing of 100 villages survey and the PODES related to the Rp/USD exchange rate

8.3 Cross-sectional Variation

Is violence more likely to arise in highly religious areas? Are stronger measures of religious intensity more strongly associated with social violence? Table 8.3 reports OLS estimates of an equation linking social violence and religious intensity:

$$V_{jp} = \beta' \mathbf{R}_{jp} + \alpha' \mathbf{X}_{jp} + \varepsilon_{jp},$$

where V_{jp} represents in columns 1 and 2 all social violence incidents from 1990 to 2001 and in columns 3 and 4 all social violence incidents with a minimum one death in any village j in province p; $\mathbf{R}_{jp}$ is a vector for village j in province p representing the percentage of Pengajian participation in a village, religious worship buildings per 1,000 population, religious schools per 1,000 population, and seminaries per 1,000 population; and $\mathbf{X}_{jp}$ represents village, geographic, and fiscal control variables (urban dummy, population, area, number of shops per 1,000 population, mean pre-crisis monthly per capita nonfood expenditures, dummies for geographic characteristics such as flat, steep, beach, forest, valley, and river, 1996–1997 INPRES funds per 1,000 population

Table 8.3
Relationship between religious intensity and social violence

	Incidents of social violence		Incidents with minimum 1 death	
	(1)	(2)	(3)	(4)
All violence (OLS)				
Pengajian participation in village, August 1998 (%)	35*	36*	11*	11*
	(17)	(17)	(5)	(6)
Religious worship buildings per 1,000 population	4**	3*	1**	1*
	(2)	(2)	(0)	(0)
Religious schools per 1,000 population	16**	14***	5*	5***
	(7)	(4)	(2)	(1)
Seminaries per 1,000 population	115***	101***	36***	32***
	(18)	(25)	(6)	(8)
R^2	0.34	0.49	0.32	0.48
N	93	93	93	93
Controls	N	Y	N	Y

Source: Social Violence data from UN Support Facility for Indonesian Recovery, "Database on Social Violence in Indonesia, 1990–2001."

Notes: Regressions are OLS regressions of 93 villages and include province-level clusters. An incident of social violence is recorded if the national news agency, *Antara*, or the national daily, *Kompas*, reported an incident with at least one victim, be it human (casualties or injuries) or material (e.g., houses, buildings, or vehicles damaged or burned). Ninety-six percent of the incidents occur between 1998 and 2001; most are communal violence, defined as social violence between two groups of community, one group being attacked by the other. Control variables are village, geography, and fiscal characteristics as listed below.

Village characteristics: Urban, population, size, number of shops per 1,000 population, mean pre-crisis per capita nonfood expenditures.
Geography characteristics: Flat, steep, beach, forest, valley, river.
Fiscal characteristics: 1996–1997 INPRES funds per 1,000 population for economic activity, building and facilities, offices and institutions, human resources, and IDT funds.

for economic activity, building and facilities, offices and institutions, human resources, and IDT, another village assistance program).

The estimates show a strong association between each measure of religious intensity and violence. The strong association remains after controlling for village, geographic, and fiscal characteristics (columns 2 and 4). Even stronger measures of religious intensity—religious schools and seminaries, and other institutions good at inculcating group identity—provide much stronger predictors of violence. Religious schools per 1,000 population and seminaries per 1,000 population are associated with violence at 1 percent statistical significance in most specifications (table 8.3, columns 1–4). The percentages of Pengajian participation and worship buildings per 1,000 population are associated with violence at 5 to 10 percent statistical significance in these specifications. These results corroborate Barron, Kaiser, and Pradhan (2004) who also find in their cross-sectional analysis of 2003 PODES data that a higher presence of faith groups is associated with higher levels of conflict.

In magnitudes, multiplying the coefficient β by the mean of the religious intensity measures sums up to the mean of the violence incidents. Thus, if one takes $\mathbf{R}_{jp}$ as exogenous, religious intensity can explain practically all the violence that occurred on average. The R^2 of the regression displayed in column 1 is 0.34, suggesting religious intensity is behind one-third of the variance of violence that occurred. The R^2 of the regression displayed in column 3 is 0.32. Columns 2 and 4 have R^2 of 0.49 and 0.48 respectively.

8.4   Reverse Causality

A possible explanation for the link between religious intensity and violence is the intensity of the religious response to social violence and not vice versa. In any empirical setup this possibility is precluded because most measures of religious intensity are relatively time-invariant and are pre-crisis measures. It is unlikely that new religious institutions were built during this crisis, so these measures can be interpreted as pre-crisis numbers. Most violence (96 percent) occurs after a crisis (figure 8.1). It is unlikely that villages build schools, seminaries, or religious buildings in anticipation of social violence.

Separately regressing violence year by year on pre-crisis religious intensity obtains the following regression:

$$V_{jpt} = \beta_t' \mathbf{R}_{jp} + \alpha_t' \mathbf{X}_{jp} + \varepsilon_{jpt}.$$

As this regression suggests, the strong relationship between pre-crisis religious intensity and social violence begins right after the crisis. Estimates are reported in table 8.4. For example, the estimates of β_t in 1993 are compared with the 1998 rise from 0.252 to 12.107 for the Pengajian participation and the rise from 1.449 to 23.659 for the seminaries (columns 1 and 3). Figure 8.3, panel a, displays the relationship between the August 1998 Pengajian insurrection and yearly social violence. Figure 8.3, panels b through d, gives the relationship between the pre-

Table 8.4
Relationship between religious intensity and year-by-year social violence

Dependent variable: Incidents of social violence	Pengajian participation (1)	Worship buildings (2)	Religious schools (3)	Seminaries (4)
1993	0.252 (0.211)	0.004 (0.027)	0.339*** (0.085)	1.449*** (0.304)
1995	−0.251 (0.244)	−0.014 (0.016)	0.032 (0.058)	−0.668 (0.748)
1996	0.252 (0.211)	0.004 (0.027)	0.339*** (0.085)	1.449*** (0.304)
1997	1.509 (1.264)	0.027 (0.160)	2.033*** (0.509)	8.695*** (1.824)
1998	12.107* (5.352)	1.504*** (0.275)	1.388 (1.447)	23.659** (6.880)
1999	7.605* (3.704)	0.682** (0.254)	2.050** (0.706)	18.988** (5.761)
2000	10.521 (5.622)	0.983 (0.613)	5.598*** (1.508)	34.414*** (8.141)
2001	4.456* (1.935)	0.220 (0.249)	2.214** (0.722)	12.534*** (3.243)
Controls	Y	Y	Y	Y

Source: Social Violence data from UN Support Facility for Indonesian Recovery, "Database on Social Violence in Indonesia 1990–2001."

Notes: Regressions are OLS regressions of 93 villages and include province-level clusters. An incident of social violence is recorded if the national news agency, *Antara*, or the national daily, *Kompas*, reported an incident with at least one victim, be it human (casualties or injuries) or material (such as houses, buildings, or vehicles damaged or burned). Ninety-six percent of the incidents occur between 1998 and 2001; most are communal violence, defined as social violence between two groups of community, one group being attacked by the other. Control variables are village, geography, and fiscal characteristics are listed below.

Village characteristics: Urban, population, size, number of shops per 1,000 population, mean pre-crisis per capita nonfood expenditures.
Geography characteristics: Flat, steep, beach, forest, valley, river.
Fiscal characteristics: 1996–1997 INPRES funds per 1,000 population for economic activity, building and facilities, offices and institutions, human resources, and IDT funds.

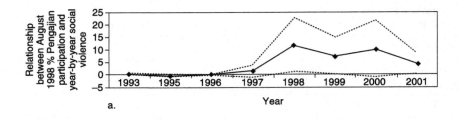

a.

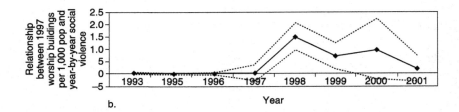

b.

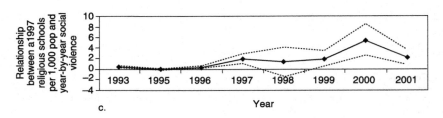

c.

Figure 8.3
(a) August 1998 Pengajian participation and social violence. (b) Pre-crisis worship buildings per 1,000 population and social violence, 1990 to 2001. (c) Pre-crisis religious schools
per 1,000 population and social violence, 1990 to 2001.

crisis per capita buildings of worship religious schools, and seminaries
respectively and the year-by-year incidents of social violence. Table 8.4
and figure 8.3 give no information for 1990 to 1992 and 1994 because
there were no reports of social violence that overlap with the Hundred
Villages Survey in those years.

8.5   Other Social Activities

Social violence is negatively associated with other social activities.
Table 8.5 gives partial correlations between social violence and each
recorded social activity. While the Pengajian is positively correlated
with social violence and statistically significant at the 5 percent level,

Table 8.5
Relationship between social activities and social violence

	Incidents of social violence (1)	Incidents with minimum 1 death (2)
All violence (OLS)		
Pengajian participation in village, August 1998 (%)	39**	12**
	(12)	(4)
Training for women participation, August 1998 (%)	−33	−9
	(30)	(10)
10 Helps for housing participation, August 1998 (%)	−50	−15
	(30)	(10)
Club for skill learning participation, August 1998 (%)	−32	−10
	(25)	(8)
Burial society participation, August 1998 (%)	−30	−9
	(18)	(6)
Sports club participation, August 1998 (%)	3	−0
	(10)	(4)
Savings club participation, August 1998 (%)	−1	−1
	(22)	(8)
Controls	Y	Y

Source: Social Violence data from UN Support Facility for Indonesian Recovery, "Database on Social Violence in Indonesia 1990–2001."

Notes: Each coefficient represents a separate OLS regression of 93 villages, conditional on controls, and include province-level clusters. An incident of social violence is recorded if the national news agency, *Antara*, or the national daily, *Kompas*, reported an incident with at least one victim, be it human (casualties or injuries) or material (such as houses, buildings, or vehicles damaged or burned). Ninety-six percent of the incidents occur between 1998 and 2001; most are communal violence, defined as social violence between two groups of community, one group being attacked by the other. Control variables are village, geography, and fiscal characteristics are listed below.

Village characteristics: Urban, population, size, number of shops per 1,000 population, mean pre-crisis per capita nonfood expenditures.

Geography characteristics: Flat, steep, beach, forest, valley, river.

Fiscal characteristics: 1996–1997 INPRES funds per 1,000 population for economic activity, building and facilities, offices and institutions, human resources, and IDT funds.

social violence is not significantly associated with any other surveyed social activity: sports groups (Olahraga), burial societies (Kematian), workshops for obtaining skills (Karang Taruna), family welfare practices (PKK and "occasional family-planning training for women"), and housing assistance (Dasawisma). These results suggest that the omitted variables associated with both religious and nonreligious social activities are not driving the relationship between religious intensity and social violence.

In sum, the estimates suggest that participation in nonreligious social activities is negatively associated with social violence. Each percentage point of Pengajian participation is associated with 0.39 more incidents of social violence, whereas each percentage point in participation in women's training, housing help, skill learning, or burial societies is associated with 0.30 to 0.50 fewer incidents of social violence.

8.6   Panel Data

The significant relationship between some measures of religious intensity and social violence before the crisis (table 8.4) suggests some unobserved environmental variables may be correlated with religious intensity (e.g., if ethnic-religious diversity is greater where there are more religious institutions, and diversity is correlated with violence, this can bias the relationship between religious intensity and social violence upward). To address this possibility, I controlled for province and time fixed effects in my examination of the relationship between Pengajian participation and social violence. Pengajian participation is the only measure of religious intensity that is time-varying. Fixed effects controls were for environmental characteristics such as religious or ethnic diversity across regions.

To construct the panel of religious intensity and social violence, I used information on Pengajian participation that is collected for three-month periods. I matched the average Pengajian participation rate of each province over a three-month period to the number of incidents of social violence for the same three-month period. Since the Hundred Villages Survey collected Pengajian participation at three different times, this gave me 8 provinces and 3 time periods for a total of 24 observations to estimate:

$$V_{pt} = \beta R_{pt} + \kappa_p + \tau_t + \varepsilon_{pt},$$

where V_{pt} represents the incidents of social violence, R_{pt} represents the percentage of Pengajian participation in province p at time t, κ_p are the province's fixed effects, and τ_t are the time-fixed effects. I show specifications with and without weighting by the number of households in the Hundred Villages Survey per province.

The estimate of about 4.4 in column 4 of panel A in table 8.6 indicates that Koran study is correlated to communal violence incidents with a minimum of one death at 10 percent statistical significance. The estimate of 5.1 in column 2 indicates Koran study is positively correlated to incidents of communal violence. The coefficient 4.3 in column 4 is smaller than the coefficient 11 in column 3 of table 8.3, one reason for which is that violence is restricted to a three-month period here whereas in table 8.3 violence was aggregated for 1990 to 2001. The estimates are roughly the same with and without population weights (columns 1 and 3).

Even with controls for fixed effects, omitted variables may be driving changes in both Koran study and violence. To the extent the economic distress that stimulates Koran study can stimulate any kind of social violence, observing the relationship between changes in Koran study and changes in other types of social violence provides a test of this possibility. When different types of violence are considered in panels B and C, the association of Koran study with other types of violence, state-community and industrial, is weaker, with coefficients of -0.11 and 0.91 respectively. The sum of state-community and industrial violence also is weakly associated with Koran study. There is not enough variation in state-community and industrial violence incidents with a minimum of one death to run fixed effects regressions. These findings lessen the concern that omitted variables drive changes in both Koran study and violence, since there is something specific about communal violence rather than violence in general that is associated with Koran study.

8.7   Alternative Explanations

One alternative explanation for the rise in social violence is that instead of economic distress, it is the political vacuum created during the crisis that allowed social violence to arise. However, between 1990 and 2001 violence as a result of difference in political views accounted for only 3.3 percent of deaths due to communal violence (table 8.2). A related

Table 8.6
Relationship between religious intensity and social violence (panel)

	Incidents of social violence		Incidents with minimum 1 death	
	(1)	(2)	(3)	(4)
Panel A: Communal violence (fixed effects)[a]				
Pengajian participation in province (%)	4.340	5.107	3.989*	4.348*
	(4.598)	(5.850)	(2.209)	(2.335)
Panel B: State-community violence[b]				
Pengajian participation in province (%)	−0.034	−0.108	n/a	n/a
	(1.090)	(1.469)		
Panel C: Industrial violence[c]				
Pengajian participation in province (%)	1.190	0.909	n/a	n/a
	(1.215)	(1.311)		
Population weighted	N	Y	N	Y
Fixed effects	Province, time	Province, time	Province, time	Province, time

Source: Social Violence data from UN Support Facility for Indonesian Recovery, "Database on Social Violence in Indonesia 1990–2001."
Notes: Regressions are fixed effects regressions of 8 provinces in each of 3 time periods, a total of 24 observations, with province and time fixed effects. Population weights are the number of households per province in the sample. Each coefficient represents a separate OLS regression of Pengajian participation rates for 3-month period on violence. An incident of social violence is recorded if the national news agency, *Antara*, or the national daily, *Kompas*, reported an incident with at least one victim, be it human (casualties or injuries) or material (such as houses, buildings, or vehicles damaged or burned). Ninety-six percent of the incidents occur between 1998 and 2001; most are communal violence, defined as social violence between two groups of community, one group being attacked by the other. n/a: Too few state-community and industrial violence incidents with minimum 1 death to run fixed effects regressions.
a. Communal violence: Social violence between two groups of community, one group being attacked by the other.
b. State-community violence: Violence between the state and the community who are expressing protests against state institutions.
c. Industrial violence: Violence that arises from problems of industrial relations.

hypothesis is that violence arises when civic or police institutions weaken and that religious institutions are correlated with the presence of civic/police institutions. This also does not appear to be the case.

Another possibility is that religious fragmentation is necessary for social violence. However, greater religious fragmentation of an area, as computed by the Herfindahl index of religious worship buildings, is not strongly associated with pre-crisis religious intensity. Nor is it the case that less violence occurs under a single religious regime when there is exactly one mosque in the village.

Since most measures of religious intensity like worship buildings, schools, and seminaries were collected before the financial crisis, the association between religious intensity and social violence appears not to be due to economic distress causing both religious intensity and social violence. If economic distress could explain the relationship between changes in religious intensity and changes in social violence, there would have been evidence of increase in state and industrial violence along with Koran study. This was clearly not the case.

8.8   Conclusion

In this chapter, I presented an analysis of data from the Hundred Villages Survey and data from the Database on Social Violence in Indonesia 1990–2001. OLS estimates show a large positive relationship between religious intensity and social violence. Because most religious intensity measures are relatively time-invariant and are pre-crisis measures and because villages are unlikely to build schools, seminaries, or religious buildings in anticipation of social violence, reverse causality does not explain this association. On the contrary, a strong relationship between pre-crisis measures of religious intensity and social violence began after the crisis. In addition stronger forms of religious intensity are more associated with the violence. To control for any omitted variables bias, I used longitudinal data on Koran study, which I tracked over time. Koran study remains associated with communal violence even after province and time-fixed effects are included, but it is unrelated to state or industrial violence.

In Chen (2005b) I show that religious intensity is linked to more social violence in regions that are more economically distressed, and this may shed light on why religious intensity and social violence are so linked. Alternative social insurance mitigates this link. To the extent that governments, international organizations, and NGOs are concerned about ideological extremism, in particular, because it can lead to religious conflict and violence, the results here and in Chen (2005a) suggest that increasing intervention in social insurance is a way to mitigate fundamentalist tendencies.

Data Appendix

The empirical analysis draws on the Hundred Villages Survey collected by the Indonesian Central Statistics Office. The panel dataset follows 8,140 households from May 1997 to August 1999, beginning before the crisis and continuing in four waves after the 1997 Indonesian financial crisis (figure 8.1). In the pre-crisis period, the survey randomly selected 120 households in each of 100 communities. However, between 1997 and 1998, the number of village enumeration areas increased from 2 to 3, necessitating a replacement of about 40 randomly selected households per village. The partial replacement of pre-crisis households is why the panel data contained 8,140 instead of 12,000 households. The survey also collected village-level information in the first wave of 1997 and 1998.

One measure of religious intensity is the response to "In the past 3 months, has your household increased, decreased, stayed the same, or not participated in the study the Koran (Pengajian)?" More precisely, the phrase is *Pengajian/kegiatan agarma lainnya*, which translates to religious activity. However, translators say the question is interpreted by native Indonesians as specifically referring to Koran study; non-Muslims may interpret the question as referring to the equivalent in their respective religion. This question was asked after the crisis, and the responses are coded as $-1/0/+1$.

The controls, X_{ij}, include pre-crisis May 1997 values of:

village characteristics—urban dummy, population, area, number of shops per 1,000 population;

geographic characteristics—dummies for flat, steep (the excluded topography dummy is slight angle), beach, forest, valley, river terrain (the excluded geography dummy is other);

fiscal characteristics—INPRES (Presidentially Instructed Program for Village Assistance, implemented during 1996–1997) funding received normalized to US$ per 1,000 population, which divides into funds used for productive economic effort, for buildings and facilities, for

Table A8.1
Descriptive statistics

Household summary statistics		Village summary statistics	
Percentage own wetland	31%	Standard deviation of village consumption shock	11.42
Percentage own dryland	66%		(1.56)
Percentage in farming	66%	During crisis (Aug 1998–May 1997) standard deviation of village consumption shock	9.22
Wetland ownership (hectares)	0.17		(2.16)
	(0.01)		
Dryland ownership (hectares)	0.72	Non-crisis (May 1999–Dec 1998) total worship buildings per 1,000 population	3.83
	(0.01)		(0.28)
Surname indicates Haj pilgrimage	1.0%	Religious schools per 1,000 population	0.12
			(0.04)
Number of children attending Islamic school	0.15	Seminaries per 1,000 population	0.01
	(0.01)		(0.01)
Monthly per capita food expenditure, May 1997	14.6	% Pengajian participation in village, August 1998	0.61
	(0.1)		(0.03)
Monthly per capita nonfood expenditure, May 1997	7.3	Credit available	0.34
	(0.2)		(0.05)
Household size	4.16	Number shops per 1,000 population	0.07
	(0.02)		(0.03)
Government worker	6%	Urban	0.20
Service worker	10%		(0.04)
Number of households (N)	8,140	1996–1997 INPRES funds in $/1,000 population	0.91
			(0.09)
		Number of villages (N)	99

Crisis summary statistics

	1998 Aug	1998 Dec	1999 May	1999 Aug
Monthly per capita nonfood expenditure, change	−4.7	1.1	−0.1	0.2
	(0.2)	(0.2)	(0.2)	(0.2)
Pengajian participation rate	61%	unavail.	67%	71%
Pengajian increase in last 3 months	9%	unavail.	7%	7%
Pengajian decrease in last 3 months	9%	unavail.	10%	11%

Table A8.1
(continued)

Violence summary statistics	
Incidents of social violence	34.65
	(3.20)
Incidents of social violence with minimum 1 death	11.26
	(1.02)
Incidents of communal violence (3-month period)	0.83
	(0.29)
Incidents of communal violence with minimum 1 death (3-month period)	0.33
	(0.16)
Incidents of state-community violence (3-month period)	0.08
	(0.06)
Incidents of industrial violence (3-month period)	0.17
	(0.08)
% Pengajian participation in village, August 1998 (3-month period)	0.66
	(0.03)
Number of provinces	8

offices and institutions, and for human resources, and total IDT (another village assistance program) funds received by the household between 1994 and 1996.

I use the entire sample of 8,140 households. Appendix table A8.1 presents some descriptive statistics.

Note

I thank Maulina Cahyaningrum, Prima Fortunadewi, and Julius Kusuma for translation assistance, and the National Science Foundation, Social Science Research Council, MacArthur Foundation, Russell Sage Foundation, and MIT Schultz Fund for financial support.

References

Abadie, A., and J. Gardeazabal. 2003. The economic costs of conflict: A case study of the Basque country. *American Economic Review* 93(1): 113–32.

Alesina, A., R. Baqir, and W. Easterly. 1999. Public goods and ethnic divisions. *Quarterly Journal of Economics* 114(4): 1243–84.

Barron, P., K. Kaiser, and M. Pradhan. 2004. Local conflict in Indonesia: Measuring incidence and identifying patterns. Mimeo. World Bank.

Chen, D. L. 2005a. Club goods and group identity: Evidence from Islamic resurgence during the Indonesian financial crisis. Mimeo. University of Chicago.

Chen, D. L. 2005b. Does economic distress stimulate religious fundamentalism? Mimeo. University of Chicago.

Easterly, W., and R. Levine. 1997. Africa's growth tragedy: Policies and ethnic divisions. *Quarterly Journal of Economics* 112(4): 1203–50.

Friend, T. 2003. *Indonesian Destinies*. Cambridge: Harvard University Press.

Irawan, P. B., I. Ahmed, and I. Islam. 2000. *Labour Market Dynamics in Indonesia: Analysis of 18 Key Indicators of the Labour Market (KILM) 1986–1999*. Jakarta: International Labour Office.

Miguel, E., and M. K. Gugery. 2005. Ethnic divisions, social sanctions, and public goods in kenya. *Journal of Public Economics* 89(11–12): 2325–68.

Tadjoeddin, M. Z. 2002. Anatomy of social violence in the context of transition: The case of Indonesia 1990–2001. UNSFIR Working Paper 02/01-E.

9 Social Identity and Redistributive Politics

Moses Shayo

9.1 Introduction

How is national pride related to redistributive politics? Why do poor Americans support less redistribution than their German counterparts? Why are they so proud to be Americans? Drawing on the results in Shayo (2005), in this chapter I suggest that well-documented processes of social identification can help clarify these and related questions. I also discuss why these relationships can differ in developing countries.

For the past three decades social identity has been the focus of intense research throughout the social sciences.[1] This chapter outlines in a nontechnical way a general framework that seeks to distill into a concise statement the more robust empirical results obtained primarily by social psychologists on what it means to identify with a group, and what factors are important for determining which groups people are likely to identify with. The framework then offers a concept of equilibrium where the profiles of actions and social identities are jointly determined.

The basic theoretical framework we propose is straightforward. A society may have many social groups—American, black, academic, middle class, and so on—but in any given situation individuals identify with only one (in a sense to be made more precise below). Given their social identities, they choose courses of action that determine the aggregate outcome. That outcome forms the social environment that in turn affects the pattern of social identities. A social identity equilibrium (SIE) is then a steady state where (1) each individual's behavior is consistent with his social identity, (2) social identities are consistent with the social environment, and (3) the social environment is determined by the behavior of all individuals.

I briefly outline an application of this general framework to a standard model of income redistribution. The application yields several new insights. It can help explain why lower income individuals tend to identify more strongly with their nation, why they may or may not vote for high redistribution, why national threats, immigration and ethnic diversity may be relevant to this outcome, and why rising inequality does not in general lead to more demand for redistribution.

Finally, the chapter points to strong but previously unexplored empirical relationships between national identification and redistributive politics: that in most advanced democracies, national identification tends to reduce support for redistribution, that the poor are more likely to identify with their nation, and that across countries there is a strong negative relationship between the level of actual redistribution and the extent of national identification.

The model relates to papers that study the possibility of multiple redistributive equilibria (e.g., Piketty 1995; Benabou 2000; Benabou and Tirole 2005) and more generally to the literature on the different welfare systems in the United States and Western Europe (see Alesina and Glaeser 2004 for a comprehensive discussion). The contribution of this model is that instead of relying on multiple beliefs or market imperfections, it highlights the effects of redistribution on the likelihood that members of that class will identify with it and behave (vote) in terms of their class membership. The model also relates to models in which voters care about issues other than their economic payoffs (Roemer 1998; Lee and Roemer 2004), but it offers an explanation of the origin of these other concerns and of how their prevalence may interact with the political outcome.

The chapter proceeds as follows: Section 9.2 presents my definition of social identity and a general model. I review some of the evidence from social psychology and experimental economics underlying this framework. Section 9.3 provides an application of this framework to the issue of redistribution and a summary of related empirical findings. Section 9.4 concludes with a discussion of how the predictions of the model can vary in a developing country setting.

9.2 Social Identity Equilibrium: A General Model and Evidence from Psychology

This section outlines the general framework proposed for analyzing social identity, and includes a brief empirical justification for its use. In

Shayo (2005) I provide a more detailed account and show how this model accounts for several behavioral regularities that are not explained by standard economic models.

9.2.1 The General Framework

The primitives of the model are as follows:

• A set of *agents*.

• A set of *social groups* or categories. These are categories that individuals learn to recognize when growing up and living in a society, much as they learn other categories such as vegetable or chair. I do not examine here the cultural or sociological process by which these social categories evolved.

• A set of available *actions* for each agent.

• A consequence or *aggregation function* that maps the individual actions into consequences (e.g., a policy outcome).

• A *material payoff* function for each agent that captures the utility familiar from standard models.

• A perceived *distance* between each agent and each social group.[2]

• A *relative status* function for every social group. Group status is the relative position of a group on valued dimensions of comparisons such as wealth, occupational status, and educational achievement (Tajfel and Turner 1986). I will generally take the relative status of a group to be the difference in mean material payoff between that group and the other groups.

From these building blocks we can formulate a definition of social identity and a solution concept for the model. However, in our case we will limit the discussion to individuals who identify with a single group, although the definition can be extended to allow for identification with several groups.

DEFINITION 1   An agent i is said to identify with social group j if his preferences over consequences are such that he prefers consequences where group j's status is higher to ones where it is lower, and he prefers outcomes where his perceived distance from group j is lower to ones where it is higher, other things equal.

In other words, identification with a group is taken to mean caring about the relative status of that group while paying a cognitive cost that increases with the perceived distance between the individual and the group. Loosely speaking identification thus implies making the group's interest part of one's own interest. Further the cognitive cost of identification implies that as long as agents identify with a given group, they will want to resemble that group: from wearing its typical clothes and symbols to imitating typical group behavior. Using revealed preference we can then infer social identities from observed choices made by individuals.

With social identification defined in terms of preferences, I now propose a solution concept that captures the endogenous determination of these preferences.

DEFINITION 2   A social identity equilibrium (SIE) is a profile of actions, one for each agent, and a profile of social identities, one for each agent, such that:

i. Each agent chooses his most preferred action (given his social identity) from the set of actions available to him.

ii. Each agent is more likely to identify with a group the higher is its social status and the smaller is the perceived distance between himself and that group.

iii. The consequence is determined by the actions of the agents, according to the aggregation function.

The first condition has to do with choice of actions under a given pattern of social identities. It is the standard Nash condition. The second condition describes the process determining the pattern of social identities and hence of preferences. The third condition requires that the social environment be determined by the actions of the agents in the economy.

Note that the SIE framework is a generalization of several existing models. First, in situations where one's actions cannot affect one's group's relative status nor one's distance from that group, an agent behaves like a standard material payoff maximizer. Second, the SIE generalizes the model proposed by Akerlof and Kranton (2000). Akerlof and Kranton focus primarily on the effects of social *prescriptions* that indicate the appropriate behavior for people in given social categories. Identification in their terminology means the adoption of such rules of behavior. Insofar as prototypical modes of behavior affect perceived distances between self and group, the SIE framework may also result in people behaving in accordance with their group's prototypical behavior. Similarly the framework can generate utility losses from nonprototypical behavior by other members of the group. However, social identity produces conformist behavior only under conditions that make identification with the group hold in equilibrium. Third, the SIE approach generalizes models that assume altruistic preferences. If the payoffs of ingroup members are positively related to ingroup status and if actions only affect the ingroup members, then we may observe altruistic behavior. However, such universal altruism disappears once actions affect members of an outgroup that competes with the ingroup for status. In that case we may observe particular altruism, benefiting ingroup members and possibly hurting outgroup members. Finally, we may even observe costly actions that decrease the welfare of ingroup members if such actions promote the ingroup's relative status (Congleton and Fudulu 1996).

9.2.2   Evidence

Consider first the following experiment. A set of agents is partitioned into two groups. Each agent knows to which group he belongs. Each agent then chooses an allocation of profits (e.g., money) between two other randomly chosen agents, one from each group. The choices are made privately and simultaneously. There is no interaction between agents, and they never know the decisions made by other agents nor who is in their group or in the other group. After all agents make their choices, payments are made in private and the experiment is over. Allocations are chosen from linear choice sets. The allocations may involve a trade-off between the ingroup member's profit and that of the outgroup member. The allocations may also be such that while both ingroup and outgroup are positively related, increasing the ingroup (and outgroup) profits diminishes the *relative* profit of the ingroup member. In any case the allocator's material payoff—the total amount allocated to him by other agents—is independent of his decision. That is to say, by standard economic models, any outcome is a Nash equilibrium.

Environments like the one just described have been studied extensively in experiments known as the minimal group paradigm (MGP) initiated in the late 1960s (see especially Tajfel 1970; Tajfel et al. 1971) and replicated hundreds of times (for reviews, see Brewer 1979; Bourhis and Gagnon 2001). The robust result is that agents that were categorized to groups based on some questionnaire or task systematically favor their ingroup member. Further a majority of subjects choose distributions that maximize the *relative* profit in favor of the ingroup member over distributions that maximize the absolute profit of both the ingroup member, and outgroup members (Brewer 1979; Tajfel and Turner 1979). I will take such categorizations into groups to be a form of exogenously affecting perceived distance from group. Most commonly, the categorizations consist of highlighting a common trait of the ingroup while contrasting it with the corresponding trait of an outgroup.

Consider now adding a second valued dimension along which groups are compared, such that the two groups are not initially equal in status. A substantial body of research, both experimental and correlational, exists on the implications. The studies consistently show that people tend to identify more with high status groups than with low status groups.[3]

By definition 1, an agent that identifies with a group prefers an outcome where his distance from that group is low over one where it is high, other things equal. In other words, the agent seeks to be similar to other members of the group. We would thus conclude from SIE condition ii that categorizing people to a group and highlighting their similarity to it would increase conformity with other members of that group. Results from the literature on social influence confirm this expectation. People are more likely to conform to views and behaviors of members of their group than to those of outgroup members. Further people conform more to ingroup norms of behavior when group concerns are highlighted, when comparisons between ingroup and outgroup are made possible and when group identity is made more salient than individual identity.[4]

Finally, we note that the SIE framework can help explain contributions to public goods. In particular, in situations where material payoff maximizers have a dominant strategy to contribute nothing to the public good, agents identifying with their group will contribute positive amounts, and contributions would increase with the contributions of other ingroup members—even in a one shot game.[5] We would thus expect contributions to increase with the factors that affect identification. Consistent with our framework, a large number of experimental results show that in keeping material payoffs fixed, we find that people tend to cooperate more with members of their group when their similarity to the group is made more salient, and when their group's performance is contrasted with the performance of an outgroup.[6] Cooperation has also been found to decrease with ingroup heterogeneity, which can be seen as tending to increase perceived distance from the group.[7]

Overall, results from social psychology and experimental economics lend strong support to the notion of social identity set forth in definitions 1 and 2. When led to perceive themselves as closer to their group, or when their group is endowed with high status, agents reveal themselves as caring about how well their group is doing in comparison to other groups, and appear to be willing to sacrifice personal material gain to promote that goal.

9.3 Nation, Class, and Redistribution

9.3.1 Applying the SIE Framework

The preceding framework is very general. I now sketch an application of that framework to a standard model of income redistribution (see Shayo 2005 for a formal treatment). My application focuses on modern industrialized democracies.

Consider then a simple general-interest redistribution setting (Meltzer and Richard 1981). The government collects an income tax at a fixed rate t and distributes back the tax revenues, minus deadweight losses caused by the distortionary tax. Thus the higher the tax rate, the more redistribution occurs and when $t = 1$, everyone has the same after-tax income. I will keep the political process as simple as possible so that the equilibrium policy directly reflects the policy preferences of the voters. This is a reasonable approach to the long-run, general-interest redistributive regimes we are interested in here. Thus agents vote directly over the tax rate and the actual tax rate t^* is determined by a pure majority rule.[8] Absent social identity considerations, the chosen tax rate is the tax rate chosen by the median income agent. The tax rate is then a function of the median to mean income: the smaller is the median income relative to the mean, the higher the chosen tax rate. This is the standard median voter result.

Consider now what happens when agents can identify with two types of social groups: their social class or their nation as a whole. Of course, these were not always prominent social categories. Indeed they are not prominent in developing countries today where local and ethnic identities are much more important and the nation is a rather vague and artificial category. However, there is little doubt that in modern industrialized countries social class is a significant source of identity that influences voting behavior. Similarly the nation has undoubtedly been an important social category in Western democracies at least since the early twentieth.[9] Let us now analyze the conditions under which voters are likely to identify with their class or with their nation, and the implications for redistributive policy.

We focus here on a simple one-nation two-class model that conveys the basic intuition. The two classes—the poor and the wealthy—are characterized by the income levels of their members. The nation is the superordinate social category that includes all the agents in the economy. We assume that the agent with median income is not in the wealthy class. To focus on the status implications of redistribution, we assume fixed cognitive distances for all individuals in a given group, and that it is cognitively very costly to identify with a group that one does not belong to (thus in equilibrium, agents will only identify with groups they belong to).

Recall that the status of a group is its relative position along valued dimensions of comparisons. The relative status of the nation can be thought of as exogenously given here, since this is a one-nation model. The qualitative results of the model are unchanged when national status depends positively on the wealth of the nation as captured by its per capita after tax income.[10] The relative status of the two classes, however, depends on their typical or mean after-tax income (and possibly also on their before-tax income). This means that the relative status of the poor class depends negatively on the before-tax income inequality as measured by the difference in mean group income, and positively on the level of redistribution as measured by the tax rate.

Let us now look for social identity equilibria. The SIE condition ii implies that in equilibrium, an agent is more likely to identify with the nation (and less likely to identify with his class) the higher the status of the nation, the lower the status of his class, the higher the perceived distance from his class, and the lower the perceived distance from the nation. Now the status of the wealthy class is never lower than the status of the poor class. Thus, for similar cognitive distance from class, the SIE condition ii implies that the poor are more likely to hold a national identity than the rich. The alternative social identity of the poor simply has a lower status.

We now turn to the determination of the equilibrium tax rate t^*. The SIE condition i says that actions must be optimal given social identities.[11] Since we do not assume that national status responds systematically to the tax level, a person identifying with the nation has the same policy preferences as in the standard model.[12] An individual identifying with the poor class, however, will prefer a higher tax rate, as he now cares not only about his own after-tax income but also about the relative position of his class. Thus, while class identification induces individuals to care more about the distribution of income, national identification shifts their social identity concerns elsewhere to the status of their nation, for example, to its importance as a power in the world or other such variables that are not necessarily clearly related to tax policies.

It can be shown that under the assumptions of the model the median voter theorem applies, with the median voter being the median income agent. Thus the equilibrium tax rate can be high or low, depending on whether the median identifies with the poor class or with the nation as a whole. But the identity of the median, in turn, depends on the relative status of the poor, which is itself a function of the tax rate.

Thus, depending on the parameters of the model we may get a unique equilibrium or multiple ones. If the perceived distance of the median from the nation is sufficiently low and perceived distance from the poor class sufficiently high, then there exists a unique equilibrium where the median identifies with the nation and the amount of redistribution is relatively low. Conversely, if the perceived distance from the nation is sufficiently high and perceived distance from the poor class sufficiently low, then there may exist a unique equilibrium where the median identifies with his class and the tax rate is high. However, as long as after-tax income matters for the relative status of the class, there exist values of the distance parameters such that there exist two stable equilibria. At the low tax rate equilibrium, the relative status of the poor is sufficiently low to induce the median voter to identify with the nation rather than with the poor even if that entails a higher cognitive cost. He then prefers a low tax rate. However, with a high tax rate the poor are not that far behind the rich in their standards of living and hence in their status. The median may now identify with the poor class and thus vote for a higher tax rate.

The first implication of these results has to do with the effect of the distance that citizens perceive between themselves and their nation. The lower is the distance from the nation, the higher is the likelihood of a low-redistribution equilibrium, other things being equal. Perceived distance may be due to slow-changing fundamentals such as ethnic or cultural diversity, but this perception is susceptible to various shocks. The experimental results suggest that a common threat, salient international competition, or a conflict with another nation can reduce perceived distance from the nation and hence, according to our model, increase the likelihood of a low-redistribution equilibrium. In particular, a salient national security danger is likely to enhance a feeling that we are all in the same boat—rich and poor alike. But a national identity means less weight on class issues and less support for redistribution. This suggests that there may be an incentive for elites to hype national threats—perhaps even to the point of going to war—in order to diffuse domestic claims for more redistribution, or to soften opposition for a reduction in the level of redistribution (see the related discussion on the supply of hatred in Glaeser 2005). In the longer run the nature of the school system—whether it fosters similarity to the nation or class distinctions—should also affect the redistributive regime (see Weber 1976; Kremer and Sarychev 1998; Gradstein and Justman 2002).

This point brings us to the second implication. Factors that decrease the sense of distance between the median and the lower class tend to increase class identification and hence support for redistribution. One interesting implication relates to the effect of ethnic diversity. As the experimental results suggest, group identification declines with heterogeneity. Suppose that ethnic diversity is concentrated at the poorer segments of society, so the nation as a whole is more ethnically homogeneous than the poor group. This will reduce the likelihood of class identification on the part of the lower class and hence that of a high-redistribution equilibrium. An illustration of this point might be the shift of significant portions of the working class in Western Europe from socialist to nationalist parties (Kitschelt 1996; Ignazi 2003; Lubbers et al. 2002). A recent survey on the resurgence of the radical right in Western Europe states that certainly the most common explanatory factor put forward for the electoral breakthrough of the radical right are immigration and the presence of immigrants (Schain et al. 2002, p. 11). Such a relationship is readily interpretable in terms of our model: immigration of foreign workers affects primarily the composition of the poorer segments of society. Categorizing oneself as part of the working class is not as self-evident anymore. Consistent with our model, Soroka et al. (2006) find a negative relationship across OECD countries between changes in social spending and immigration flows in the 1970 to 1998 period.[13]

Third, a high relative status of the nation also tends to increase the likelihood of national identification and a low-tax equilibrium. President Ronald Reagan once said he hoped history would remember him on the basis that "I wanted to see if the American people couldn't get back that pride, and that patriotism, that confidence, that they had in our system. And I think they have."[14] If indeed they have, by our model it helps explain the popularity and political success of his tax policies even among blue-collar workers.

Finally, an interesting question arises as to the effect of *before-tax* inequality. Note that we have two different measures of before-tax inequality that can affect the result: the median-to-mean ratio and the interclass difference. Locally around the equilibrium points the effect of an increase in before-tax inequality is unambiguously to increase redistribution, as in the standard median voter result. However, consistent with several empirical studies, it is not clear that an economy with high before-tax inequality will in general be at a high-tax equilibrium.[15] This is so because as the interclass income difference increases, the status of the poor falls, making class identification and a high-tax equilibrium less likely, and a nationalistic low-tax equilibrium more likely. Thus an exogenous increase in income inequality that substantially hurts the status of the poor may actually promote a shift of the poor toward supporting *less* redistribution.

More generally, the model suggests that we may observe rather different levels of redistribution among economies with similar before-tax income distributions and similar political institutions, and it points to several factors that can cause such differences. However, the proposition also suggests that we may observe different levels of redistribution even when all these factors are held constant, as different levels of redistribution serve to reinforce the identification patterns that gave rise to these levels of redistribution. That is, even if the lower class Swedes, say, were just as diverse as the lower class Americans and their nation had the same relative status as the United States, in equilibrium they could still identify less with their nation simply because of the relatively high status of their class due to the (historically given) high degree of redistribution. As a result they would continue to support the high level of redistribution. Historical contingencies can thus have a lasting effect on the redistributive system.[16] So empirically we should expect to find higher levels of national identification the lower is the level of redistribution, and vice versa.

9.3.2 Evidence: National Identity and Redistribution

From the preceding application of the SIE framework several new predictions concerning national identity and redistribution in democracies can be made:[17]

1. Given social identity, support for redistribution is decreasing in income. Further, for given income, support for redistribution decreases with national identification among the nonwealthy.

2. The poor are more likely to identify with their nation.

3. Across countries, democracies should exhibit a negative correlation between levels of national identification and levels of redistribution.

Both micro and cross-country data seem to support these predictions, at least in advanced democracies. I briefly summarize here the main empirical results from Shayo (2005).

The micro data come from two sources: the World Values Survey (WVS, Inglehart et al. 2000) and the International Social Survey Program (ISSP: National Identity 1995). Each survey covers more than twenty democracies during the 1990s. The ISSP 1995 provides better measures of national identity. However, it does not contain data on attitudes toward redistribution. The WVS contains a cruder measure of national identification but includes measures of preferences for redistribution. Finally, to measure the extent of redistribution at the national level (third prediction), I use data on the difference between before-tax and after-tax income distributions, obtained from the household income surveys included in the Luxemburg Income Study (LIS). I limit the analysis to democracies, but use a relatively lax definition of democracy.[18]

Before I discuss the main results, I will address the issue of measuring social identity out of the lab. My definition of social identity requires that an agent care about the status of his group. In experimental studies, such preferences can be directly inferred from behavior (e.g., ingroup favoritism in allocation decisions that do not affect own payoffs). In larger empirical studies, survey questions are used. Ellemers et al. (1999a) show that ingroup favoritism in allocation decisions is captured by questions on commitment to the group, meaning the desire to continue acting as a group member. These consist of agreement to such statements as I would like to continue working with my group or I dislike being a member of my group. On the other hand, ingroup favoritism is not captured by mere self-categorization statements such as I am like other members of my group.

The WVS contains a question asking: "How proud are you to be [e.g., French]?" answered on a scale of 1 to 4 (very proud, quite proud, not very proud, and not at all proud). This question seems reasonably well suited to capture our concept of national identity. The WVS also asks respondents to rank on a scale from 1 to 10 whether "incomes should be made more equal" or whether "we need larger income differences as incentives for individual effort." This question captures preferences over the type of policies that we have assumed in the model, namely ones that make incomes more *equal* (e.g., as opposed to policies designed to secure a minimal standard of living for the poor). These data can be used to examine the first prediction.

Two major patterns emerge from these data. First, within both the group of those professing to be very proud to be members of their nation and the group that includes the rest, support for redistribution is generally decreasing with household income in most surveys. Second, in most advanced economies[19] people who identify more strongly with their nation prefer a lower level of redistribution than people with low levels of identification and similar income. Figure 9.1 presents the particularly stark results from the United States in 1990. Outside the industrial world, however, there is usually no clear difference between the two groups in their support for redistribution, once the study controls for income (see next section for a discussion). Similar results emerge from regressions of the support for redistribution on log income and dummies for level of national pride, controlling for sex, age, years of education, and log of household size. There is a strong negative relationship between income and preferences for redistribution in almost all countries. Further people who profess to be very proud of being members of their nation appear to support redistribution significantly less than people who profess to be not proud or not at all proud, controlling for log of income and years of education. The point estimates are negative in 23 out of 27 available surveys—and appear very large when compared to the effect of income. If taken literally, the point estimates imply that moving from not being proud to being very proud of the nation is equivalent in terms of attitudes toward redistribution, to having one's household income multiplied by a

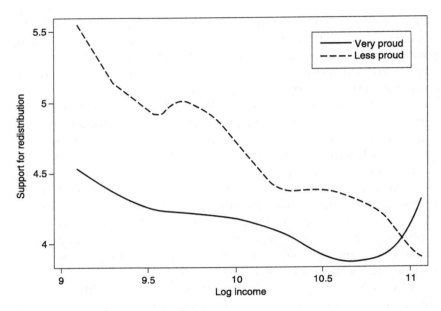

Figure 9.1
Support for redistribution by national identity and income: United States, 1990 WVS
data. Locally weighted regressions with quartic kernels. See Shayo (2005) for details.

factor of between 1.5 and 3 in most Western democracies. The relationship between national pride and preferences for redistribution is statistically significant in most industrialized countries but weaker in the
less advanced countries.

Available data seem to support the prediction that national identification is negatively related to support for redistribution—at least in
advanced economies. But who are the nationalists? The model predicts
that low-income individuals, having less to be proud of in their immediate social group, will in general tend to identify more strongly with
the nation. To test this prediction, I used detailed micro data from the
ISSP 1995 National Identity module. The ISSP 1995 includes surveys
from 22 democracies (using our broad definition of democracy based
on political rights). The surveys include six items that seem to capture
the notion of national identity.[20]

For each country and each of the six national pride items, I estimated
an ordered probit model with the national identity variable as the dependent variable and with log of income, log of household size, sex,
and age as independent variables. I also looked at a national identity

scale, which is just an unweighted sum of the six items taking values from 0 to 24. I then repeated this procedure with controls for years of schooling. The data seemed overwhelmingly supportive of the notion that poorer people tend to identify more strongly with their nation. A negative relationship between income and the national identification scale is apparent in all countries surveyed. The relationship generally holds even when controlling for years of education.

Finally, on the overall levels of redistribution and national identification, according to the model in equilibrium we should expect high levels of redistribution to be accompanied with relatively low levels of national identification, and vice versa. To measure the extent of actual redistribution I used the share gain of the bottom quintile, defined as the difference between the share of the bottom quintile in factor income (before taxes and transfers) and disposable income (Milanovic 2000). To measure the extent of national identification I used both the median of the six-item national identity scale constructed from the ISSP, and the estimated fraction of the population in each country professing the highest level of national pride from the WVS.

Figure 9.2 presents the main results.[21] In both panels a clear negative relationship appears. It is noteworthy that the negative relationship is not just driven by cross-Atlantic differences but also holds within Western Europe. To get a sense of the strength of the association, the R^2 from regressing the share-gain on measures of national identification alone is 0.72 in the sample using the ISSP measure and 0.6 using the WVS. Note that this pattern holds despite the commonly held view that the welfare state makes Europeans proud of their country: the more redistributive countries are actually characterized by *less* national pride. Note also, in panel b, that most of the negative relationship comes from cross-country variation and not variation within countries over time. Movements within countries—in both dimensions—are very small relative to the differences between countries. This suggests rather stable equilibria.

It is, of course, possible that the cross-country correlation is driven by some other factors (or fixed effects) that affect both national identification and levels of redistribution, without the direct link between the two postulated by my model. However, the micro level results presented above limit the relevance of this possibility. As I have showed, the relationship between national identification and redistribution also holds at the individual level: within almost every Western

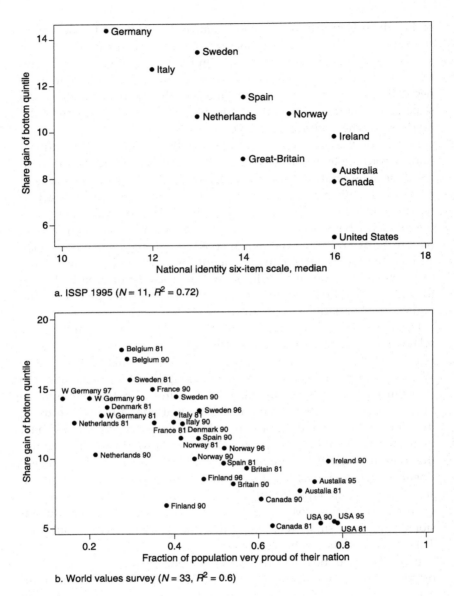

a. ISSP 1995 ($N = 11$, $R^2 = 0.72$)

b. World values survey ($N = 33$, $R^2 = 0.6$)

Figure 9.2
Redistribution and national identity. National identity scale from ISSP 1995. Fraction very proud from WVS waves 1 to 3. Share gain from LIS (Milanovic 2000). Data are taken from the LIS household income surveys closest to the WVS or ISSP surveys. The transition economies of Eastern Europe are excluded. See Shayo (2005) for details.

democracy, people who identify with their nation support less redistribution than people who do not. And in almost every country, poverty seems to encourage nationalism. If the grand, long-run redistributive system reflects voters' preferences, then it is indeed puzzling that the cross-country patterns had not reflected the micro results. Overall then, for advanced and well-established democracies, the data lend strong support to the model.

9.4   Concluding Remarks on Developing Countries

I conclude by making a few conjectures on how the social identity framework might apply to developing countries. There are several reasons to think that applying the social identity framework to developing countries can yield very different results. Consider first the result presented above, that the poor are more likely to hold a national identity. This result hinges on two important assumptions. First, that the social status of the wealthy class is primarily a function of its economic achievements. Second, that perceived distance from the nation is similar for all agents, and in particular, is not systematically related to class. These assumptions are reasonable for today's industrialized nation states. But consider eighteenth- and nineteenth-century Europe where productivity resided with the bourgeoisie but status still resided to a significant extent with the aristocracy. Further at the early stages of industrialization and urbanization much of the poor population lives in rural areas, often separated from the rest of their nation by cultural, linguistic, and geographic barriers. Perceived distance from the nation was thus higher for the rural poor than for the urban middle class. The following (quite representative) passage from Eugen Weber's (1976) study of nineteenth-century France is rather revealing:

In 1864 a school inspector in Lozère was incensed to find that at one school he visited not a single child could answer questions like are you English or Russian? or what country is the department of Lozère in? Among most of these children, the inspector added bitterly, thought doesn't go beyond the radius of the poor parish in which they live. Every year, reported Bodley shortly before 1914, there are recruits who had never heard of the Franco–German war of 1870. He quoted a 1901 survey in which an average of six out of every ten recruits in a cavalry squadron had never heard of the war. A similar inquiry among recruits of 1906 revealed that 36 percent were unaware that France was vanquished in 1870 and barely half knew of the annexation of Alsace–Lorraine. Indeed, only one man in four could explain why July 14 was a national holiday (Weber 1976, p. 110).

Under these conditions the urban middle class is likely to be more nationalistic than the rural poor. Indeed, at the time of the French revolution, "Grégoire's correspondents noted sadly that 'there is no patriotism in the countryside.' Only 'the more enlightened' could conceive the notion. Patriotism was an urban thought" (Weber 1976, p. 98). Similar conditions appear to have been held in colonized countries where the local elites did not enjoy as high a status as they would based solely on their domestic economic position, and also in developing countries where much of the poor population is concentrated in rural areas.

Second, in many developing countries the important social categories are often based on locality or ethnicity rather than class and nation. As was noted in the previous section, in less advanced countries there usually is no clear difference in the support for redistribution between those respondents who are very proud of their nation and those who are not. Interestingly the only *advanced* economies in my sample where the relationship between national identity and support for redistribution was not apparent are Belgium, Italy, and Spain. This may be related to the fact that (Switzerland notwithstanding) Italy, Spain, and Belgium have the strongest ethnic-regional cleavages among the Western democracies. This suggests that the model may need to be adjusted when a strong regional identity is available. If the predominant immediate social group is not the class but the region, then it is not clear that a shift to a national identity will in general mean less support for redistribution. Northern Italy or Catalonia, for example, are relatively rich regions and hence shifting from a national to a regional identity in these areas will likely reduce support for redistribution.

Third, grand schemes of redistribution (as opposed to transfers to specific groups) change very slowly, and it is only in the long run that we can expect them to reflect the preferences of the voters, as a median-voter framework implicitly assumes. The application I discussed above should thus account for long-run equilibria in established democracies—but not in transition economies or in emerging democracies. Consistent with this expectation, adding the transition economies of Eastern Europe to the cross-country analysis presented in figure 9.2 should reduce the strength of the association between national identification and the extent of redistribution.

However, the model of this chapter does suggest that as national identification becomes more prevalent in the process of development—either due to the destruction of local linguistic and transportation barriers or due to an enhanced national status—it can help reduce intranational class or ethnic struggles (see Miguel 2004 for evidence). At the same time, as both my general framework and Western history suggest, national identification can also promote international competition for relative status, and this can have obvious adverse effects.

Notes

This chapter is a nontechnical companion paper to Shayo (2005). In writing this chapter I benefited enormously from discussions with Roland Benabou, Anne Case, and Thomas Romer. I would also like to thank seminar participants at Ben-Gurion, Carnegie Mellon, George Mason, Hebrew, Princeton, and Tel Aviv Universities and at the CESifo Workshop on Political Economy and Development.

1. As Jenkins (1996) puts it, "identity" has become one of the unifying frameworks of intellectual debate in the 1990s. Everybody, it seems, has something to say about it: sociologists, anthropologists, political scientists, psychologists, geographers, historians, philosophers. For surveys of the social psychology literature, see Brown (2000), Ellemers, Spears, and Doosje (1999b, 2002), and Hogg and Abrams (2001). For a sociological perspective, see Jenkins (1996). The political science literature on gender, class, national, ethnic, and other social identities is immense. Classic references include Anderson (1991), Gellner (1983), and Horowitz (1985). Akerlof and Kranton (2000) proposed a way to integrate some of this research into economics. As will become apparent, my approach generalizes the model they proposed.

2. The key to categorization decisions in the cognitive psychology literature is the perceived difference between the stimulus that is to be categorized, on the one hand, and the features of the available categories, on the other. The larger the distance in psychological space (Nosofsky 1986, 1992) between stimulus i and category j, the lower is the probability that the stimulus would be categorized as a member of j. Following Turner et al. (1987), I adopt this approach to the process of categorizing *oneself* into a group.

3. See, for example, Ellemers et al. (1988, 1992, 1993, 1999a), Guimond et al. (2002), Hogg and Hains (1996), Mael and Ashforth (1992), and Roccas (2003). A meta-analysis of 92 experimental studies with high-status/low-status manipulation confirms that high-status group members favor their ingroup over the outgroup significantly more than do low-status group members (Bettencourt et al. 2001).

4. See Mackie and Wright (2001), Spears et al. (2001), and Cialdini and Goldstein (2004) for recent reviews on social influence as it relates to social identity.

5. See Fischbacher et al. (2001), Frey and Meier (2004), Gaechter (2005), Holt and Laury (2005), Ledyard (1995), and Zelmer (2003) for experimental evidence on such behavior.

6. See, for example, Brewer and Kramer (1986), De Cremer and Van Vugt (1998, 1999), Kramer and Brewer (1984, 1986), Orbell et al. (1988), Sausgruber (2003), Solow and Kirkwood (2002), and Van Vugt and Hart (2004).

7. See Ledyard (1995), Polzer et al. (1999), and Zelmer (2003) for experimental results. For field studies, see Alesina et al. (1999) on the relationship between ethnic homogeneity

and provision of public goods across US localities, and Costa and Kahn (2003) on the relationship between company heterogeneity and cowardice in the Union Army.

8. That is, agents vote directly and sincerely over tax rates and the tax rate adopted is the Condorcet winner if it exists.

9. See Evans (2000) for a survey of the evidence on class voting. The literature on the prominence of the nation as a social category is immense. See, for example, Anderson (1991), Billig (1995), and Gellner (1983). While I will discuss how ethnic diversity can affect the results, I do not model ethnic identity directly in this chapter.

10. Indeed the main results are strengthened in this case. Nationalists prefer less redistribution not just because of how redistribution affects class status, but also because high taxes harm the overall wealth of the nation (due to deadweight losses). My results, however, do not rely on a negative effect of taxation on national status.

11. In the current context this condition means that when forming policy preferences, agents take their social identities as given. That is, they do not take into account the possibility that as taxes change, they may stop caring about the group they currently identify with and start caring about some other group. Consequently they may come to have policy preferences different from the ones they currently hold. On voters' tendency to overestimate the stability of their political positions, see Lowenthal and Loewenstein (2001).

12. In other words, my results do *not* depend on nationalists willing to sacrifice material payoff because they recognize a negative effect of redistributive taxation on national strength.

13. The idea that support for redistribution increases as identification with the group that benefits from it increases, and that such identification is related to distance along ethnic dimensions, is also supported by Luttmer (2001). Based on the American GSS, Luttmer reports that support for welfare spending increases as the share of local welfare recipients from the respondent's race increases. The model also appears consistent with the evidence presented by Alesina et al. (2001) and Alesina and Glaeser (2004), on the relation between racial heterogeneity and the extent of redistribution, but it points to the importance of heterogeneity within the poor and middle classes—and not in society as a whole.

14. Reagan to Barbara Walters, quoted in *The New York Times*, June 6, 2004.

15. This is consistent with most of the empirical studies reviewed in Benabou (1996) and Alesina and Glaeser (2004). See, however, Milanovic (2000).

16. Such contingencies may well be factors included in my model, such as the heterogeneous-immigrant composition of the American working class in the early twentieth century, or the absence of wars from Swedish history after the Napoleonic era.

17. I stress the national identification side of the model and not the class identification side for two reasons. One is practical: in contrast with data on national identification, data on class identification are harder to obtain. While many surveys (e.g., the GSS, Eurobarometer, WVS) ask respondents what social class they belong to, this is at best a self-categorization question, similar to asking to which nation do you belong? It tells us little about identification as I defined it (more on this below). Second, the effect of class identification seems less contentious. It is not too surprising to find that low-income individuals with a strong working class identity desire more redistribution than their comrades with weak class identification. It is also hardly startling to find that working class iden-

tity is more common in Western Europe, where there are higher levels of redistribution, than in the United States (see Evans 2000). The predictions regarding national identification however appear more in need of empirical verification.

I will not revisit here the effects of ethnic fragmentation. The effect of national threats, and the interaction of domestic policy with the incidence of war are also beyond the scope of this chapter.

18. Specifically I look only at what Freedom House (2003) defines as political rights: a measure of the existence of free, open, and fair elections that determine who actually rule. I do not use the other component—civil liberties—to filter out nondemocracies.

19. Economies are divided into advanced and less advanced according to whether real GDP per capita (PWT 6.1, Heston et al. 2002) is less than 50 percent of the US real GDP per capita.

20. The questions were worded as follows:

How much do you agree or disagree with the following statements? [1. Agree strongly; 2. Agree; 3. Neither agree nor disagree; 4. Disagree 5. Disagree strongly]

1. I would rather be a citizen of (R's country) than of any other country in the world.
2. There are some things about (R's country) today that make me feel ashamed of (R's country).
3. The world would be a better place if people from other countries were more like the people in (R's country).
4. Generally (R's country) is a better country than most other countries.
5. When my country does well in international sports, it makes me proud to be citizen of (R's country).
6. (R's country) should follow its own interests, even if this leads to conflicts with other nations.

While all items gauge feelings of national pride, items 2 and 5 are conditional on transitory conditions (things about my country today), and are thus less suitable to capture commitment to the group.

21. I exclude here the transition economies of Eastern Europe because they had not yet reached equilibrium by the time of these surveys. Adding these countries would weaken the strength of the association, although the R^2 should remain high (46 and 49 percent using ISSP and WVS respectively).

References

Akerlof, G. A., and R. E. Kranton. 2000. Economics and identity. *Quarterly Journal of Economics* 115(3): 715–53.

Alesina, A., R. Baqir, and W. Easterly. 1999. Public goods and ethnic divisions. *Quarterly Journal of Economics* 114: 1243–84.

Alesina, A., and E. L. Glaeser. 2004. *Fighting Poverty in the US and Europe: A World of Difference.* Oxford: Oxford University Press.

Alesina, A., E. L. Glaeser, and B. Sacerdote. 2001. Why doesn't the US have a European-style welfare state? Harvard Institute of Economic Research Discussion Paper 1933.

Anderson, B. 1991. *Imagined Communities: Reflections on the Origin and Spread of Nationalism*, rev. ed. New York: Verso.

Benabou, R. 2000. Unequal societies: Income distribution and the social contract. *American Economic Review* 90(1): 96–129.

Benabou, R., and J. Tirole. 2005. Belief in a just world and redistributive politics. NBER Working Paper 11208.

Bettencourt, B. A., K. Charlton, N. Dorr, and D. L. Hume. 2001. Status differences and ingroup bias: A meta-analytic examination of the effects of status stability, status legitimacy, and group permeability. *Psychological Bulletin* 127(4): 520–42.

Billig, M. 1995. *Banal Nationalism*. London: Sage Publications.

Bourhis, R. Y., and A. Gagnon. 2001. Social orientations in the minimal group paradigm. In R. Brown and S. Gaertner, eds., Intergroup Processes: Blackwell Handbook in Social Psychology, vol. 4. Oxford: Blackwell, pp. 89–111.

Brewer, M. B. 1979. In-group bias in the minimal group situation: A cognitive-motivational analysis. *Psychological Bulletin* 86: 307–24.

Brewer, M. B., and R. M. Kramer. 1986. Choice behavior in social dilemmas: Effects of social identity, group size, and decision framing. *Journal of Personality and Social Psychology* 3: 543–49.

Brown, R. J. 2000. Social identity theory: Past achievements, current problems and future challenges. *European Journal of Social Psychology* 29: 634–67.

Cialdini, R. B., and N. J. Goldstein. 2004. Social influence: Compliance and conformity. *Annual Review of Psychology* 55: 591–621.

Congleton, R. D., and P. Fudulu. 1996. On the rationality of mutually immiserating coercion. *Journal of Economic Behavior and Organization* 30(1): 133–36.

Costa, D. L., and M. E. Kahn. 2003. Cowards and heroes: Group loyalty in the American Civil War. *Quarterly Journal of Economics* 118(2): 519–48.

De Cremer, D., and M. van Vugt. 1998. Collective identity and cooperation in a public goods dilemma: A matter of trust or self-efficacy? *Current Research in Social Psychology* 3(1): 1–11.

De Cremer, D., and M. van Vugt. 1999. Social identification effects in social dilemmas: A transformation of motives. *European Journal of Social Psychology* 29(7): 871–93.

Ellemers, N. 1993. The influence of socio-structural variables on identity management strategies. In W. Stoebe, and M. Hewstone, eds., *European Review of Social Psychology*, vol. 4. New York: Wiley, pp. 27–57.

Ellemers, N., B. J. Doosje, A. Van Knippenberg, and H. Wilke. 1992. Status protection in high status minority groups. *European Journal of Social Psychology* 22: 123–40.

Ellemers, N., P. Kortekaas, and J. W. Ouwerkerk. 1999a. Self-categorisation, commitment to the group and group self-esteem as related but distinct aspects of social identity. *European Journal of Social Psychology* 29(2–3): 371–89.

Ellemers, N., R. Spears, and B. Doosje, eds. 1999b. *Social Identity: Context, Commitment, Content*. Oxford: Blackwell.

Ellemers, N., A. Van Knippenberg, N. de-Vries, and H. Wilke. 1988. Social identification and permeability of group boundaries. *European Journal of Social Psychology* 18: 497–513.

Ellemers, N., R. Spears, and B. Doosje. 2002. Self and Social Identity. *Annual Review of Psychology* 53: 161–86.

Evans, G. 2000. The continued significance of class voting. *Annual Review of Political Science* 3: 401–17.

Fischbacher, U., S. Gachter, and E. Fehr. 2001. Are people conditionally cooperative? Evidence from a public goods experiment. *Economics Letters* 71(3): 397–404.

Freedom House. 2003. Freedom in the World Country Ratings 1972 through 2003 ⟨http://www.freedomhouse.org/ratings⟩.

Frey, B. S., and S. Meier. 2004. Social comparisons and pro-social behavior: Testing 'conditional cooperation' in a field experiment. *American Economic Review* 94(5): 1717–22.

Gaechter, S. 2005. Conditional cooperation: Behavioral regularities from the lab and the field and their policy implications. Mimeo. CESifo.

Gellner, E. 1983. *Nations and Nationalism*. Ithaca: Cornell University Press.

Glaeser, E. L. 2005. The political economy of hatred. *Quarterly Journal of Economics* 120(1): 45–86.

Gradstein, M., and M. Justman. 2002. Education, social cohesion, and economic growth. *American Economic Review* 92(4): 1192–1204.

Guimond, S., S. Dif, and A. Aupy. 2002. Social identity, relative group status and intergroup attitudes: when favourable outcomes change intergroup relations ... for the worse. *European Journal of Social Psychology* 32(6): 739–60.

Heston, A., R. Summers, and B. Aten. 2002. Penn World Table Version 6.1. Center for International Comparisons at the University of Pennsylvania (CICUP), October.

Hogg, M. A., and S. C. Hains. 1996. Intergroup relations and group solidarity: Effects of group identification and social beliefs on depersonalized attraction. *Journal of Personality and Social Psychology* 70, 295–309.

Holt, C. A., and S. K. Laury. 2005. Theoretical Explanations of Treatment Effects in Voluntary Contributions Experiments. In C. Plott and V. Smith, eds., *The Handbook of Experimental Economics Results*. Amsterdam: North-Holland.

Horowitz, D. L. 1985. *Ethnic Groups in Conflict*. Berkeley: University of California Press.

Ignazi, P. 2003. *Extreme Right Parties in Western Europe*. Oxford: Oxford University Press.

Inglehart, R., et al. 2000. *World Values Surveys and European Values Surveys, 1981–1984, 1990–1993, and 1995–1997*. ICPSR version. Ann Arbor, MI: Institute for Social Research.

International Social Survey Program (ISSP). 1995. *National Identity*. ICPSR release. Köln, Germany. 1998. *Zentralarchiv fuer Empirische Sozialforschung*. Ann Arbor, MI: Interuniversity Consortium for Political and Social Research.

Jenkins R. 1996. *Social Identity*. London: Routledge.

Kitschelt, H. 1996. *The Radical Right in Western Europe*. Ann Arbor: University of Michigan Press.

Kramer, R. M., and M. B. Brewer. 1984. Effects of group identity on resource use in a simulated commons dilemma. *Journal of Personality and Social Psychology* 46: 1044–57.

Kramer, R. M., M. B. Brewer. 1986. Social group identity and the emergence of cooperation in resource conservation dilemmas. In H. Wilke, D. Messick, and C. Rutte, eds., *Experimental Social Dilemmas*. Frankfurt am Main: Verlag Peter Lang, pp. 177–203.

Kremer, M., and A. Sarychev. 1998. Why Do Governments Operate Schools? Mimeo. Harvard University.

Ledyard, J. 1995. Public goods: A survey of experimental research. In A. Roth and J. Kagel, eds., *The Handbook of Experimental Economics*. Princeton: Princeton University Press, pp. 111–94.

Lee, W., and J. E. Roemer. 2004. Racism and redistribution in the United States: A solution to the problem of American exceptionalism. Cowles Foundation Discussion Paper 1462.

Lowenthal, D., and G. Loewenstein. 2001. Can voters predict changes in their own attitudes? *Political Psychology* 22: 65–87.

Lubbers, M., M. Gijsberts, and P. Scheepers. 2002. Extreme right–wing voting in Western Europe. *European Journal of Political Research* 41(3): 345–78.

Luttmer, E. F. P. 2001. Group loyalty and the taste for redistribution. *Journal of Political Economy* 109(3): 500–28.

Mackie, D. M., and C. L. Wright. 2001. Social Influence in an Intergroup Context. In R. Brown and S. L. Gaertner, eds., *Blackwell Handbook of Social Psychology: Intergroup Processes*. Oxford: Blackwell, pp. 281–300.

Mael, F., and B. E. Ashforth. 1992. Alumni and their alma mater: A partial test of the reformulated model of organizational identification. *Journal of Organizational Behavior* 13: 103–23.

Meltzer, A. H., and S. F. Richard. 1981. A rational theory of the size of government. *Journal of Political Economy* 89(5): 914–27.

Miguel, E. 2004. Tribe or nation? Nation-building and public goods in Kenya versus Tanzania. *World Politics* 56(3): 327–62.

Milanovic, B. 2000. The median-voter hypothesis, income inequality, and income redistribution: An empirical test with the required data. *European Journal of Political Economy* 16: 367–410.

Nosofsky, R. M. 1986. Attention, similarity and the identification-categorization relationship. *Journal of Experimental Psychology: General* 115(1): 39–57.

Nosofsky, R. M. 1992. Similarity scaling and cognitive process models. *Annual Review of Psychology* 43: 25–53.

Orbell, J. M., A. J. Van-de-Kragt, and R. M. Dawes. 1988. Explaining discussion-induced cooperation. *Journal of Personality and Social Psychology* 54: 811–19.

Piketty, T. 1995. Social mobility and redistributive politics. *Quarterly Journal of Economics* 110: 551–84.

Polzer, J. T., K. J. Stewart, and J. L. Simmons. 1999. A social categorization explanation for framing effects in nested social dilemmas. *Organizational Behavior and Human Decision Processes* 79: 154–78.

Roccas, S. 2003. The effects of status on identification with multiple groups. *European Journal of Social Psychology* 33(3): 351–66.

Roemer, J. E. 1998. Why the poor do not expropriate the rich: An old argument in new garb. *Journal of Public Economics* 70: 399–424.

Sausgruber, R. 2003. Testing for team spirit—An experimental study. Mimeo. University of Innsbruck, Department of Public Economics.

Schain, M., A. R. Zolberg, and P. Hossay, eds. 2002. *Shadows over Europe: The Development and Impact of the Extreme Right in Western Europe*. New York: Palgrave.

Shayo, M. 2005. Nation, class and redistribution: Applying social identity research to political economy. Mimeo. Hebrew University.

Solow, J. L., and N. Kirkwood. 2002. Group identity and gender in public goods experiments. *Journal of Economic Behavior and Organization* 48(4): 403–12.

Soroka, S., K. Banting, and R. Johnston. 2006. Immigration and Redistribution in a Global Era. In S. Bowles, P. Bardhan, and M. Wallerstein, eds., *Globalization and Egalitarian Redistribution*. New York: Russell Sage Foundation, pp. 261–88.

Spears, R., T. Postmes, M. Lea, and S. E. Watt. 2001. A side view of social influence. In K. D. Williams and J. P. Forgas, eds., *Social Influence: Direct and Indirect Processes*. Philadelphia: Psychology Press, pp. 331–50.

Tajfel, H. 1970. Experiments in intergroup discrimination. *Scientific American* 223: 96–102.

Tajfel, H., M. G. Billig, R. P. Bundy, and C. Flament. 1971. Social categorization and intergroup behavior. *European Journal of Social Psychology* 1: 149–78.

Tajfel, H., and J. C. Turner. 1979. An integrative theory of intergroup conflict. In W. G. Austin and S. Worchel, eds., *The Social Psychology of Intergroup Relations*. Monterey, CA: Brooks/Cole, pp. 33–48.

Tajfel, H., and J. C. Turner. 1986. The social identity theory of intergroup behavior. In S. Worchel and W. Austin, eds., *Psychology of Intergroup Relations*. Chicago: Nelson Hall, pp. 7–24.

Turner, J. C., M. A. Hogg, P. J. Oakes, S. D. Reicher, and M. S. Wetherell. 1987. *Rediscovering the Social Group a Self-categorization Theory*. Oxford: Blackwell.

Van Vugt, M., and C. M. Hart. 2004. Social identity as social glue: The origins of group loyalty. *Journal of Personality and Social Psychology* 86(4): 585–98.

Weber, E. 1976. *Peasants into Frenchmen: The Modernization of Rural France, 1870–1914*. Stanford: Stanford University Press.

Zelmer, J. 2003. Linear public goods experiments: A meta-analysis. *Experimental Economics* 6(3): 299–310.

Index

Printed in the United States
by Baker & Taylor Publisher Services